Shotgun STUFF

by Don Zutz

Published by
SHOTGUN SPORTS, INC.

Published by Shotgun Sports, Inc.
P.O. Box 6810
Auburn, California 95604

Library of Congress Catalog No.: 91-067655
ISBN 0-925012-01-7

Manufactured in the United States of America. Distributed to the book and sporting goods trade by Shotgun Sports, Inc., P.O. Box 6810, Auburn, California 95604. To order this book and others from this publisher, call (916) 889-2220 or FAX (916) 889-9106. Dealer inquiries welcome. For subscription information on *Shotgun Sports* magazine, call (916) 889-2220.

Any and all loading information presented in this book should be interpreted carefully and used with caution. Since they have no knowledge of or control over the reader's choice of guns, components or actual loadings, the author, publisher and the various firearms and components manufacturers mentioned assume no responsibility for the use of this information. Always consult comprehensive reference manuals and bulletins for details on proper requirements, procedures and safety precautions before attempting any reloading.

Front Cover: Photo by Walter L. Rickell

Preface

If you have ever wanted to pick the brain of the man who writes all those great articles in *Shotgun Sports* about reloading, gun collecting, improving your performance on wild game and wild targets and choosing and fitting the right gun, here's your chance! Don Zutz has taken pen in hand and provided us with a book covering all the facets of shotgunning.

Don's over 40 years of hunting and shooting experience is summarized in this book. He tells us which shot to use and when and which gun to use for the shot. In addition, he gives us some great recipes for loads to get the best from any gun and provides us with a little insight into the beginnings of the way we hunt and some of the equipment we use.

If you are a beginner with a shotgun or just getting into reloading, Don gives you advice to save you lots of time and trouble. If you are an experienced hunter or clay-target shooter, you can find tons of tips to help improve your performance with your smoothbore and get it to do more than you thought it could.

We've waited a long time for a book like this, one covering all the angles of shotgunning for those of us who are not into just one kind of shotgun sport. Don shows how versatile the shotgun really is, and you may just find some new ways to enjoy your shotgun after reading this book.

Frank Kodl
Editor/Publisher
Shotgun Sports Magazine

About The Author

At the age of 12, Don Zutz missed a sitting starling — twice! He took a critical look at his .410 shotgun, began patterning into a snowbank to see why he had missed and has been at it ever since. His life has been an ongoing fascination with shotguns, shotgun performance, bird hunting and competitive clay-target shooting.

Now, at the age of 60 (and still running 2 miles every other day when when he's not hunting), Don has written his sixth book. He just returned from South America, where he tested many different patterns on millions of doves. In 1990, he won the Hunter Event at the United States Sporting Clays Association's National Championship, and after a lengthy layoff from skeet, returned to win his 1991 county skeet title with a 99x100 using a release trigger to overcome the flinch he acquired through his years of heavy shooting.

Prior to launching a second career as a free-lance writer, Zutz spent 15 years teaching and coaching at the high school level. He holds a B.A. degree in Latin, English and history, plus a master's degree in history from the University of Wisconsin. In addition to shotgunning, he enjoys fishing and gourmet cooking with wild game and plans to never retire!

As the years pass, Don gets more enthusiastic about shotgunning and writing. In preparation are two more books, one in partnership with Dr. Michael J. Keyes covering competitive shotgunning, and another to be called *Shotgunning — Let's Get Technical*. And don't be surprised if *Shotgun Stuff II* follows at a later date!

Other books by Don Zutz include: *Handloading For Hunters, The Double Shotgun, Modern Waterfowl Guns And Gunning, Shotgunning Trends In Transition* and *Wine Seasoning And Wild Game Cooking*. To order any of Don's books, contact Shootin' Accessories, Ltd., P.O. Box 6810, Auburn, CA 95604, Phone (916) 889-2220 or FAX (916) 889-9106.

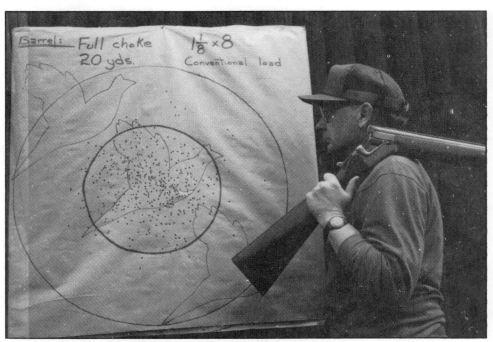

The author at work. Don Zutz spends many hours shooting and patterning with shotguns to gain the knowledge he shares in his writing.

Contents

INTRODUCTION

This book is something like a shot charge that has come through an open-choked barrel – the topics are spread liberally about. Subjects range from the value of clay-target shooting for hunters to the science of shotgunning; from wing-gunning technique to observations about patterning; from comments about special field guns and loads to the mental aspects of executing a shot without botching it because of anxiety; and from the subtleties of gripping to the effects of changes in gun weight.

Don't expect to be told something so simple as to use 6's as an all-around pellet or that Full chokes shoot tight patterns while Cylinder bores scatter 'em around. The topics covered herein go a step beyond the basic and casual. I believe shotgunners deserve more than the syrupy stuff found in books and magazines that spoon out the bland fundamentals over and over again. I want to dig deeper into pertinent topics, rather than brush past them in a rush.

A note about the reloading recipes in this book. As I have always warned handloaders, all reloading data should be used with caution. Use only recipes for which there is published data. Do not try to make the recipe fit the reloading components you have on hand; first find the data for the kind of load you want and then acquire the proper components. Always start with reduced loads and make sure they are safe in each of your guns before proceeding to the highest loads listed. Since the publisher and I have no control over your choice of reloading components, guns or actual loads, we nor the various firearms and components manufacturers cannot assume any responsibility for the use of this data. Always consult comprehensive reference manuals and bulletins for details on proper requirements,

procedures and safety precautions before attempting any reloading.

Handloaders should also be aware of whether pressures are listed as p.s.i. or l.u.p. They are *not* the same! In general, p.s.i. (pounds per square inch) values will be higher for any given reload than the l.u.p. (lead-unit pressure). As a very rough rule of thumb, p.s.i. readings tend to be approximately 1,000 units higher than l.u.p. readings. Some handloading manuals use l.u.p. and some use p.s.i., so you may find different pressures listed for the same load. Just watch the initials following the pressure figure, and remember there can be differences between test guns and equipment that can also affect these readings.

This book is not an attempt to cover every possible nook and cranny of shotgunning. Such overall coverage can't be done in one book unless it is the size of the Sears, Roebuck & Company catalog of the 1920s, and that is not economically feasible these days. The topics covered here are pertinent to modern shotgunning and hunting, and I can't help but believe they'll appeal to anyone who is into shotguns, bird hunting, trapshooting, Sporting Clays or reloading. I have tried to add another dimension to your pleasure in the shotgun sports without merely repeating what has been printed before. Indeed, this book is no rehash. It takes the information you have read in the excellent articles in *Shotgun Sports* magazine and expands on it.

If enough of you are interested in this sort of in-depth shotgunny stuff, I just might make this an annual thing. I could call the next one *Shotgun Stuff II* – what's Rambo got that I haven't?!

Don Zutz
1991

1

Does Clay Target Shooting Really Relate To The Field?

Although I am an ardent, perhaps obsessed, clay-target shooter, there was a time when I seriously questioned whether skeet, trap or even behind-the-barn hand-trap practice did me any good as a hunter. My initial loss of faith occurred one Saturday morning when I started the ruffed grouse season with a 28-gauge Remington Model 11-48 skeet gun I had been wielding reasonably well in skeet tournaments. Less than a half hour into the season, I sat down heavily on a huge boulder to enjoy the babbling of a nearby trout stream. . .and to wonder just why in the hell I had missed my first two birds with a total of four shots! Hadn't I learned anything from those thousands of rounds I had launched at skeet and trap clays during the summer?

Sometimes the cerebral gears turn slowly, and as I sat there pondering, I let the misses replay on the slow-motion equipment in my mind. The first had been a straightaway, something like the Low-Seven target in skeet, except it had flushed 10 to 12 yards ahead instead of at my elbow. I tried to use a skeet move on it, and — *Bang! Bang!* — I punched two holes in the brambles directly below the bird. The second had come off a hillside, angling down and away in the manner of the High-Two target in skeet. I tried the High-Two picture — *Bang! Bang!* — nuts! Not a feather drifted down. I slid off the boulder and left the tinkling of the stream without understanding those misses. Another hour of hunting netted naught.

Later, on a tote road spotty with clover, I had a surprise flush from almost directly underfoot. The grouse had apparently laid under the outer tips of a young pine as I approached, and when my toe came down within inches of it, it burst wildly. I had no time to equate it with a skeet shot — 15 yards away was the dense wall of a cedar swamp — the 28 cracked, the bird arched down, trailing feathers, and collided with sprigs of the first cedar. Without trying to analyze the shot, I quickly went to retrieve the bird. Just as I stepped from the tote road, a second grouse flushed behind me and slammed its way upward through some light birch cover to top an abrupt rise. The 28's pattern caught it cleanly in its sharp rise, and it folded and dropped softly into the leaves and laid with its white belly up — an easy mark and recovery.

Suddenly, I had made two centered hits with two shots, and I hadn't even considered the mechanics of skeet shooting. For a short time thereafter I questioned the value of skeet or any other type of practice shooting as they related to actual field gunning. Mightn't a hunter do just as well skipping all that practice and trusting to "instinctive" shooting?

I must confess that, for a time, I leaned

toward the instinctive side. Looking back, I could think of some pretty good outings during those years before I shot my first round of skeet. My high school and college years were financially lean, as were my first couple years out of college, and I didn't step onto a skeet layout until I was in my mid-20's. For more than a decade, however, I bagged plenty of ruffed grouse, pheasant, cottontails, Hungarian partridge and waterfowl without any clay-target shooting. Oh, every now and then, a buddy and I would buy a case of clays and throw them with a hand-held gizmo, but that probably happened no more than once a summer, and shooting at 50 to 60 clays a summer can hardly be called "grooving" the swing.

A couple other things happened to weaken my belief in clay-target shooting as a necessary stepping stone to results afield. First, a friend who was quite a good skeet shot simply walked away from the game. Money wasn't a factor — he was loaded — his problem was, in his opinion, the mechanical aspects of skeet were upsetting his duck shooting, and duck shooting was extremely important to him. Each year he and some friends spent at least two weeks in Canada hunting ducks and prairie grouse, and anything that even remotely seemed to impinge upon his enjoyment of this annual pilgrimage was eliminated *posthaste*. He said he knew the fundamentals of shotgun shooting, wasn't bad at putting them into effect (even after a 50-week layoff), and he didn't want to spend the first week of his hunting trip unlearning the "groove" of skeet.

The second thing that again made me wonder about the value of skeet and trap for a hunter was a comment from a dog trainer. His main interest was the retrieving breeds, and he was a respected man in his field. There were thousands of birds shot on his training grounds each year, and I spent several afternoons with him after I got out of college because I was looking for a dog but hadn't decided between a retriever or a pointer. When I mentioned I spent the preceding Sunday

Does clay-target shooting really relate to the field? Of course it does! This chap swinging on a high-tower bird on a Sporting Clays' layout isn't doing anything different than...

...this hunter, who is lining up on some geese coming over his pit blind. The important thing is understanding that the same swing must be employed on game as on clays.

afternoon shooting skeet, the trainer said, "Why? The only way to learn to shoot live birds is to shoot live birds. No pheasant ever flushed as fast as a clay target." The way he and his boys dropped birds ahead of dogs without the benefit of skeet training made it all sound convincing.

PRACTICE

I still believe the old dog trainer, who has long since gone to his reward, was absolutely right: The best way to learn bird shooting is to shoot birds. You don't become a champion golfer by spending your time at the bowling alley, do you? Through the years, however, I have come to realize it is unlikely I will have the chance to shoot hundreds or thousands of birds each year unless I happen to be a Persian prince with countless oil wells pumping for me or a successful dog trainer who releases birds that are paid for by his clients. So, what can we mere mortals do to improve our lot with the shotgun?

We can shoot clay targets, of course, but with an entirely different frame of mind than the dog trainer, my friend or I had when we were critical of clay saucers for training and practicing. I am no longer skeptical about the role of clay targets in the honing of wing-shot skills; they indeed will serve the purpose if you have your head on straight and go into skeet, trap, Sporting Clays or behind-the-barn hand-trapshooting knowing fully what to expect and what you wish to achieve.

BEWARE THE MECHANICAL SWING

The biggest mistake you can make as a hunter is letting yourself be duped into taking a tournament shooter's mechanical view of the clay-target games. That was the mistake I made on that fateful morning when I tried to equate my first two grouse of the new season with skeet stations so I could apply skeet techniques. I believe it was also my friend's mistake when he tried to visualize skeet leads on highballing Canadian ducks. The grooved, mechanical swings of an inanimate-target contest are not especially effective afield where you get all sorts of unexpected angles and unknown distances; that sort of mechanical approach is useful mainly in tournaments, where you must repeat the same moves all day with the measured cadence of a metronome.

This doesn't mean hunters can't benefit

Another example of how similar field and target shooting are. This Sporting Clays' shooter is starting after a pair of targets heading behind a tree like a brace of grouse. His moves will be the same...

The added necessity of mounting under pressure lessens your chances of becoming a groove gunner because it lengthens the physical aspects of the shot.

What about the artificialities of clay-target fields and the high starting speed of the targets? You must always understand that no practice field can ever perfectly match actual bird hunting. At best, even the most realistic layout will be limited in its ability to simulate game, and it will throw targets significantly faster than wild game can fly. The purpose of the practice is to stress your technique and refine it by making you move swifter than you ever have before. This emphasis on enhanced reaction time and movement speed should carry you to an advanced level of performance. It's like an Olympic sprinter training by dashing downhill to get the experience of doing it faster than he feels on the level and learn to coordinate under extreme pressure so the same moves can be

from clay-target shooting. Far from it. What it means is a field shot must work his clays using the gun-handling routine and more-upright stance of field shooting. You should start with your gun down, initiating the mounting move only when the target is airborne, and you are better off if you don't try to establish a mathematical lead, but rather swing each target as if it were an entirely new challenge. By so doing, you will find your clay-target practice closer resembles the moves you make afield. The process is more realistic, and therefore, helps to create coordination, timing and smoother overall gun handling.

...as those of this hunter who just flushed a bird that's curving around a bush toward heavier cover in the background. Both are starting gun-down — and both have to hurry!

made more gracefully at conventional speeds.

Sports psychologists have learned that improvement comes with pressure to reach a new level; it doesn't come gradually by practicing the same old laggardly moves. Thus, a hunter using low-gun practice at skeet Stations Two and Six will surely improve his upland gun-mounting technique, and a duck hunter who starts with a lowered gun on skeet Stations Three, Four and Five will learn the physical and mental rhythm of taking crossing shots. Grouse and quail may not fly the exact angles of skeet clays, and ducks will definitely be farther out much of the time, but the swing technique will be fundamentally the same.

DISCOVER F.I.T.A.S.C.

Hunters who are looking for one game that equates to much of the shooting found afield will want to try F.I.T.A.S.C. I won't elaborate on it here; Chapter 11 will handle it in more detail. If any game delivers hunting ranges, distances and myriad of angles, it is F.I.T.A.S.C. In rapid succession, I shot a F.I.T.A.S.C. tournament and a whitewing dove hunt in Mexico, and there was little

difference between many of the flying targets in the F.I.T.A.S.C. tournament and those doves in the Mexican sorghum fields.

THE ANSWER?

So, does clay-target shooting *really* relate to the field? Yes, but you must know what the clay targets can and cannot provide. They will not cackle like a pheasant, quack like a duck, honk like a goose or cluck like a sharptail. They are, pure and simple, moving marks that give you a chance to mount and swing. If you employ the basic stance and style you use afield, you will benefit from the experience. If you keep an open mind, you will know you are practicing gun work, not stacking up meat, but if you start to crouch like a tournament skeetman or begin with your gun up and hugged tightly like a trapshooter, you will derive little benefit for your field shooting.

Game shooting is rapid and varied, demanding quick reactions to new challenges. Shooting clays with a gun-down starting position can help you hone your gun-handling skills for the field, and F.I.T.A.S.C. does it best of all.

A sensibly set rabbit trap in Sporting Clays can help hunters learn how to handle low targets.

2

When Did Wing Shooting Really Start?

It is often said that the age of wing shooting didn't really get underway until the invention of percussion ignition by the Reverend Alexander Forsythe of Belhevie, Aberdeenshire, around 1806. And so it might seem, as percussion ignition simplified, speeded up and weatherproofed the vital ignition step in shotgunning, working an almost revolutionary advancement into the sport compared to the troublesome and inefficient ignition of the matchlocks and flinters. The enhanced speed of ignition obviously made it easier to time shots at flying targets with a swinging gun than it had been with the variously delayed ignition of the flintlocks, which invariably upset a shooter's timing.

Modern shooters can appreciate the chemical achievement made by Forsythe. Today gun tinkerers make very high-speed shotgun locks, and many trapshooters insist upon having them. I have heard one lock with an ultra-fast tumbler fall can get the load out of the barrel before another slower lock can even pop the primer! We speak in terms of milliseconds, whereas the old flintlocks ignited with an initial "*poof*!" in the firing pan followed by the "*whoosh*" and "*whomp*" of the black powder moving out of the long barrel. Some people toy with flinters in trapshooting these days, mostly folks who like the old-time guns and gather together for buckskin events, but the value of percussion ignition goes unquestioned. Indeed, I see very few flinters betting their dollars against a modern Perazzi or Ljutic!

The question is, however, did wing shooting start with Forsythe's invention around the time of the War of 1812 or were hunters already swinging on flying birds by then? It didn't take much delving into history to learn that the skills for shooting moving targets were already being practiced long before Forsythe entered the picture. I have not found every book on the subject of shotgunning, of course, but those I have uncovered indicate wing shooting was being tried as early as the 16th century.

EARLY BEGINNINGS

The *Weidmannslied*, which dates to 1560, reflected basically European trends and indicated shooting birds on the wing was already a practice prior to *its* publication. On the other side of the world, a Japanese author, Nagasawa Shagetzuma, wrote *The Book Of Firearms* in 1612 which showed that younger Japanese shot at flying birds while riding at full gallop on horseback. Talk about your macho stunts!

From extant literary sources, it is apparent

Wing shooting was established well before percussion ignition, perhaps as early as the 16th century.

the Europeans were ahead of the British in both wing shooting skills and gunmaking at this time. As Charles Trench reflects in his 1972 publication, *A History Of Marksmanship*, "Exiled [British] Cavaliers were astonished at the skill of the Continental gentry, and no wonder when Louis XIV, for example, once killed 32 pheasant on the wing with 34 shots."

Trench cites another English author who, in 1717, was wowed by the French in particular, noting that, "It is as rare for a professed marksman of that race to miss a bird as it is for one of ours to kill one."

By the late 17th century, the British were catching on, however. The concept seems to have taken hold, or at least been recognized in England between 1677 and 1686. In 1677, Nicholas Cox wrote a book entitled *The Gentleman's Recreation*, and wing shooting wasn't mentioned; when the second edition was printed in 1686, however, illustrations showed sportsmen shooting at flying partridge.

According to those who research shotgunning literature, this 1686 edition of Cox's book bore the first-ever instructions for shooting on-the-wing as well as the first endorsement of the method. Cox wrote:

"It is now the mode to shoot flying, as being by experience found the best and surest way, for when your game is on the wing it is more exposed to danger; for if but one shot hits any part of its wings so expanded, it will occasion its fall, although not to kill it, so that your spaniel will soon be its victor."

To that point, Cox did just fine, but thereafter the reader begins to think Cox himself must have done little more sport than play cricket, as his next advice sends shivers up and down my spine:

"The gun most proper for this sport should be about four and a half foot

long in the barrel and of a pretty wide bore, something under a musket. You should have your gun always cocked in readiness, with your thumb over the cock for fear of its going off contrary to your intention, so that when you meet with any game, you must be quick, and having got an aim to your mind, let fly with all expedition."

I wonder how many hunter-education teachers today would endorse Cox's idea of walking about with a hammer gun cocked at all times!

I also question the advice penned by Cox in his discussion of whether or not to lead flying birds:

"Some are of the opinion that you must shoot something before the fowl, otherwise it will be past before the shot will meet it; but that is vulgar error, for no game can fly so quick but that the shot will meet it; for the shot flyeth as wide as about the compass of a bushel, if rightly ordered in the charge."

Again, this proved to be controversial commentary. History disputes Cox's idea that you don't have to lead moving marks. Even patterns that open to the size of a bushel basket don't compensate for the target's speed. At least the discipline had been started in England, and writers after Cox refined matters, just as British gunsmiths refined the break-action double once they picked it up from the French.

While early British writers struggled with the theory and practice of wing gunning, a Frenchman, Magné de Marolles, was busy setting down another version succinctly stating the very basics we know today.

"The real way not to miss crossing game, on the wing or running [the hare was, and still is, very much a part of British and European hunting], is not only to swing forward, but even more, to avoid involuntarily stopping your swing at the moment of pulling the trigger, as do most unskilled shots; because then the hand stops swinging to fire and in that instant, however brief, the bird, which does not stop, passes the line of aim and

is missed behind. It is essential to accustom the hand to follow the game without stopping."

In the 250 years or so since Magné de Marolles wrote this, no truer words have been spoken!

In the early 18th century, it was still as common to write in meter and verse as it was to write in prose, and those who wrote about wing shooting were no exceptions. A 1727 book called *The Art Of Shooting Flying* employed poetry to discuss the techniques for taking different angles of game birds on the wing. Here are excerpted verses which cover, in order, the incoming shot, straightaway and crosser.

When a bird comes directly to your face,
Contain your fire awhile and let her
    pass,
Unless some trees behind you change the
    case.
If so, a little space above her head
Advance the muzzle, and you strike her
    dead.
Ever let shot pursue when there is room;
Marks hard before thus easy will
    become.

But when the bird flies from you in a
    line,
With little care I can pronounce her
    thine;
Observe the rule before, and neatly raise
Your piece till there's no open under-
    space
Betwixt the object and the silver sight;
Then send away, and timely stop the
    flight.

The unlucky cross mark, or the traverse
    shoot,
By some thought easy (yet admits
    dispute,
As the most common practice is to fire
Before the bird) will nicest time require.
For, too much space allowed, the shot
    will fly
All innocent, and pass too nimbly by;
Too little space, the partridge, swift as
    wind,

*Will dart athwart, and bilk her death
behind.*

I'm certain few publishers today would run their how-to features in meter and verse, but in the 1700s the practice was in vogue and these verses were undoubtedly accepted by the hunters who read them. Of course, we no longer advocate letting incoming birds pass before shooting as in the first verse above, but that is a matter of the evolution of techniques. The point is, the art of wing shooting was obviously established well before the advent of percussion ignition.

THE TRANSITION

We can, however, interpret Forsythe's invention of percussion ignition as the transition from the beginning of wing shooting to our modern practices — the pivot point, let's say. Forsythe may have been a clergyman, but he was also a waterfowler, and in his hunts he noticed ducks and geese often flared upon seeing the flash of a flintlock's ignition system and scattered before the main ignition took place. Flashpans were exposed to the elements and moisture, not an uncommon factor in waterfowling, hindered positive ignition, and sometimes the wind blew the powder from the pan. Being a learned man for his age, Forsythe applied his observations and chemical knowledge to the problem.

Forsythe knew about chlorate of potassium and fulminate of mercury and that they produced a hot, sharp flash when ignited, so he first used them in the flashpan of his flintlock for improved ignition, but they did not generate enough force when set off by the sparks from a flintlock device. He then went further and studied chemicals that detonated with greater energy when unleashed by percussion. The rest is history — how he incorporated the mixture into a lock of his own design and fought the government red tape and how his

Before percussion ignition, hunters were plagued with moisture hindering ignition, wind blowing powder from the pan and ducks bolting at the sight of the flash of the ignition.

percussion-ignition system was at first rejected, even by the British military.

Finally, Forsythe, frustrated in his attempts to *give* the idea to the British army, teamed up with James Purdey to produce percussion muzzleloaders. However, the harsh hand of British tradition came down heavily in criticism of the project. One British publication, *The Gentleman's Magazine*, editorialized against percussion ignition as a way to get more-positive ignition in bad weather by opining that, ". . .gentlemen do not go sporting in that sort of weather." Ah, tradition!

Editorials could not overcome the common sense of hunters, thank goodness, and in a short time the tandem of Forsythe and Purdey was changing the course of shotgunning. Eventually, they came up with the idea of enclosing the new priming mixture in a small tin cup rather than pouring it into a detonating chamber to receive the hammer blow. The primed cup was positioned atop an anvil, and the rotating tumbler compressed the mixture between itself and the anvil to produce a very sharp explosion. The muzzleloading percussion gun was thus carried a step further, and the whole idea of a breechloading gun became possible.

Hunters had been wing shooting for perhaps 250 to 300 years before modern percussion ignition came along, but I'm sure glad it did. Aren't you?

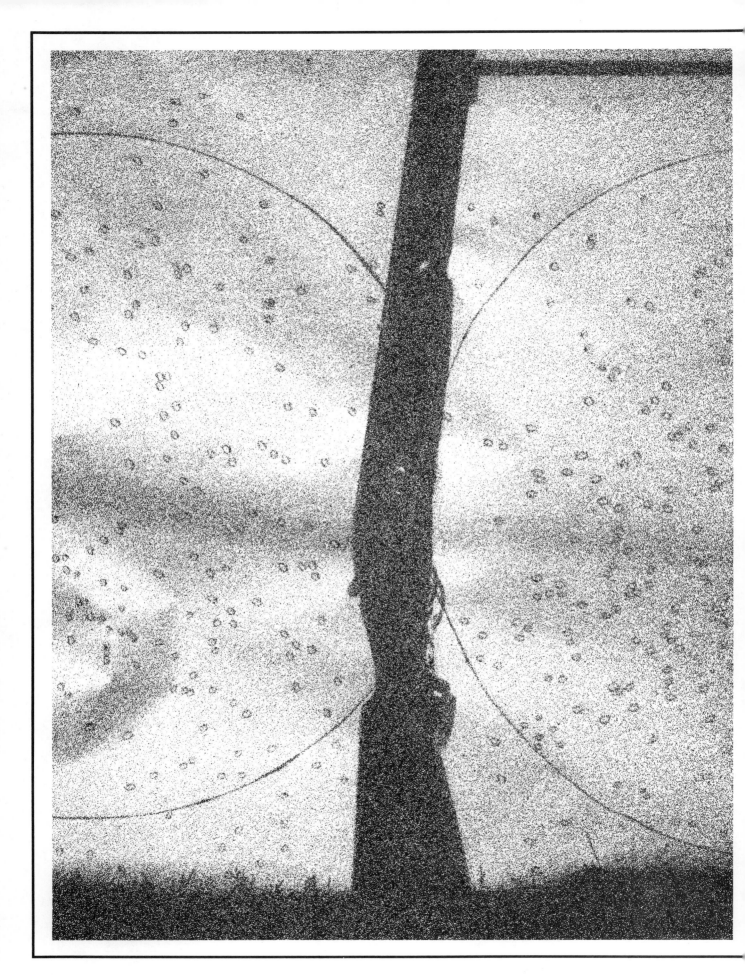

3

What Makes A Scattergun Scatter?

Here we are, all experienced shotgunners, and I begin this chapter by asking a silly, simple question like that! What produces the various scattering effects that take place when a shot charge leaves a smoothbore's muzzle? The typical answer is something called "choke," meaning a narrowing of the bore at or near the muzzle. Heck, it's common knowledge Full chokes hold the tightest shot strings, Modifieds are for medium ranges and Improved Cylinders (IC's) are for close-flushing birds. There are a couple of other constrictions: Improved Modified (IM) which splits the difference between Modified and Full as a trapshooting specialty and, in recent years, a pretty good choice for steel shot; and Skeet choke, which can be a variety of open-patterning configurations that give wider close-range clusters than Improved Cylinder. We all know about those things, so why bother to ask?

The concept of choke has been around since about the time of the American Civil War. Research into the subject even finds mention of choke boring as early as the 1700s, but there is still a question as to who actually invented it.

I don't think we will ever know who was the first gun tinkerer to chomp down on the muzzle-end of a smoothbore in an attempt to control shot distribution. Americans often point to Fred Kimble, an Illinois duck hunter, as the first to master choke in the late 1860s, but even those who knew and admired Kimble agree the *idea* was around prior to Kimble's use of it.

One of those who is said to have used choke boring earlier than Kimble was Jeremiah Smith of Rhode Island, whose choke work has been traced back to the late 1820s. On a patent basis, American inventor Sylvester Roper was the first to file for rights to a shotgun choke system in April of 1866. The Roper Choke was, believe it or not, a screw-on system threaded to the muzzle! Talk about being ahead of your time. A gunsmith in England named Pape filed for a choke patent about six weeks after Roper did stateside.

It appears, then, that shotgun chokes have been around for a long time. As a concept, it is generally understood and accepted, but how and why does it all work? Why would a shot charge that is run through a full-choked barrel hold a tighter pattern than one that is shot through an IC choke when there is just a measly difference of 0.030″ between them?

Generally, Full chokes have diameters of 0.040″ down to about 0.035″, while IC's have anywhere from 0.005″ to 0.010″ of constriction. That paltry difference of 0.030″ to 0.035″ simply can't firm up a shot charge meaningfully — it just can't! Therefore, choke

Wads don't just cushion against pellet deformation and prevent powder-gas seepage; modern plastic wads influence pattern density and shot-string length, depending upon their design. Slit petals like these open and act as brakes to slow the wads and prevent them from ramming the pellets.

constriction alone doesn't explain pattern development; it is merely a part of a more-complex system. The next question is: How does it fit into the overall phenomenon of pattern development?

A DYNAMIC DUO

There is, indeed, more to pattern development than just the degree of choke in a shotgun's muzzle segment. Choke constriction plays an important role, but in reality, it is a static part of the system; equally vital are a pair of dynamic forces which work in concert with the choke constriction to actually shape the shot charge as it enters free flight. These forces are: 1) the pressure of the wad on the base of the shot charge as it clears the muzzle and 2) the air resistance (drag) that works against the pellets once they are in free flight away from the urging of the wad and powder gases.

For many shooters, the inclusion of air resistance as a factor in pattern development will be a surprise. Many shooters think only of a tight choke narrowing the shot string and an open choke letting the pellets out in a pancake mass. As I just tried to show, however, the difference in the diameter of a Full choke and an IC isn't enough to affect such shot string formation by itself. The actual mathematical difference between a bona fide Full and an IC choke is significantly less than the diameter of a #10 pellet. The real work of shaping up the in-flight pattern is done by the wad pressure and air-drag factor.

THE AIR-RESISTANCE FACTOR

The force imposed by air molecules is not taken into consideration by most casual hunters and shooters. It is hardly noticeable as you stand on a trap field's handicap stripe nor does it worry a hunter as he walks up behind a quivering pointer. That is because humans encounter air at a low speed, but when you are driving along in your car and stick your hand out the window while doing 60 m.p.h. you notice a definite force pushing your hand backward. That's air resistance, and it works harder against a shot charge and each individual pellet than it does against your hand because the pellets are moving a lot faster.

A 3-drams equivalent trap load with a velocity around 1,200 f.p.s., for instance, is moving at something like 800 m.p.h., while a high-brass, 3¾-drams equivalent hunting load with 1¼ ounces of 6's in the 12 gauge is reaching just beyond 900 m.p.h. Even at 40 yards, those 6's are still doing around 500 m.p.h.; thus, they bump into substantially more air resistance than your hand does at 60 m.p.h.!

Just like the air moves your hand around and pushes it backward, so does it alter the flight of pellets, causing them to scatter and string out depending upon the impact the wad had at the muzzle. Let's take a closer look at the wad's role in shaping the shot string.

THE BATTERING RAM

Shooters think of a wad as just being something that cushions the pellets against deformation and seals against powder-gas seepage. Wads do provide those services, generally speaking, and some do it better than others, but there is one more thing a wad does, and that is influence pattern density and shot-string length as it rams variously into the shot charge at the moment of emission.

A wad being pushed through the bore by thousands of pounds of gas pressure will not stop abruptly at the muzzle and fall down – *kerplunk*! – no way. Because of gas pressure still on its tail and its own momentum, the wad keeps moving.

In the old days when wad columns were still comprised of nitro-card overpowder discs and heavily waxed fillers, they would shoot into the shot charge like a battering ram and force the interior pellets to the outside, resulting in a blown or "donut" pattern. This battering-ram effect has been moderated substantially by the use of plastic shotcup wads that have slit petals that open and act as air

brakes to slow the wad and keep it from shooting through the pellet mass. Wad pressure is, nevertheless, still a factor in shot charge shaping, as there is some wad/shot impingement at exit.

Now that you know about the wad's influence on the shot charge, you can put it all together and see how wad pressure, choke constriction and air resistance work to form patterns and shot strings.

PUTTING IT ALL TOGETHER

In your mind's eye, conjure up a slow-motion picture of a shot charge rambling up the bore of a shotgun. It is encased in the shotcup of a plastic wad, which is sealing powder gases and is being driven to constantly higher velocities. It takes a shot charge about 0.003-second to go from a static mass in the chamber to the muzzle, in which time it accelerates to at least 1,200 f.p.s. That's a wheel-spinning start, and it puts momentum into both the wad and pellets, which is an important thing to remember.

Now we come to that split instant when the pattern begins to shape up. The wad/shot tandem encounters the choke taper and more happens here than just a narrowing of the shot charge, which alone doesn't amount to much. We have already discussed this above, but when a shot charge goes from the 0.729″ diameter of a standard 12 gauge to the 0.695″ diameter of a full-choked barrel, it really isn't being swaged down meaningfully. What is more important is how the choke taper impacts the wad.

A tighter choke pinches down on the wad, slowing it and letting the shot charge escape with little or no wad pressure. At the other extreme, a cylinder-bored barrel or light Skeet choke let the wad pretty much slide through without deterring it, meaning it can remain up against the base of the shot charge. Between those extremes we have IC, which pinches the wad just slightly; Modified, which applies a heavier hand on the wad; and IM, which comes down almost as hard as a Full choke on the wad. Thus, the way the choke constriction

A Modified choke (left) slows pellets more than a Cylinder bore but less than a Full choke (right). There is enough wad pressure and air resistance to flatten the string into a wide pattern. In contrast, pellets spurt through a Full choke to give a longer string that stays together for a tight pattern.

slows the wad determines, at least in part, how the shot charge emerges. At the point of emergence, we encounter air resistance.

THE PANCAKE EFFECT

You have probably heard the expression about being caught between a rock and a hard place. Well, that's the way a shot charge must feel when it bursts from the muzzle of a shotgun. Behind it are thousands of pounds of gas pressure; ahead of it is air resistance. Because air resistance works harder against fast-moving objects than it does against slower ones, the immediate impact of air resistance is felt by the pellets, and they slow abruptly during their first few feet of travel.

Pattern and shot string formation now depend upon how powerful the rear-end wad pressure is. If it is fierce, as in the case of a cylinder-bored barrel, the shot charge is virtually pancaked between the opposing forces of wad pressure and air resistance and the pellets spread sideways as the wad bumps them and air drag slows them, resulting in a wide pattern.

In a Full choke, the wad is slowed more noticeably. The choke constriction retards the wad and the pellets narrow down to squeeze through the narrow opening. Pellets tend to spurt through a Full choke because the narrowing is a minor obstruction, so they escape in a longer line and, because the wad is delayed by the choke taper, the pellets continue on a straighter course despite air resistance because they are not being rammed from behind as in the case of a Cylinder bore.

Initially, a Full choke shows a longer shot string than a Cylinder bore, and photos of emerging shot masses prove this. Downrange, however, the reverse becomes true; Cylinder bore has a longer shot string than the Full choke. Why? The wide distribution of a Cylinder bore exposes most pellets individually to air resistance right from the start of their free flight, whereas in a long, stringy full-choke mass, a lot of pellets don't feel air resistance due to the windbreaking effect of the leading pellets. This is something like the windbreaking role of the leading runner in a foot race or the leading goose in a wedge. They create a vacuum in which the air-drag factor is lowered, and the trailing pellets can retain more of their initial velocity.

Because the trailing pellets of a full-choked load can clip along with somewhat less air drag slowing them, they also tend to remain bunched together; their energies are used to go forward, not at an outward angle to the bore axis. The full-choke pattern develops because there is less wad pressure on the base of the shot charge at exit thanks to the slowing effect of the tight constriction and because air resistance impacts fewer pellets initially. The full-choked string isn't pancaked between a hard-driving wad and stiff air resistance like that of a Cylinder bore.

WHAT ABOUT MODIFIED CHOKE?

Modified choke, known to the British as "half choke," has about half as much constriction as Full choke, say, 15 to 22 points. It varies from maker to maker, of course, but what this tells us is that the wad is being slowed more than it is in a Cylinder bore or Skeet choke but less than in a Full choke. The result is some pellets escape without being hammered from the rear, and these, like those of a Full choke, tend to remain in the core of the cluster and break wind for the trailing shot.

The lower layers of shot are bumped by the emerging wad, as the modified-choke constriction isn't enough to thwart the wad entirely. These lower layers are sort of pancaked like those of a Skeet choke, so they angle outwardly and feel air resistance individually. The pellets which escape first in a modified-choked gun will fill the core of the pattern, while those emerging last will be influenced by the trailing wad and will be urged to the outside to contribute to a somewhat broader spread than with the Full choke at closer ranges between 20 to 35 yards.

HIGH-ALTITUDE PERFORMANCE

If anything proves the importance of air resistance in pattern development, it is testing at high altitude. The air is lighter a mile above sea level, and because the 1968 Olympics were held at Mexico City some tests were run to learn how shotguns perform in lighter air. The results were tighter patterns across the board for each gun/load combo checked.

The 1990 United States Sporting Clays Association (USSCA) National Championships were shot on a mountainside near Colorado Springs. At that altitude, the light IC choke I was using with a 5-point constriction broke birds decisively at distances well beyond what you might equate with IC patterning. My assumption is the lighter air, which also made people gasp as they climbed, had a tightening effect on the patterns.

It has been theorized that a Cylinder bore shot in a vacuum would deliver 100-percent patterns all day long thanks to the absence of air resistance. The pellets could travel straight ahead, outrunning the wad's disastrous impact from behind. Choke, then, is important only as it retards or does not retard the wad and how it shapes the shot charge for its impact with air resistance. Wad pressure and air resistance are what make a scattergun scatter.

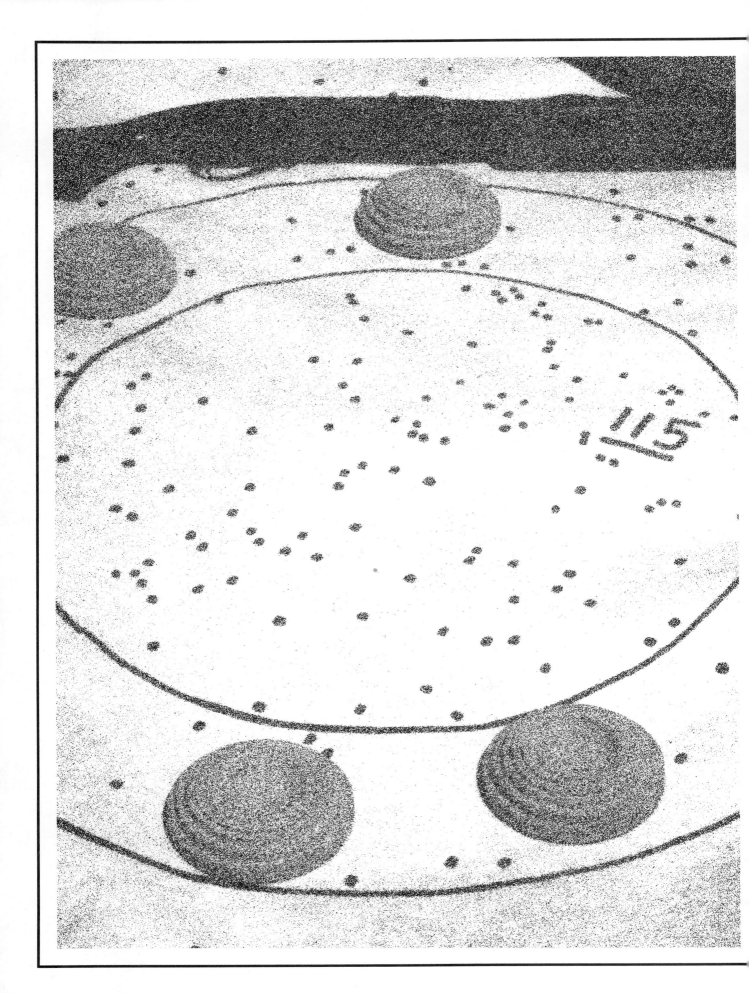

4

Practical Patterning

Shotgun patterning is sort of like the weather – everybody talks about it, but no one ever does anything about it. Screw-in choke tubes have made hunters and clay-target shooters very conscious of choke/pattern changing, but most shotgun owners don't have the foggiest idea what those tubes do with the loads fired through them. Indeed, most talk about patterns takes far too much for granted, since each choke/load combination can pattern differently. I just finished running some pattern tests through a modified-choked barrel with a 19-point (0.019″) constriction, and the variety of reloads I ran through that gun gave patterns which ranged from snug Improved Cylinder (IC) to early Full choke.

There's more to patterning than merely finding percentages and distributions. There is also the simple matter of determining accuracy, namely, learning if your gun is shooting where you're pointing it. Although we like to believe the gun we've just bought is perfect in every detail, there are times when that isn't exactly so!

PATTERNING FOR ACCURACY

When we were fresh out of high school, a friend of mine blew one of his first paychecks on a new 12-gauge autoloader, had a Poly-Choke attached and took it out to the local gun club's annual merchandise shoot. They were holding ten-shot events in skeet and trap,

and my friend stepped right into a skeet round and missed nine out of ten shots! Well, he had to get used to the new gun, didn't he? He twisted the Poly's collar to Cylinder bore, signed up again and missed another nine targets. Well, maybe skeet wasn't his game.

He switched to trap. After tightening the Poly to Full choke, he picked up right where he had left off in skeet and missed them all! What the heck was wrong?

Knowing he wasn't that bad of a shot, I suggested he pattern his new gun. One of the club members had a few sheets of cardboard, so we slipped away with the Poly still set on Full choke and shot directly into the center of that cardboard from 40 steps. You can imagine my friend's frustration when we found only a few pellet holes nipping the cardboard's right edge! His gun was shooting markedly to the right, practically missing the entire area of the cardboard.

After a gunsmith straightened that barrel, my friend did extremely well with it. He was lucky, really; if he had taken the gun hunting without ever patterning it for accuracy, he could easily have wasted a whole season.

I once had a similar thing happen with an imported side-by-side (SxS) 20-gauge Magnum. Doubles are generally regulated to superimpose their patterns at 40 yards, so when I got that cutie home I set up a patterning sheet at 40 yards and proceeded to test my 3″ reloads. The gun proved to be cockeyed. It sent the left barrel's shot string well to the right and the right barrel's cluster put only its fringe pellets on the left side of the sheet at 40 yards. I would have had a fine time shooting mallards 45 to 50 yards high with that gun regardless of the patterns' densities. Obviously, it went back to the maker *posthaste*!

Manufacturing mistakes do occur and can be a factor in shotgun accuracy. We may not aim scatterguns *per se*, but your guns should at least deliver patterns to the correct point. The most natural eye/hand coordination in the world can miss if the gun doesn't shoot where your eye is looking! If for no other reason, then, you should at least pattern your guns to learn their respective points-of-impact.

SHOOTING SLUGS WITHOUT SIGHTS

Many hunters go deer hunting with slugs using just their bird guns without any sighting devices other than the gun's rib and/or beads. This is wrong! Shotgun slugs and loads of fine shot or buckshot don't invariably print to the same point-of-impact. A shotgun which centers its birdshot loads just fine when you line up the front bead with the matted receiver top will often punch its rifled slugs to some other point because slugs have different velocities and vibrational patterns than shot charges.

All gun barrels vibrate as a load fires and moves through the bore, and loads will exit while the muzzle is at different points in its vibrational movement. In my experience, shotguns without sights can shoot low with 1 to 1¼-ounce slugs. I had several autoloaders that sent slugs 12″ to 15″ low when I aimed with the front bead in the matted receiver top, while an identical hold with birdshot rounds centered the pattern. Don't believe your old duck gun is automatically a precise slug gun just because you line up with a squinty-eyed hold; barrel vibration patterns and different exit velocities can cause marked discrepancies in points-of-impact between slugs and shot loads in the same gun.

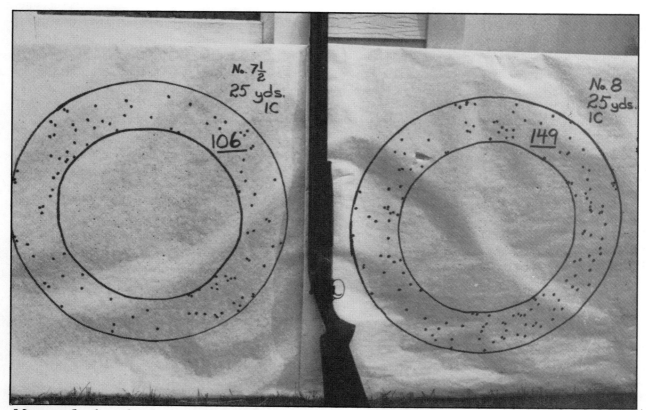

Most gun/load combos have ample core density at average ranges; the outer ring is where they differ. These patterns were shot by the same barrel/choke. Which would you prefer for Sporting?

SIMPLIFIED PATTERNING

In Chapter 7, I write about the vagaries of gun/load performance, and anyone who bothers to do a thorough job of pattern reading according to the scientific steps of the Berlin-Wanasse or Thompson-Oberfell methods knows such vagaries can be subtle or blatant. However, few hunters and clay-target shooters even consider doing a detailed study of their gun's patterns. If they pattern at all, they want to know the simplest method, and the more I pattern, the more I have begun to see the advantages of using a less-elaborate system.

One simplified patterning method I have come to enjoy is based on an analysis of the so-called "annular ring" of patterns. To explain the concept of an annular ring, let me begin by saying experts anticipate finding two different distributions in any shotgun pattern. One of these is the "core" of the pattern, which is the center; the other is the "annular ring," also known as the "outer ring," which is the area between the core and the main 30″-diameter circle. In other words, it looks like a big donut. The cores in my patterns have a diameter of 20″, which means the annular ring occupies the outer 5″ strip surrounding the core.

The reason the outer ring is so important is twofold. First, a shotgun's main purpose is to provide a wide hitting area, and if you want to utilize your shotgun for optimum effectiveness, it is the outer ring which will provide that quality. Indeed, what is the value of a scatter-gun if it doesn't provide a beneficial scatter? Second, despite the popular idea a shotgun invariably spreads its shot charge around, we know there is a tendency for shotguns to hold a lot of pellets in the center of their shot strings. This happens because pellets which remain round generally fly relatively straight routes to the target and eventually strike on the core, leaving the outer ring sparsely popu-lated and weak. This tendency toward high center density is increased with such things as hard, high-antimony lead shot which with-stands setback pressures; copper or nickel-plated shot; and steel shot, which doesn't de-form at all. Thus, even open-bored guns –

Cylinder bore, Skeet choke and Improved Cylinder – can and do hammer dense cores without filling out the annular ring efficiently. If you want to get the maximum benefit from a given degree of choke, it should provide clean-killing coverage in the annular ring as well as the core.

ASSESSING THE ANNULAR RING

Although the industry's standard patterning range is 40 yards into a 30″-diameter circle, that is not always the most practical way to do it. To assess the quality of any gun/load combo's annular ring, you should figure your average working range and test over that distance. A skeet shooter, for instance, is better off patterning at 17 to 20 yards than 40 yards or even 21 to 25 yards, because most skeet clays are snapped up before they reach the center of the field, which is 21 yards according to NSSA dimensions. A trapshooter could pattern at 32 to 35 yards for 16-yard events and 40 yards for optimum handicap distances. Hunters who find their average shot at woodcock is 15 yards can use that figure, while goose hunters who take long shots over 55 yards should measure off that yardage for their testing.

Once the distance is established and the patterning sheet is set up, the shot should be fired into a blank sheet of paper or cardboard. There can be a centered aiming point, of course, but the 30″ and 20″-diameter circles should not be drawn prior to the shot. They are inscribed only after the blast around the area of greatest density. This is done because shotguns aren't accurate enough to center their patterns in pre-drawn circles.

The point of emphasis becomes the annular ring. Assuming your choke selection has been appropriate for the range, the 20″-diameter core will almost invariably be dense enough throughout for effective hits. In the most prac-tical and simplified sense, your goal is to learn which of several potential loads puts the most pellets into the annular ring and spreads them evenly over the most area. The first part of your goal should be self-explanatory; the more pellets the annular ring picks up, the better the

Most patterns look pretty good to the eye, and many hunters would say this one is okay, but when you place clay targets in the pellet-free patches...

pattern's ability to find the target's vital areas if it's a game bird or make a positive break if it is a clay bird. Multiple hits are the key to efficient shotgunning.

The second part of your goal may require some further elaboration. Although we blandly talk in terms of 30″ patterns, actual shooting proves a full 30″ spread of shot at working range is often mythical. The outer 2″ to 3″ of an annular ring are seldom dense and virtually never even. It is very important to eyeball the position of the hits within the annular ring, as a mere tally doesn't tell the entire story. I have seen patterns with heavy annular-ring counts where practically all the holes were within 2″ to 3″ of the core circle, while the outer 2″ to 3″ of the 30″ circle were bare. Indeed,

my own feeling is modern shotguns and loads do a far better job of filling out 27″ to 28″ of pattern and the 30″-concept is rather absurd. There is a need to eyeball the annular-ring

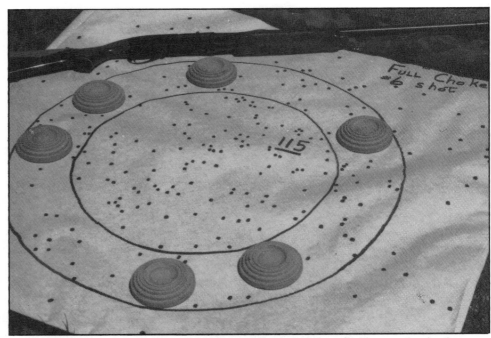

...you get this — a pattern with plenty of potential to feather and cripple on annular-ring hits. A clay target is about the size of many game birds' vital areas.

distribution critically for evenness of coverage as well as density when judging a load.

HOW MUCH IS ENOUGH

How many pellets are needed in the annular ring? That's really a moot question. My answer could be you should have as many as possible, especially for hunting, because I firmly believe hunters hit more frequently with the annular ring than they do with the core. Exactly what this means in terms of numbers depends upon the target and pellet size, of course. For minimum effectiveness, I might venture a guess that three pellets are needed in every area that can be covered by a clay target, since a clay target is about the size of the vital area of most game birds. Having that density would put at least two to three pellets on target. Frankly, I would prefer more

pellets for optimum shock and a better chance to impact the vital spots, but the fringe weakness I have seen tells me it's difficult to reach this ideal.

To check for effective pattern density, then, place a clay target flat on the pattern and slide it around in the annular ring. If there are places where it covers less than three to four pellets, the pattern can be judged variously weak.

After checking just a few patterns in this manner, you will gain a new respect for the inherent foibles of shotguns, because you will find them less than potent as they open into the extremities of the annular ring. You will see that various loads can be entirely different in the way they populate the annular ring, and you will be glad you started patterning to find a combination which gives you the best density *plus* distribution.

The Fringe Factor

If you were to do all your patterning into a 20″-diameter circle, you would find practically every gauge, including the dinky .410 bore, can generate enough density for clean kills on game. This is especially so with full-choked guns and a lot of those marked Modified. Characteristically, in-flight shot strings keep the round, relatively undeformed pellets in the core, while pellets suffering from deformation flare outwardly. Even with low-antimony shot, such as those around two to three-percent antimony, there tends to be enough upper-end pellets to produce adequate center density.

Once you get beyond the 20″-diameter core of a shotgun pattern, however, you begin to see weaknesses in the form of low density and/or pellet-free patches. It is this area between the 20″-diameter core and the outer ring of the 30″-diameter circle, known as the annular ring, which causes a lot of crippled and lost birds.

My own penchant for the 12 gauge isn't based on overall load weight but rather on the fact the 12's heavier shot charges have the potential to fill out the annular ring and fringe areas better than the lighter loads of the

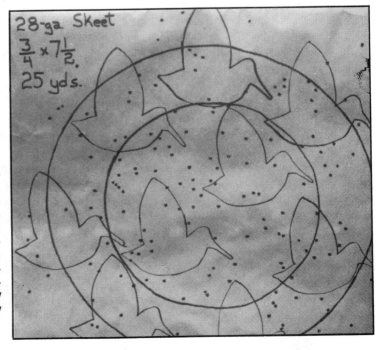

Many hunters talk about patterns but have never really seen or analyzed one critically. Although the center 20″ of most patterns can be effective on game, the outer ring is often weak and the fringe of the main 30″ circle is prone to crippling birds or chipping clay targets. This picture of a 28 gauge's 25-yard pattern with #7½ shot shows how thin the pattern can be outside the 20″-diameter core. Note how few pellets some of the woodcock silhouettes have picked up — they would be cripples for sure!

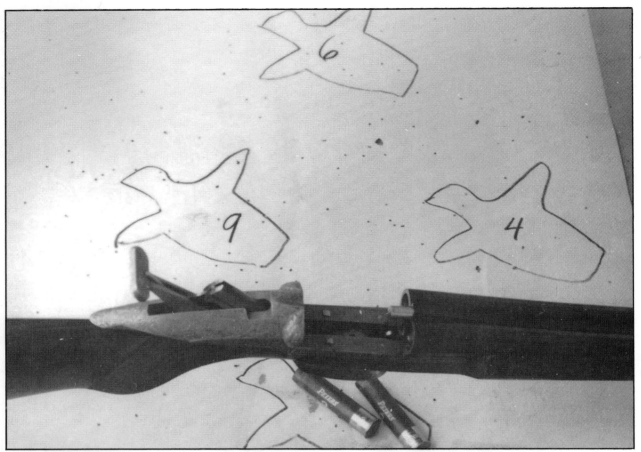

Here's another 28-gauge pattern shot against quail outlines. Check how few hits recorded in each outline and note the distance between pellets.

smaller gauges and .410 bore. If a hunter were able to work only with the center 20″ of a pattern, he could be totally indifferent to gauge. As I said, practically any of them with the right load can do the job on game birds, hares or rabbits; it's when you miss with the 20″ core that crippling and wastage occur.

TALES OF WOE

These conclusions have not been based on sheer patterning. Much of my original patterning was done to determine why I did not drop birds when I saw feathers fly. The answer proved to be that there were places inside the vaunted 30″-diameter patterning circle where less than killing pellet counts were evident.

A few seasons back, for example, I had a new .410 over & under (O&U) on consignment, and the only way to get a good idea

about how such a gun works is to take it hunting, right? This stackbarrel was bored Modified and Full but tended to pattern at full-choke levels from both barrels, giving pretty dense 20″ cores. Miss with that core, however, and the picture on the paper indicated very few pellets contacted the target.

I put in 3″ loads of 6's and went after a mixture of pheasant and chukar on a hunting preserve because the regular bird seasons had already closed. By some quirk, I dropped the two planted cock birds cleanly. Then came the chukar, and it was a different ball game.

The first chukar was a rising outgoer, and I saw it flinch slightly at the shot. The range was about 20 long strides, and I watched the partridge rise steeply, set its wings and sail over a hill. "We'll look for it later," my partner said, "Mark its line of flight." So doing, we worked on and came in behind another point. This chukar ran down some sorghum rows before it, too, flushed well out. The .410 spat from both tubes, and minimal rump fuzz fell away as the bird planed after the first one. We changed direction and followed the pair.

We had no idea where the birds came down, so we walked slowly and let the Brittany do its thing. Along the edge of a sorghum field, the dog began making the game. Finally, it made a solid point, but no bird went up; the Brit relocated, but still no flush. Finally, the spaniel dove into the growth and came up with a chukar that simply wouldn't fly. Later investigation showed us it had taken one pellet from the .410's fringe into its body cavity and had been weakened by the loss of blood. Had we not followed, it might have died as waste.

Try as we might, we couldn't locate the other chukar I had also visibly wounded. After a considerable expenditure of time, we headed back toward the clubhouse; halfway there the Brittany went on point in the distance. It was locked solidly at the base of the hill over which the birds had flown, and there in an open grassy area was the first chukar, stone dead with its wings outstretched. It, also, had taken some pellets into its posterior but had not felt enough shocking power to fold immediately. It apparently died in flight as it neared a landing.

The point is, of course, lack of pattern density caused the crippled and nearly lost birds. Probably one to two more pellets per bird would have dropped them immediately, but those pellets weren't present in the .410's fringe. This is my objection to many light loads in small gauges: Their fringes lack adequate density for clean kills when you miss with the 20″-diameter core of the shot string. To be very realistic about it, no one ever centers every target perfectly; sooner or later, the fringe will come into play, and at that point the gauge and load with the best potential for filling the annular ring will do the most humane job.

Birds hit by the fringe of a shot string may not look as if they have been hit, so conservation-minded hunters will follow them and check their landing sites; they may bleed out in flight and be dead on landing.

.410 STUFF AND NONSENSE

One of the biggest bits of nonsense in shot-gunning is the popular belief that with the .410 you either miss cleanly or kill cleanly. The center of a .410 pattern can knock down birds with amazing authority and suddenness, but that business about always missing cleanly — no way! Many birds that appear to be whiffed cleanly actually pick up only a solo pellet from the .410's ring or fringe, and that pellet can cause a slow death.

The same is often true of the 28 gauge, which can be a mini-powerhouse when you center a bird or bunny with its ¾-ounce load, but outside the 20″-diameter core, the 28 gauge has ample crippling potential. Luckily, a lot of people who use the 28 also have retrievers that make the little 28 look good. Moreover, it is easier to center a bird with the 28 than the .410 because the 28 is a heavier gun in most instances and, therefore, swings smoother. Lightweight .410's don't possess the momentum needed for smooth strokes and positive follow-throughs, so there is a lot of inaccurate pattern placement due to the sub-smallbore's whippy qualities. When you combine a whippy fowling stick with a weak pattern ring and fringe, the results can be disastrous.

Anyone who needs proof of the .410's weak fringe should shoot a round of skeet or trap with one. It will make no difference what the choke is or if you use 7½'s or 9's, during the course of the round some targets will be merely chipped or split by one-pellet hits. This is a result of the weak fringe. On clay targets it won't make any difference, of course, since any visible chip scores a dead bird, but the same rinky-dink hit on game, you must realize, can lead to a crippled and lost game bird or rabbit. Indeed, on many one-pellet hits the impact may not even be seen; you may think it is a total miss, and that's a tragedy.

It is not a case of hit or miss with the .410; the cigarette-sized shotshell has a weak and/or patchy fringe and is a crippler. Unfortunately, many sportsmen consider the .410 a "sporting" gun because they believe it gives the game a chance, but what is sporting for the hunter can be agony for game that is plinked by only one or two pellets and dies a lingering death in the weeds.

A .410 got these ringnecks but didn't anchor some chukar that flew 300 yards before landing. The .410 has a weak fringe that can cripple with one-pellet hits that look like misses.

THE BIG GUNS

This is not to say the .410 is the only bore that causes crippling — every gauge and pattern has a fringe. The point is, a heavy shot charge has a greater chance to put more pellets into the annular ring and fringe for better performance. The 1¼-ounce shot charges from the 12, 16 and 20 gauges sweeten the annular ring and increase the potential for clean-killing saturations on birds. The heavier the annular ring density, the broader the sure-kill hitting area, and the broader the sure-kill area, the better your chances of grassing targets solidly.

One of the best runs I ever had without losing a crippled bird was when I carried a Remington Model 1100 skeet gun with 1½-ounce short Magnums with 6's or 5's for ringnecks. That pattern gave me a reasonably even distribution of relatively heavy pellets at 15 to 30 yards, and I went for two seasons without a cripple. Then one day I swung too aggressively through a rising rooster and just raked him along the back, cutting only a feather or two; he went down, but his running gear was still in good order and I never saw him again. I'm not certain the pellet that

made contact even touched muscle; things get dicey for every pattern as you get away from the core.

I have a hunch one reason steel shot has a reputation for crippling is because steel loads tend to pattern very tightly and few hunters can center their ducks with a mere 20″-diameter core. So, they barely nip the duck with the outer fringe of their steel-shot cluster and, unless it's a lucky head/neck hit, the bird sails on or folds and swims away into the rushes. In the case of woodies or divers, they will splash in and dive from sight. When a hunter centers his ducks with steel, however, it's a dramatic kill. Hunters must begin to understand steel alone is not the culprit; pattern placement is important, and poor shooting has a lot to do with crippling. Neither lead nor steel can stop 'em cold when they're nipped only by the fringe.

Some seasons ago, I was grouse hunting with a friend who was using 3″ loads in a 20 gauge. There was snow on the ground and grouse tracks were everywhere. Along the edge of an alder and willow clump, he jumped a big cock bird which flew straight away from him

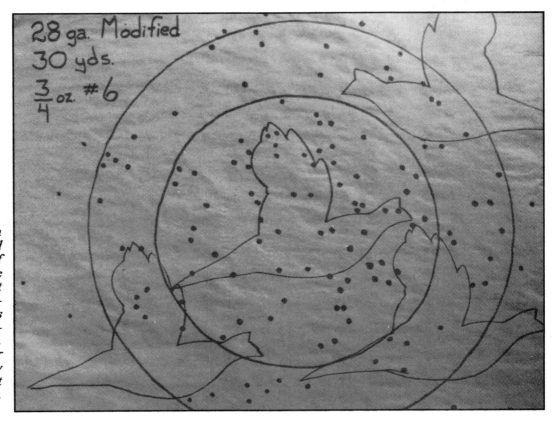

A bird as big as a ruffed grouse should absorb a lot of pattern, but these grouse profiles didn't all pick up clean-killing pellet counts from a modified-choked 28 gauge. The two lower birds would probably be cripples and not easy retrieves.

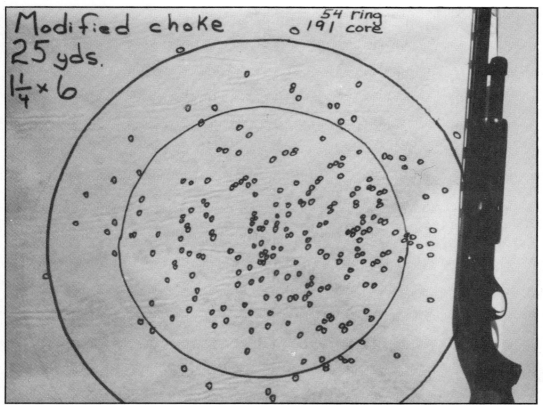

They say Modified choke is an all-around tube, but this Modified pattern shot at 25 yards shows the annular-ring area can nip a bird with only one pellet for a crippling hit.

and stayed quite low as it crossed a field of marsh grass headed for the pines. He shot twice, both times with the bird in acceptable range, but at no time did the bird give the appearance of being hit. After uttering a few expletives that I will delete here, he said, "It came down next to that tall pine on the edge. We can pick up its trail after we've worked out this edge." It sounded like a good plan.

When we got over to the tall pine, we saw no grouse tracks. We thought the bird may have flown past. I hunted into the pine and birch stand but couldn't pick up any prints. Then my partner, who had begun circling the pine, called, "Here he is!" The big cock grouse was already stiff; he had laid there, wings outstretched, while we hunted in the alders. When my partner cleaned the bird that evening, he found a pair of pellets had driven into the body cavity but hadn't caused enough shock or immediate damage to drop the bird. It apparently had bled to death as it sailed. If we hadn't marked it and tried to pick up its trail, we would not have found it and the bird

would have been a waste. We could have chalked up another one to a weak fringe hit!

MAKE SURE YOU MISSED

The moral to all of this should be obvious. You may love bird hunting, wing shooting and shotguns, but you must realize a shotgun's pattern is less than 100-percent effective! This is true whether it's the pet Purdey that cost you $30,000 or the hand-me-down pump gun with which dear ol' grandfather killed more game than you'll ever see. The fringe areas of patterns are potential cripplers regardless of gauge, choke or shot size. Every pattern I ever shot, and there have been thousands, has had weak spots; miss with the core density, and you can have a cripple on your hands.

The important thing for you to realize is this potential exists. Follow up birds that have been shot at but don't seem hit despite the fact they were easy chances and looked good over the gun. You may have struck the

Whatever the gauge, there are usually enough pellets to give an effective 20" core, but when loads get lighter the annular ring and fringe become weak and prone to crippling.

bird as I did in the above examples. Watch where the bird comes down and make a point of hunting it out; look for signs of a hit, like loose feathers and/or tiny blood spots. It's something every sportsman and conservationist should do now that you know about the inevitable weaknesses in your shotgun patterns' fringes.

6

The Two Faces
Of Full Choke

Full-choked shotguns are supposed to shoot tighter patterns than those bored Improved Cylinder (IC) or Modified (M), and in most instances they do just that. The comparative adjective "tighter" is a relative term, however, not an absolute, and it leaves us with an important question: How tight is tight?

After decades of patterning with numerous Full (F) chokes and myriad ammunition types, I still find it impossible to answer that question. Practically every full-choked gun varies its performance depending upon the load. These performances take on two different characteristics: Some loads ram ultra-tight center densities which are useful mainly for trap handicap and very long hunting shots; other loads give patterns which, although still bona fide full-choke clusters of 70 percent or better, are somewhat broader and have more pellets outside the core for better effectiveness on 16-yard trap and game beyond 30 to 35 yards but not extreme shotgun range. When I checked different shotshells in full-choked guns at the patterning board, I found the ol' Full choke has two faces.

THE TWO FACES OF FULL

Several years ago, I spent a considerable amount of time with a single-barreled trap gun

that had a definite full-choke constriction, and during that time I had patterning averages as low as 58 percent at 40 yards and some up around 80 percent. That's a significant difference! A pattern that does 58 percent with 7½'s is putting about 197 to 200 pellets into a 30″ circle at 40 yards, while a pattern receiving 80 percent of a 1⅛-ounce load of 7½'s is picking up roughly 270 to 275 pellets. The difference is around 75 pellets, and that can mean a lot on the trap line or in the uplands. I'll gladly take another 75 pellets in my pattern any time!

This is not to say Full chokes that throw broader patterns automatically drop their percentages; they don't. I have had Full chokes that printed 75 percent or better at 40 yards while distributing pellets throughout the 30″-diameter circle; on the other hand, some Full chokes shot only 70 percent and bunched pellets into the very center of the pattern to give little more than 24″ of effective hitting area.

It is the pellet-distribution factor, *not* just overall pattern percentages, we are discussing here. It is a useful discussion, because the trapshooter who finds a load that will fill out the full 30″ circle at 35 to 40 yards without sacrificing percentages will have a lethal 16-yard and short-handicap gun/load combo; ditto for the hunter whose longest shots come between 35 and 45 yards. Conversely, a

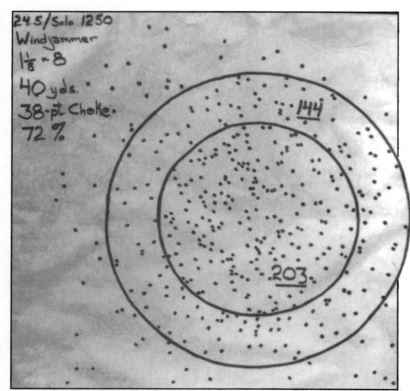

Handwritten on image:
24.5/Solo 1250
Windjammer
1⅛ × 8
40 yds.
38-pt Choke.
72%
144
203

A Full choke can perform differently while reaching its density of 70+%. This photo shows a bona fide Full can top 70% but give less center density with another load.

bore diameter and a choke constriction of 0.038″. That is Full choke by any industry standard, and introductory patterning showed that barrel generally slammed ultra-tight center densities with commercial target loads and reloads assembled with fast-rate powders. That gun gave pattern averages over 80 percent with hard 7½'s in the following reload.

> Remington Premier hull
> Remington 209P primer
> 19.0/Green Dot
> Remington TGT-12 wad
> 1⅛ ounces hard #7½ lead shot
> Pressure: 7,300 p.s.i.
> Velocity: 1,145 f.p.s.

The last three-pattern string I shot with that recipe averaged 84 percent, the 20″-diameter core was solidly packed and there were very few pellets in the peripheral area 2″ to 3″ inside the outer ring. The pellets were all in or around the core. That's tight!

trapshooter who finds a tight-patterning load for his Full choke will have an advantage from the longer handicap stripes, as will the hunter whose sharptail flush at 30 to 35 yards on a windy day.

Finding loads that produce these two different characteristics in patterns from the same Full choke isn't always easy. It may take some trial-and-error testing, but when the loads are found you will gain some versatility. One load can handle your 16-yard trap-shooting, and simply by switching ammo you can make the same gun do Extra-Full (XF) duty for handicap and/or the second target of trap doubles. Hunters can chamber one of the wider-shooting loads for the first shot afield and put tighter-shooting rounds in the magazine for follow-up shots.

RECENT VARIATIONS

Recently I did some patterning with Scot Powder Company's line of Solo propellants in reloads fired through a barrel with a 0.727″

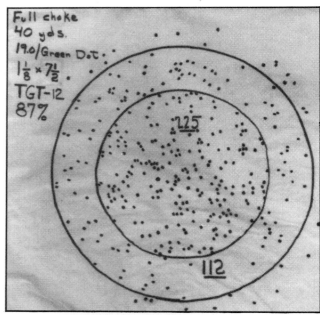

Handwritten on image:
Full choke
40 yds.
19.0/Green Dot
1⅛ × 7½
TGT-12
87%
225
112

Another full-choked gun/load combo gave a tight center density and weak annular ring with an 87% effort. Only by patterning do you really know which full-choke pattern your gun/load gives.

Then I began patterning with Solo 1250, which is a moderate-rate powder that generates reasonably low chamber pressures even in full 3-drams equivalent loads. When I tested the following reload made with Solo 1250, the full-choked gun changed its patterning characteristics — lowering the core count and sending considerably more pellets into the outer reaches of the 30″ circle for much better target coverage outside the core.

Winchester AA hull
Winchester 209 primer
24.5/Solo 1250
Windjammer wad
1⅛ ounces lead shot
Pressure: 7,400 l.u.p.
Velocity: 1,200 f.p.s.

Initial shooting with that reload powered by Solo 1250 was with 7½'s, but when its tendency toward broader pellet distribution appeared, I tried some hard 8's and found it gave an ideal 16-yard cluster. This reload continually gave wider, more-even pellet distributions through the Full choke that had tight-shooting tendencies. Why? I don't know, but the fact is it happens. Interestingly, Scot Powder Company's primary target powder, Solo 1000, didn't alter the tube's tight shooting style, but also punched snug center densities with weak outer rims.

Here is another reload that tempted more-open patterns from that 38-point Full choke:

Winchester AA hull
Winchester 209 primer
22.0/Unique
Remington RXP-12 wad
1⅛ ounces lead shot
Pressure: 8,700 p.s.i.
Velocity: 1,200 f.p.s.

It didn't fill out the last couple inches of the main 30″ circle as well as the load with Solo 1250, but it gave wider distributions than the other loads tested. Trial-and-error testing uncovered reloads that produced two different performances from the same full-choked barrel.

The reloads above with 19.0/Green Dot and 24.5/Solo 1250 are among the best for your early experiments toward getting high center densities or broader distributions from full-choked barrels. They may not work to perfection in all shotguns because shotguns are physical laws unto themselves, but they are worth trying when you begin work with a new gun.

Green Dot propellant gave some of the tightest core densities from full-choked field and trap guns. It's especially good for trap handicap and long-range dove shooting.

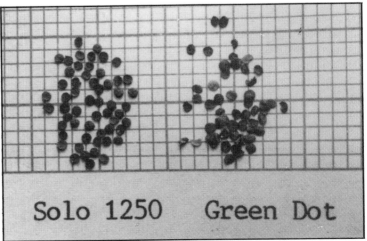

Solo 1250   Green Dot

Two powders that can give opposite results from full-choked 12 gauges. Solo 1250 can give more annular-ring density while Green Dot often gives exceptionally high core densities.

THE VELOCITY QUESTION

There are some armchair theorists who maintain velocity is the deciding factor in patterning and others who think chamber pressure plays the most important role. We often hear that low chamber pressures and/or velocities invariably give tighter patterns and that increasing velocity/pressure values can open patterns.

Sorry, but I can't prove that as a universal truism. Some high-velocity loads print exceedingly tight patterns, while some 2¾-drams equivalent target loads give wider, more evenly distributed patterns. Seeing is believing — anyone can speculate on theory.

If we accepted that theory, we would believe 3-dram equivalent trap loads don't pattern very tightly or at least shoot looser than 2¾-drams equivalent rounds. However, I have had excellent results with the following round for optimum pattern density.

Remington Premier hull
Remington 209P primer
21.0/Green Dot
Remington TGT-12 wad
1⅛ ounces lead shot
Pressure: 8,800 p.s.i.
Velocity: 1,200 f.p.s.

The pressure in this load is higher than that of the Solo-1250 reload, and its velocity is beyond that of the 19.0-grain reload of Green Dot noted for its tight patterning properties, yet the 21.0/Green Dot reload does tremendously well for trap handicap and dove because it holds snug core densities. Comparative ballistics don't automatically forecast patterning results.

JUDGING PATTERNS

The best way to judge the value of a full-choke pattern is with two steps. First, figure the basic percentage by dividing the number of hits in the 30″ circle by the total number of pellets in the original load, then compare the number of pellets in the outer ring. The outer ring is the area between the 20″-diameter core and the outer 30″-diameter circle.

The basic percentage figure will tell you if the gun is an honest Full choke, which means the average pattern should be 70 percent or more, preferably more. The outer-ring count will help you form the basis for distribution, as the gun/load pairing that puts the most pellets into the outer ring without dropping below 70 percent has qualities that recommend it for 16-yard trap and hunting over moderate 30 to 45-yard ranges. At the opposite end, the pairing which delivers high center densities with low outer-ring counts while still being above 70 percent is promising for long-range wing shooting and 25 to 27-yard handicap. I would also suggest true long-range loads be checked for patterning beyond 70 percent, as 80 to 85 percent is far better when ranges exceed 40 yards.

ADDITIONAL RELOADS

Handloaders who would like to take advantage of the two faces of Full choke for increased versatility may have a difficult time coming to a conclusion about which reloads to try beyond those mentioned above. The following recipes should help you further with your project. Each reload has a brief comment in parentheses explaining its tendencies and applications.

Federal Gold Medal hull
CCI 209 primer
21.5/PB
Federal 12S4 wad
1⅛ ounces lead shot
Pressure: 6,400 l.u.p.
Velocity: 1,150 f.p.s.
(Tends toward high center densities for trap handicap; especially good in 32″ to 34″ barrels.)

Federal paper Champion hull
Federal 209 primer
19.5/Green Dot
Winchester WAA12 wad
1⅛ ounces lead shot

(*recipe continued*)

Knowing exactly how a gun/load tandem patterns from a full-choked barrel or screw-in tube can benefit trapshooters tremendously. Loads with heavy core densities can be used for handicap and the second shots on doubles, while patterns that place more pellets into the annular ring can be chambered for the first bird of doubles and 16-yard singles.

Pressure: 9,000 p.s.i.
Velocity: 1,200 f.p.s.
(Delivers high core densities for handicap and also tightens Modified and IM chokes; seems excellent with 7½'s in most guns. Use only in once-fired hulls for best ballistics.)

———————————————

Winchester AA hull
Winchester 209 primer
17.5/Solo 1000
Winchester WAA12SL wad*
1⅛ ounces lead shot
Pressure: 7,900 l.u.p.
Velocity: 1,125 f.p.s.
(A lite load that concentrates shot into the core; interesting selection for mild-recoiling trap loads for handicap and second shots on doubles.)

*The Winchester WAA12 wad can be substituted safely.

———————————————

Winchester AA hull
Winchester 209 primer
23.0/Hi-Skor 800-X
Federal 12S4 wad*
1⅛ ounces lead shot
Pressure: 7,700 l.u.p.
Velocity: 1,190 f.p.s.
(Although a "boomy" powder with light shot charges, 800-X can give tight full-choke patterns.)

*The WAA12 wad can be substituted safely here.

———————————————

Remington Premier hull
CCI 209 Magnum primer
23.5/Solo 1250
Remington FIG 8 wad
1⅛ ounces lead shot
Pressure: 8,600 l.u.p.
Velocity: 1,200 f.p.s.
(Often will give broader pellet distribution in full-choke patterns; Use #8 or #8½ shot for heavier outer-ring density.)

Remington Premier hull
Remington 209P primer
24.5/Solo 1250
Windjammer wad
1⅛ ounces lead shot
Pressure: 8,000 l.u.p.
Velocity: 1,200 f.p.s.
(Parallels the performance of the AA-loading above; tends to fill out the annular ring with 8's and 8½'s.)

Winchester AA hull
Winchester 209 primer
20.0/Super-Lite powder
Winchester WAA12SL wad*
1⅛ ounces lead shot
Pressure: 9,100 p.s.i.
Velocity: 1,200 f.p.s.
(Tends toward pattern filling with #8 or #8½ shot.)

*Can safely interchange the WAA12 wad.

Remington Premier hull
CCI 209 primer
19.5/Super-Lite powder
Remington RXP-12 wad
1⅛ ounces lead shot
Pressure: 10,000 p.s.i.
Velocity: 1,200 f.p.s.
(Patterns similar to the preceding load in the AA case; sometimes opens well in IM chokes.)

All load data should be used with caution. Always consult comprehensive reference manuals and bulletins for details of procedures and techniques. Use only the load combinations specified in the recipes, and do not exceed the loads listed. Do not indiscriminately substitute components. Keep safety foremost in your mind whenever you are reloading. You can get the performance you want from your Full choke if you understand how it works and use the right loads.

7

The Patterning Characteristics
Of Some Gauges And Loads

It is quite common to hear exaggerated claims about the patterning prowess of certain cherished shotguns. One old-time rabbit hunter proudly told me his Winchester Model 97 hammer pump in riot persuasion would ". . .spread 'em all over the cottontail thicket," while another hunter, a dedicated waterfowler, boasted his hand-me-down mail-order double was choked so tightly, "She'll put 'em all into a soup plate at 50 yards!" And so the stories go. . .totally out of touch with reality.

We've all heard the claims and brags, of course, but how often have they been proven on paper — patterning sheets, that is — over measured distances with the pellet holes honestly counted, percentages figured and distributions analyzed? In most instances, never. Indeed, most of the super patterns I've heard of tend to be figments of somebody's overactive imagination rather than scientific fact.

Those of us who pattern all our guns and loads know better than to believe the extreme claims we hear — seeing is believing. Far too often a lucky one-pellet hit on a high mallard is mistakenly converted into stories of a gun that "shoots like a rifle," while in reality the pattern was dicey and the solo hit was mere chance. The fact is, a one-pellet head shot can look like dynamite even if the single BB came from a Cylinder (C) bore, rather than a Full (F) choke.

Shotgun patterning has been described as the study of gun/load individuality, which it definitely is. As I have often repeated, each gun and barrel is a physical law unto itself. Patterning is a complex topic, and it would be wrong to try to guesstimate any given outfit's performance based only on such things as degree of choke or potency of the load. Nothing can be taken for granted.

All of the following commentary about shotgun/load performance characteristics, therefore, must be accepted as only generalizing; nothing is carved in stone. After decades of critical patterning, however, I believe I can make some general statements about the patterning characteristics of certain gauges, chokes and loads. Taken in that general context, the information here may help casual hunters and shooters assemble effective gun/load pairings faster than if they simply accept old adages and popular fictions.

BUCKSHOT

Let's start with buckshot and which choke jibes best with it. My patterning indicates Modified (M) choke gets the job done quite well with buckshot. The best constrictions run from about 16 points of choke to roughly 22 to 23 points in the 12 gauge. Just recently, I patterned Winchester's 9-pellet 12-gauge load of #00 buckshot, and a Modified choke with 18 to 19 points of constriction virtually repeated 100-percent densities.

Why does Modified choke work so well with buckshot? I can answer that question best by explaining why Full choke, Improved Cylinder (IC), Skeet (S) and Cylinder bore fail to hold most buckshot loads in tight clusters the way hunters would like. Most sportsmen use buckshot for big game or varmints and need tight patterns to concentrate the buckshot for a better chance of making a hit to a vital area.

Full choke apparently flops with buckshot because it pinches down too hard on the robust, speeding charge of bulky lead balls. Buckshot does not flow smoothly through the narrow full-choke constriction, but instead is deformed as it swages down to squeeze through; consequently, it loses the best aerodynamic shape and can take some wild flights. Too, buckshot can take on a spin as it runs up a Full choke's incline, and the spin can make it curve away from the bore axis after exit. Finally, there is always the potential for

pattern disruption when the massive balls begin to bump into each other like so many billiard balls in a Full choke.

Despite some popular claims, open-bored guns don't seem to provide enough choke control to make buckshot loads hold tight patterns. The pellets, huge though they are, tend to scatter individually without a choke constriction. That's where Modified choke comes in.

With a constriction about half that of a Full choke, Modified apparently puts some control on buckshot loads without pinching down hard enough to cause substantial deformation or spin. Yet, Modified offers adequate constriction to hold the big spheres together reasonably well, or at least it does in my patterning.

The use of buffer to reduce buckshot deformation and expedite a more-fluid flow contributes markedly to the patterning qualities of buckshot. Under the pressure of surging powder gas, buffering materials compact around the individual spheres to encase them and deny them expansion room in which to deform. Although a close look will reveal that lead buckshot is hardly perfectly round to begin with, it is nevertheless more likely to emerge in better aerodynamic form from a buffered charge than from a naked one; thus, the combination of Modified choke and buffered buckshot is a good place to start building the tightest hunting patterns with these coarse pellets.

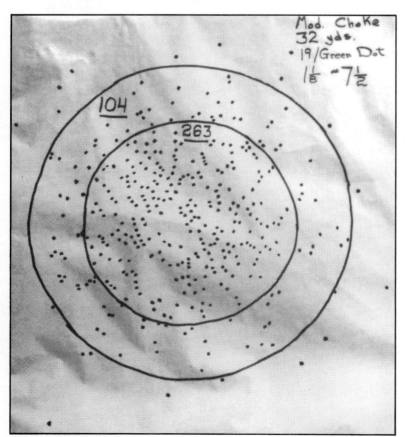

To tighten a Modified choke's pattern, Green Dot is the author's favorite propellant. Note the extreme center density plastered by a 19.0-grain charge of Green Dot with #7½ shot — this is virtually a full-choke performance. Compare it to the center density of the Solo-1250 load to see the difference powder, chamber pressure, etc. can make in gun/choke/load performance.

TIGHT PATTERNS
AND THE 20 GAUGE

When Sir Gerald Burrard wrote his classic volumes, *The Modern Shotgun*, he noted in Volume III that a very skillful barrel regulator once informed him it was ". . .easier to get a 70-percent pattern out of a full-choke 20 bore than out of a full-choke 12." This situation probably has been negated by the development of plastic wads and the wider use of over-boring and lengthened forcing cones in the 12 gauge, but the 20 can indeed still be brought to very high pattern percentages with equally high center densities. Hunters who use the 20 for long-range upland shooting, such as prairie grouse on windy days, will appreciate every percentage point, too!

My own shooting with full-choked 20's indicates the best patterns come from the slowest powders, such as Blue Dot, IMR-4227 and Hodgdon H-4227. I find #5 and #4 copper-plated shot jibes nicely with these pro-pellants. When lead shot was still legal for waterfowl, I could often make a double bored IC/M give actual patterns of M/F by using various reloads powered by these powders. One reason for the efficiency of such powders, especially in the 3″ 20-gauge Magnum, is the very bulky charges seem to absorb some of the primer's bump and thus reduce the severity of setback. Various manuals list data for reloads with these powders, and I have listed some as a start for interested handloaders.

Winchester AA-type 3″ hull
Winchester 209 primer
34.5/Hercules 2400
Remington RP-20 wad
1¼ ounces lead shot
Pressure: 9,600 p.s.i.
Velocity: 1,240 f.p.s.

Winchester AA-type 3″ hull
Federal 209 primer
39.0/IMR-4227
Remington RP-20 wad
1¼ ounces lead shot
Pressure: 10,900 l.u.p.
Velocity: 1,185 f.p.s.

Winchester AA-type 3″ hull
Winchester 209 primer
25.0/Blue Dot
Remington SP-20 wad
1¼ ounces lead shot
Pressure: 11,500 p.s.i.
Velocity: 1,190 f.p.s.

Federal paper-based 3″ plastic hull
Winchester 209 primer
45.0/Hodgdon H-4227
Remington RP-20 wad
1¼ ounces lead shot
Pressure: 8,400 l.u.p.
Velocity: 1,300 f.p.s.

(This reload suggested for once-fired hulls only to ensure a firm crimp; use in barrels of 28″ or longer for best results.)

THE MODIFIED-CHOKED 12

Many hunters buy Modified chokes as an all-around concept, believing they give patterns which split the difference between Improved Cylinder and Full. In fact, however, Modified choke can be quite fussy about which loads it will handle in that theoretical manner.

I have long been interested in Modified chokes and their performances, and my substantial patterning with them indicates they will frequently meet their basic percentage levels of 55 to 65 percent but not fill the pattern's annular ring very well. Like many other chokes, Modified constrictions can print snug center densities while leaving the outer fringes variously weak and spotty. Since Modified patterns do not automatically spread evenly and in a linear manner, you must devote some time to getting picture-perfect patterns from Modified chokes. In my opinion, it is the testiest choke of the bunch and can be very difficult to make shoot even patterns that are distributed throughout the 30″ patterning circle the way casual hunters and shooters think a Modified choke should.

One of the very best propellants I have found for Modified choke is Scot Powder Company's Solo 1250. It tends to give better pellet distribution in 12 and 16-gauge Modified chokes than most other powders.

Solo 1250 is a single-based, porous-type powder with no chemical burning deterrent. Its burning rate is controlled by the amount of air in each disc, and it is classed as a moderate-rate powder akin to Unique and SR-7625. As such, it generally has a low chamber pressure and its recoil is manageable. It is quite possible Solo 1250 gives excellent modified-choke patterns because it retains higher bore pressures and, thus, may force the wad against the base of the shot charge at emission to compact the emerging mass for broader clusters. Whatever. . .the point is, Solo 1250 does nicely in Modified chokes, and these are some of my favorite reloads with it.

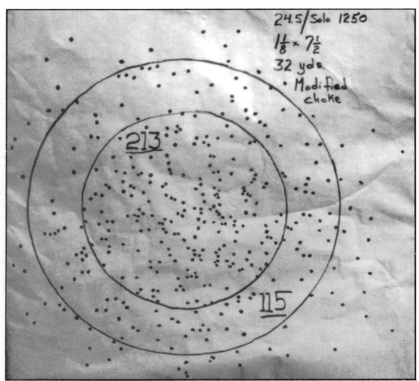

Solo 1250 is a powder that tends to give reasonably good to excellent pellet distributions from Modified chokes.

Winchester AA hull
Winchester 209 primer
24.5/Solo 1250
Windjammer wad
1⅛ ounces lead shot
Pressure: 7,400 l.u.p.
Velocity: 1,200 f.p.s.
(Excellent trap load in Modified choke.)

Federal Gold Medal hull
CCI 209 Magnum primer
26.0/Solo 1250
Federal 12S3 wad
1⅛ ounces lead shot
Pressure: 10,100 l.u.p.
Velocity: 1,255 f.p.s.
(Solid hunting load for Modified choke.)

Remington Premier hull
CCI 209 Magnum primer
23.5/Solo 1250
Remington FIG 8 wad
1⅛ ounces lead shot
Pressure: 8,600 l.u.p.
Velocity: 1,200 f.p.s.
(Gives good trap and hunting patterns.)

Winchester AA hull
Winchester 209 primer
27.0/Solo 1250
Winchester WAA12R wad
1¼ ounces lead shot
Pressure: 10,900 l.u.p.
Velocity: 1,275 f.p.s.
(Excellent field load in Modified choke.)

TIGHTENING UP
A MODIFIED CHOKE

There are times when hunters or trap-shooters who use Modified chokes would like tighter patterns that rise to about 70 percent or so for a full-choke performance. This isn't always possible, nor is it easy to find loads which tighten Modified patterns. In my patterning, however, I have learned that Green Dot will frequently coax full-choke densities from a modified-choked gun, especially when held to a reasonably low chamber pressure. A couple such loads are:

Remington Premier hull
Remington 209P primer
19.0/Green Dot
Remington TGT-12 wad
1⅛ ounces lead shot
Pressure: 7,300 p.s.i.
Velocity: 1,145 f.p.s.

Federal paper Champion hull
Federal 209 primer*
19.5/Green Dot
Federal 12S3 wad (or 12S4 if 12S3
    bulges the crimp)
1⅛ ounces lead shot
Pressure: 7,400 p.s.i.
Velocity: 1,145 f.p.s.
(Use only once-fired hulls to ensure a
firm crimp.)

*Winchester 209 or CCI 209 primers can be substituted safely.

A QUICK-OPENING
SPREADER LOAD

Sometimes it is advantageous to have a load that opens quickly from a tightly choked gun — I know. I've always loved to use my Merkel over & under in the uplands, but when

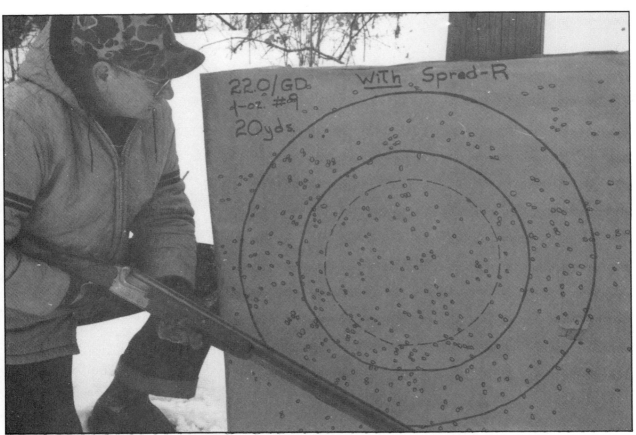

With a Spred-R wad in place and using the reload listed here, the author's Full choke blossomed into a yard-wide spread at 20 yards!

I first got it, the barrels shot Full and Extra-Full (XF) with normal 12-gauge field loads, which was a bit snug for woodcock at 12 to 15 yards! After experimenting with various scatter-load concepts, I found the one devised by Jay Menefee of Polywad, P.O. Box 7916, Macon, Georgia 31209, to be the easiest to reload. It also functions nicely when the shot charge is held to reasonably light levels, such as 1 ouncers in the 12 bore.

Menefee's idea is the Spred-R wad, which looks like a little plastic toadstool. It has a disc-like top with a long post beneath; the post is shoved down into the shot charge and the disc-like top covers the upper layers of shot, then the crimp is snugged down over the device's top. The idea is to cause a forward obstruction of the emerging shot charge so the pellets must climb around it and, therefore, fly outwardly as soon as they pop from the muzzle. A free-floating top wad doesn't do this as effectively because the shot charge can simply blow it away.

The Polywad can't be brushed aside as easily because its long plastic shaft is imbedded in the shot load and doesn't work free until the entire charge clears the muzzle, so the obstruction remains in place.

The idea works splendidly with 1-ounce loads of fine shot — like 7½'s, 8's and 9's in full-choked 12's and 20's, and my selection for close-in woodcock and quail would be:

Winchester AA hull
Winchester 209 primer
22.0/Green Dot
Winchester WAA12 wad
1 ounce lead shot
Pressure: 10,000 l.u.p.
Velocity: 1,300 f.p.s.

The Spred-R wad is pushed into the shot charge just before crimping, and the overall fit of components to hull is quite good. It's just the thing for those times when you need a wide pattern from your ol' Full choke. Polywad has additional data for different gauges and charge weights.

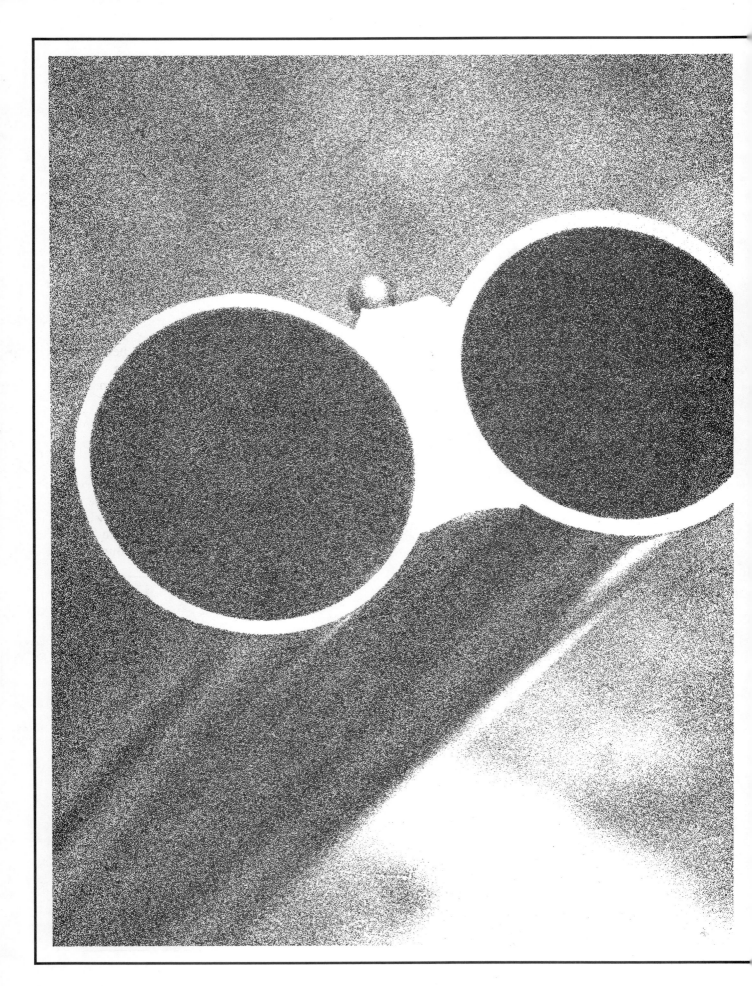

The "Swamped" Rib

I could hardly believe my eyes recently when I assembled a sample over & under (O&U) sent to me by Armsport, Inc. of Miami, Florida. Their Model 2750 boxlock was handsomely sideplated, and when shouldered, it placed before me the kind of rib I have always loved to use but which, sadly, is not found on many new guns these days, especially not O&U's. It's called a "swamped" rib.

For my money, this rib comes closer to perfection than any other rib design. The swamped rib got its name from the way its middle section swoops lower than its extremities; it is not straight and flat but is bellied, the depth of the belly varying with the gunmaker. Viewed from the side, a swamped rib resembles a swale between two hills.

THE PURPOSE OF A RIB

The beauty of a swamped rib is, when you mount the gun, it virtually disappears below your line of vision. There is nothing between your eye and the muzzle to clutter up the foreground or attract your eyes. It lets your eyes

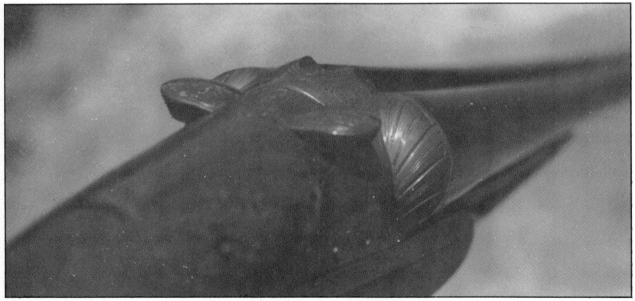

The swamped rib is a European design that generally starts high at the breech, as on this Darne shotgun, then swoops down quickly to disappear from your line of vision.

sweep over the gun to the target, which is the way it should be done — shotguns should be pointed and swung, not aimed like rifles.

Using a high, straight, ventilated rib like a rifle sight is totally wrong. In expert shotgun pointing, the rib's only role is to lead your eye to the muzzle area, and this is done primarily in peripheral vision in hunting or the low-gun games, such as Sporting Clays and International Skeet. When your eyes are well beyond the muzzle and focused sharply on the target, there is no further use for the rib, and the rib will only hinder you thereafter if you look back at it. High or wide ribs can indeed attract your eyes improperly, but the lowered center portion of the swamped rib eliminates such potential distractions.

A swamped rib often finishes very low, sometimes between the muzzles with a bead no higher than the muzzle tops, as in this photo of the Darne's business end.

WHY A SWAMPED RIB?

The swamped rib is actually quite old. It was written of by W. W. Greener in the 19th century editions of his massive tome, *The Gun And Its Development.* Historically the swamped rib has been applied to side-by-sides (SxS's), and finding it on the Armsport O&U was a pleasant surprise — I can't recall ever seeing it on a stackbarrel before.

At one time the British employed a "false rib," which was a brief solid rib jutting over the chamber area to get the eye started toward the muzzle without adding the same weight as a full-length rib. That worked well, too, and like the swamped rib, it gave visual direction while leaving a definite gap the eye could easily jump to establish eye-muzzle-target alignment without encountering distractions.

One of the fastest-pointing doubles I have ever owned was a French Darne. It had a

swamped rib that started high at the breech then swept low in a concave manner and ended below the muzzle top; in fact, the metal front bead was just about flush with the muzzle top. Anyone who knows how to use eye/hand coordination in scattergunning would find that arrangement extremely effective — nothing got in your eye's way. It was just a matter of looking at the target, mounting the gun and having no temptation whatsoever to let your eye drift or dwell on a close-in sighting appendage.

In many respects, the swamped rib resembles what you saw when you looked over a Browning Auto-5 or Remington Model 11 without a rib. These plain-barreled guns had high receivers, and when you got your head down, there was only the muzzle blob out front, and a plain-barreled A-5 or M/11 is still a fast-pointing shotgun. Many early skeet shooters used them with bulbous Cutts Compensators *sans* rib — who really needs a rib when his master eye can so readily pick up the muzzle blob of a Cutts?

I long ago began to believe many ventilated-rib designs are detrimental to good shotgunning, especially field shooting and some Sporting Clays' work. They attract your eye or obstruct it, and the important thing in good wing shooting is establishing alignment between the eye, muzzle and target. Beads or ribs that tempt you to look at them are anathema to smooth, natural pointing and swinging.

I enjoy hunting with plain-barreled shotguns and have a much-used, unribbed barrel outfitted with a screw-in Walker "full-thread" choke for my Model 1100 Remington. This unribbed barrel has a lighter feel than normally ribbed Remington barrels, and I find it very responsive on game and snappy Sporting Clays.

The swamped rib made the Armsport Model 2750 O&U a joy to shoot. My hope is more gunmakers will start to use swamped ribs rather than the straight, flat type. A swamped rib makes the muzzle stand out more

A straight-edged yardstick is inverted on a swamped rib to show how much the rib sinks — the yardstick is touching the receiver and muzzles.

prominently, thus putting more emphasis on the essential point-of-reference rather than cluttering up the receiver-to-muzzle area with unnecessary accouterments.

WHY ANY RIB?

This discussion brings up another interesting question. If a swamped rib is so great because it disappears from view as the gun is mounted, do we need any sort of rib at all? What's the difference if the rib disappears or just isn't there? It's a legitimate point that deserves a chapter of its own in this book (See Chapter 9).

This rib on a Browning A-500R is the opposite of a swamped rib, which is made to disappear and not clutter up the gun's upper pointing surfaces.

Baubles, Bangles And Beads:
A Discussion Of Shotgun Sights

Anyone who has delved into ancient and modern literature on wing shooting knows classic technique is, first and foremost, predicated upon eye/hand coordination. In theory, a hunter focuses on the bird and keeps his eyes centered throughout the entire mount-swing-lead-fire-shoot-and-follow-through sequence; there should be no peeking back at the gun to "aim" the shot by aligning the front bead with the matted receiver top, nor should the shot be lined up with the rib, middle bead or whatever appurtenance sits atop the muzzle midway on the rib. You should just look at the winging mark, let your hands work coordinately with your eyes and. . .Voila! Dead bird; fetch 'em up!

In theory, wing shooting is done about the same way Larry Bird shoots a basketball — he focuses just over the rim of the hoop and flicks his famous one-hand shot without aiming over the ball or squinting like he would over a pair of rifle sights. The same is true of Ted Williams, the last man to hit over .400 for a big league baseball season. Williams may have brought eye/hand coordination to its peak in that sport, never once looking at his bat to align it but instead trusting solely on his eyes for guidance into the target. Nor do professional bowlers, like Earl Anthony and Mark Roth, have sights on their bowling balls; they merely find their "spot" on the lane and go for it with eye/hand coordination.

Whenever I encounter budding wing shots handling new smoothbores in a sport shop, however, I continually hear them discussing the little baubles, bangles and beads that are often termed "sights" on shotguns. "I don't like the metal bead," one hunter told me recently, "I'd sooner have a bright orange one that stands out." Another hunter informed me he would never have missed the three geese he whiffed one morning if he had had a middle bead set in his gun's rib. "If I'd had that middle bead, especially a white one, I could really have lined up on them," he assured me. An ardent woodcock hunter I met at a gunsmith's insisted on having a white Bradley-type bead put on the muzzle of his over & under (O&U) so he could see it more plainly against the greens of early fall foliage.

WHEN DID IT ALL START?

Hunters today practically insist on having a raised rib of some sort on their bird guns, which is just the opposite of what it was like when I was a kid. Back then, the guns on the local hardware store's racks had plain barrels; even the first O&U's I saw had plain barrels, like the Remington Model 32, Marlin Model 90 and Savage Model 420. About the only shotgun then that regularly sported a rib was the side-by-side (SxS), and it generally had a trim, innocuous rib that filled a gap between tubes.

Indeed, it really wasn't until the 1950s rolled along that ventilated ribs became popular among hunters, and if I were to point to any one gun that started the trend, it would be the Remington Model 870, which in its early going offered a very economical rib. The Browning Auto-5's were also a contributing factor to a degree. The sustained economic growth of the 1960s allowed people to add another $20 or so to the price of their bird guns for this little nicety. In the early going, however, few hunting-grade repeaters were sold with ribs.

WHY DO WE HAVE THEM?

That brings us to a very important question. If the old-timers did such great wing shooting with their Winchester Model 97's and Remington 11's *sans* ribs and colorful beads, do we really need them now? Is the ventilated rib really necessary, and how about those brilliant front beads and cute little middle beads? Must the top of a repeating gun's receiver always be matted, and is that matting intended as a sighting device the way many hunters use it? What is it with all these supposed sighting gizmos on scatterguns?

BEADS

Let me begin with the oft-told tale of the skeet shooter who was on a hot streak and had broken 75 straight targets; all he needed was a perfect 25x25 on his last field for a 100-straight. While waiting to shoot that last round, he accidentally bumped his gun against a gun rack but thought nothing of it because he was only concentrating on the task ahead of him. He went out and shot that final 25x25 and received the congratulations of his squad members for getting a perfect century. When it came time to put his gun away, he saw that the front bead was gone. "It came off when you bumped the gun rack," said a fellow squad member, "but I didn't mention it because I didn't want you to think about it and lose your concentration." The fellow had broken his last 25 targets without his front bead and hadn't even noticed it! He was too busy doing what he should have been doing, namely, focusing on the targets and letting eye/hand coordination do the rest.

This is the way I believe a hunter should approach barrel beads — ignore them. If you can't ignore them totally, try to use them only as subconscious reference points fuzzily seen in your peripheral vision. Never look at them, and never, never try to aim with them as if

There are all sorts of beads for shotguns, but none of them are really important. Eye/hand coordination is what counts; your eyes should be looking at the target and nothing else.

they were rifle sights. The human eye cannot simultaneously focus sharply on objects both near and far. If you look at the front bead, the bird will go out of focus and you will lose eye/hand coordination to the target.

Experts in the field of vision tell us there is a phenomenon called "physiological diplopia" which pops up when we focus far or near. The result of diplopia is a double image opposite the point of focus. You can observe diplopia for yourself by doing this test: Take a trim object, such as a ballpoint pen or your thumb, and hold it up at arm's length aligned with some object in the distance; focus sharply on the pen or your thumb while, in the fuzziness downrange, you notice what happens to the far image — it should double, splitting left and right. Now reverse things and focus on the downrange object while also remaining aware of the nearer object — it should split and become a dual image.

This is what happens when you are focusing close-in on a shotgun's front bead; the far image splits, and you are actually pointing, or trying to point, at two images and wondering which is the real thing. Moreover, if you shift your focus back to the distant bird, the front bead will become double and worthless as an alignment feature.

The best move, then, is to focus where eye/hand coordination will be aided the most, which is on the target. Look back at the bead, and you are often lost. The hunter who says, "How could I have missed? I had the beads right on him," is answering his own question, although his lack of understanding leaves him dangling for an explanation. The fact is, any-one who sees his shotgun's sights clearly while making a shot is likely to miss because he is focused too close in.

Some shots can be pulled off by focusing on the bead, but the reason normally stems more from a bit of luck, the help of a spreading pattern or the shot being relatively close in. Just try handicap trapshooting or Sporting Clays while focused sharply on your gun's front bead and see what it will get you!

I have three barrels I use for skeet and Sporting Clays. One has a white front bead, the other a red bead and the third a sizeable metal bead. Frankly, I don't see any difference between them because I don't look at them. I believe I could score as many skeet targets without a bead as with one.

At best, the bead on a shotgun serves merely to show you where the muzzle is. The muzzle, after all, is virtually the front sight on a shotgun, and it should team with your eye, which is the rear sight, for alignment. If your eye gets hung up on clutter between it and the target, you will have a problem putting the best shotgunning theory to work. Look *through* the front bead and concentrate totally on the target. If you are aware of the front bead at all, it should be only as a vague, subconscious reference point that you recall *after* the shot as you replay the slow-motion event in your mind.

What about those fancy middle beads that seem to turn a lot of hunters on? They are the best sales gimmick in the sporting world. Put a two-bit metal bead in the middle of a rib, and you can charge hunters another $5 to $10 — they are far better for the national economy than they are for field shooting. If it's wrong to focus on a front bead, it surely is terribly wrong to bother with a middle bead! It not only throws your sports vision all out of shape, but even if you could manage to focus on two beads and a bird at the same time, it would be a slow process.

The middle bead is primarily effective on target-grade guns, especially trap guns, where it gives you a chance to check for alignment and against canting before calling for your target. However, trapshooters should actually be focusing downrange before calling their birds, which renders the middle bead useless during the actual point-and-swing when the target is in the air.

RIBS

What about the effectiveness of the rib on a hunting gun? When ribs were first devised, their purpose was simply to guide the shooter's master eye to the muzzle so he could get quick eye-muzzle-target alignment. In other words, the rib was to be a pathway for the eye to streak along; it wasn't meant as an aiming device at all. In fact, if you get your head down correctly on a game gun with a straight, flat rib, as on a classic field or game gun, you don't even see the rib because it is depressed below the level of the receiver or standing breech. All you should do is look out *over* the rib. Looking sharply at the rib is as wrong as looking at the front bead; the rib is just a raceway for your eye to get to the muzzle on a hunting gun.

Observant hunters look at skeet and trap guns, point to their gargantuan ribs and ask why these target-grade guns have such radical ribs if they are nothing more than aids to finding the muzzle. The fact is, ribs on target guns *do* serve other purposes, not the least of which is to diffuse rising heat waves. The extremely wide ribs on some skeet and trap barrels are designed to push the heat waves farther off to the side so the viewing plane straight down the barrel will be as free as possible from "mirages." Hunting seldom generates enough shooting heat to produce such heat waves.

The high-sitting ribs on skeet and trap guns also elevate the viewing plane while depressing the bore axis and that, in turn, generates a straight-line recoil thrust which moves below the stock's comb and tends to reduce sensible

recoil. By depressing the barrel, you get a recoil effect akin to that of an O&U's lower tube, which is straight back, as contrasted with the upper tube's inclination to buck upwards against your cheekbone.

Hunters really don't need such radically tall ribs, as they are generally more supple than rigidly upright trapshooters; therefore, their supple bodies soak up recoil energy more readily. If you shoot five swinging shots at ducks, you normally don't notice the kick, but if you shoot five shots at trap with the gun solidly mounted before the target appears, you begin to feel the recoil energy on your shouldering area. Target shooters can use the recoil reduction of a high rib; hunters, as just noted, don't really need it.

The ultra-high rib also gives target shooters greater target visibility. When trap clays come up from ground level, there is a tendency for the gun to blot out the low clays, and lofty ribs leave more space between the wide muzzle and rib's top so the clay can be more readily seen and tracked without becoming obscured by the muzzle. The so-called "unsingle" trap

Ribs were invented to guide your eye to the muzzle for quick eye-muzzle-target alignment. They were never meant for aiming. Focusing on the rib is just as wrong as aiming with the front bead.

gun, which is essentially an O&U with the upper barrel removed and a rib set in, is a manifestation of the things being done with ribs these days to enhance target visibility and keep the recoiling barrel low relative to the comb line.

I have done some trapshooting with guns that had ribs sitting up like the Golden Gate Bridge, and I had to make some adjustments in my coordination. It simply seems unnatural to have my hands so far below a bulky beavertail forend while my master eye works above a lofty rib. The best advice for hunters is to keep the rib low so it runs through or very close to your leading hand's palm for natural, not mechanical, pointing. Trap-shooters can adjust to the mechanical stuff through practice on grooved targets, but

hunters must react to all sorts of different target speeds and angles immediately, which is where natural pointing comes in.

CONCLUSION

Through the years, there have been a lot of "sights" advertised to improve wing-gunning. I won't elaborate on all of them because they are mostly a lot of poppycock. Let me just say your master eye is the rear sight of a shotgun and the muzzle is the front sight; get your head down with your eye squarely behind the receiver looking directly over the muzzle, because that's how you obtain field-gun pointing accuracy. All the other stuff is worthless baubles, bangles and beads.

This is the "picture" a shotgunner should see — a fuzzy gun with the target sharply in focus, not vice versa.

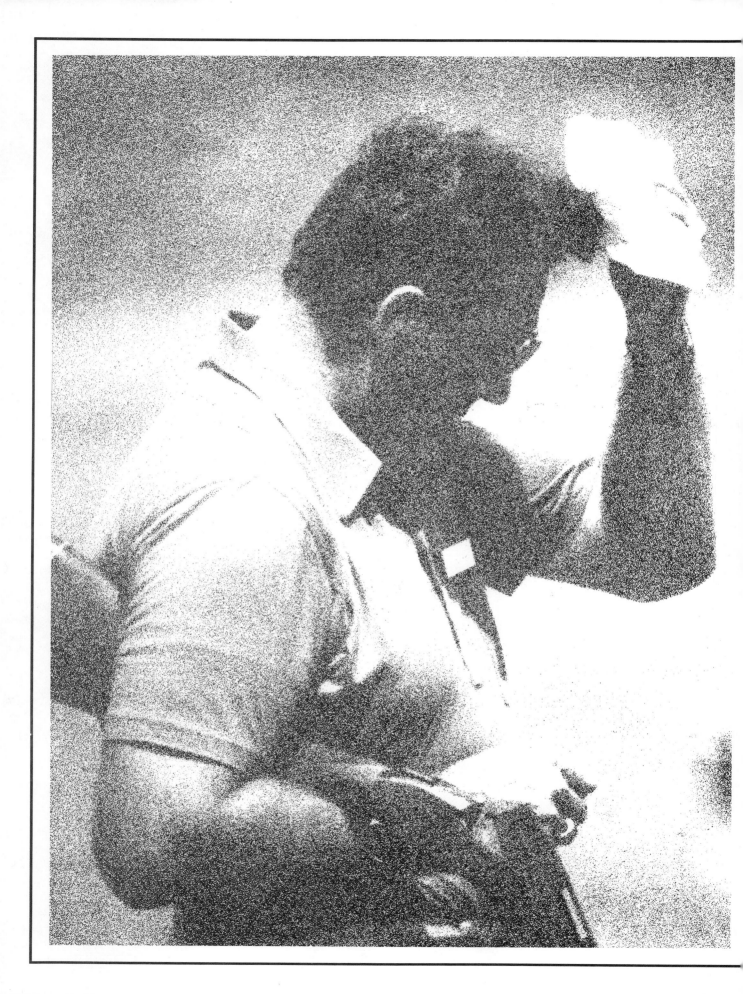

Breaking Through To Higher Levels Of Performance

There has long been a theory that improving one's ability takes constant practice, so you should shoot virtually every day and then blast some more if you want to get better scores. It is believed constantly doing a thing will eventually cause you to catch on and you will find your performance rising markedly.

Around here, guys who took clay-target shooting seriously used to say, "I wish there was a club open every evening so I could shoot at least 100 targets a day for a month straight." Many such shooters were brought back to earth by the cost of daily gunning, however. They began to fantasize about becoming shooters in the armed forces' marksmanship units and thought they understood why such soldiers could take world and national championships — they could shoot every day — who couldn't be a good shot if he practiced all the time on the taxpayers' money?

Lots of current trapshooters believe daily practice is still the way to better scoring. In theory, it seems to work. "Pros" who follow the trap circuit and shoot practically every day at the major tournaments are thought to do well because of their constant shooting, which adds up to hundreds of targets a day.

THE CASE FOR LOTS OF SHOOTING

Far be it from me to argue that a lot of shooting doesn't do any good. For beginners, it's almost a necessity if you want to become familiar with your guns and the sport in general. Indeed, it's difficult for beginners to learn solely by visualizing because they haven't yet learned how a good, repeated swing feels, how targets fly under varying conditions, how their bodies must deliver good timing and how a whole bunch of other stuff falls together. In fact, they must shoot a lot just to begin to feel comfortable and confident on the line.

Some shooters who have become comfortable, though, have not found that element of comfort bringing them higher scores. They may feel totally relaxed and among friends on the line, but they are not breaking the serial 25's necessary for good competitive results.

How do we explain it when constant shooting doesn't improve a shooter's scores, but leaves him struggling at some level short of improvement and certainly short of challenging for trophies? Will increased practice help? Should the shooter now shoot 200 targets every evening instead of just 100, or is a steady diet of shooting, shooting and more shooting actually hurting the gunner's chances for improvement?

WHEN EVERYDAY SHOOTING IS NOT ENOUGH

The answer seems to be that, after you have shot enough to build a base of familiarity and strong fundamentals, a steady diet of everyday shooting won't help you develop quickly or solidly. Coaches and sports psychologists now believe there is a better way than day-in and day-out practicing.

Shooters who don't advance even though they are shooting regularly must realize something is wrong with their training. It may be their physical technique, mental game or a combination of the pair, but just plain blasting away won't solve the problem; repetition is

good only if you are repeating the right stuff!

More importantly, repetition is good mainly if you give your body and mind time to absorb the new techniques you have practiced and which can generate higher scores. In a scientific sense, improvement occurs when you put stress on your mind and body and then rest briefly to let your mind and body adjust to the changes the stress has forced you to make. After hard work that causes you to rise to a new level of performance, your body needs time to rebuild itself before it can cope with further stresses.

New thoughts on rapid improvement in sports performance emphasize extreme pressure to improve over short intervals followed by periods of rest to allow your body to rebuild and avoid burnout. Once you are beyond the beginner stage, continuous

Shooters who don't advance even though they shoot regularly must realize something is wrong with their training.

New ideas on improving your game suggest stressing yourself for a short period of time then giving your body a chance to adjust and rebuild. In time, the right moves become routine.

shooting that fails to force changes in your physical and/or mental game can lead to naught; day-in and day-out blasting with no specific purpose, and especially with no advanced technique or mental aspects, can be counterproductive.

HOW TO APPLY STRESS FOR IMPROVEMENT

What do I mean by stressing your abilities and practicing for a specific purpose? Essentially, it means to do more than merely continue doing what you have always done. You can equate it with a college student going into and through examination time. The student has been going to classes, listening to lectures, reading books and discussing materials in a routine manner throughout the semester. Now he is suddenly faced by the final examination, and he knows to get an "A" he must go beyond the knowledge he has so far acquired and put to use in his daily routines. He has to reach a higher level because there are things he hasn't understood or hasn't stashed away in his mind yet, so he puts heavier pressure on himself and "crams" for the exams.

Cramming, of course, is forcing your mind to cope with all sorts of new stuff, from simple facts and insights to applications of those facts and insights. For a short time, the student is driven to new heights of concentration and application. Once the examinations are over, he relaxes, but from then on, he is working on a new level because the cramming elevated his level of knowledge.

After a period of rest, the student often has better use of the new facts and insights than he did during the exams. The cramming caused a change in the person, a change that would not have occurred if he hadn't been stressed by the intense studying prior to the final examinations. The change is a positive one, of course, and gives the student a new base that allows him to advance even further the next time he goes through an intense study/practice period. After such intensity, however, the mind apparently needs a period to adjust to the stress of change.

The same concept of intense practice followed by rest to let the body catch up is employed in the physical sense among athletes. Take weightlifting as an example. The standard practice in weightlifting is to have a heavy workout of certain muscles one day and then let them rest for a day or two so the cells can rebuild. Trying to lift maximum weights every day only tires the body and may have a negative effect on it; instead of improving, the body can go stale.

Trapshooters would do well to learn this

stress/relax training technique and dump the idea that daily practice is the way to improve. To go beyond your current level of performance, you must stress your mind and body so they learn to do better. You get nowhere practicing what you already know.

WHY SHOULD YOU STRESS YOURSELF?

I know many shooters who don't want to stress themselves. "I shoot for fun," they argue, "and I don't want to work harder at my trapshooting than I do at my job. I'm here to relax." Fine. . .great. . .enjoy, but also realize improvement doesn't come on the heels of fun.

For a short time, improvement *is* work, at least until your body adjusts to the greater demands. You have to stress yourself for a short period before your mind and body can advance. After the stress of learning something new, you reach a higher level of performance and can relax. Shooting is still fun, but your scores are higher!

Look at it this way — the reason you are not shooting championship scores is you are doing something wrong. Your technique is lacking, your fundamentals are sour or, perhaps, your mental game is weak. The key is finding what is wrong and making mental demands upon your overall shooting to right those wrongs. It doesn't happen automatically by popping 100 caps an evening. No gymnast or figure skater ever became a champion because they lucked into the right moves during casual, after-work practice on a relaxed level. Champion gymnasts and figure skaters work a million times harder than trapshooters do to improve their skills.

The element of stress is a vital factor in this type of training. You can fire a 500-target, 16-yard or doubles' marathon and not stress yourself or learn a thing, and you can come away from that blasting relaxed and entertained because you had fun, but do you have a competitive score? A shooter who strives to improve his competitive scores with intense practice may find himself stressed after just 100 targets on which he applied the correct technique to improve his score.

I have watched shooters come into evening

leagues with excellent tools for trapshooting — sharp-focusing eyes, snappy reactions and quick, well-coordinated movement times — and begin shooting scores in the 20's immediately. Three years later, however, those same shooters are still in the same leagues shooting virtually the same scores of 22x25 or 23x25. They never stress themselves to put it all together, to hone a proper technique or reach a higher level that would give them 25x25. If that is their idea of fun in trap, so be it.

The final step to becoming a complete shooter doesn't result from doing what comes naturally; it is a stressful step that you must consciously take to carry yourself to a new level of performance. Once your body adjusts to the new level, the whole thing becomes easier again. Your body goes through a positive change, and your performances tend toward higher scores. You don't have to stress yourself to reach that level every time out. High scoring becomes routine because your body and mind have adjusted to the new techniques, but it's work on the way to those

Many trapshooters think daily practice is the way to better scores, but repetition is good only if you work on improving the technical and mental aspects.

higher scores because your body must make changes in nerve conduction, reaction, muscles, etc.

If your body isn't given time to change, it can get all fouled up. So, too, can your brain, which also needs time to refine its reflexes after tough, intense practice. Books on modern training techniques, sports psychology and sports medicine call this the "delayed effect," meaning your body adjusts to a new level of performance after the fact, not during the practice session. (The term used to describe improvement *during* practice is called the "immediate effect.") This perhaps is why some shooters who were only mediocre at the tag-end of a season will begin the next season at a significantly higher level; their bodies adjusted to the demands made in the preceding season during the lull between seasons. The practice didn't pay off on the spot but showed up down the road; that's the key to a breakthrough in this work/rest type of training.

You needn't go out and shoot every evening in hopes of somehow mysteriously becoming a good shot just by repetition. Repetition was a part of educational psychology in the past, but new concepts have outmoded it as an effective training tool. Standing on Station Five shooting wide rights won't make you a better trapshooter unless you stress yourself to hit that target using the right technique in a short, intense training period and then let your body relax and adjust to the new proficiency so the right moves become routine.

Good, stiff practice sessions on weekends *can* develop you into an improved trapshooter. The week lets you adjust to the rigors of using the demanding new technique so the following weekend your mind and body will have adjusted to the new demands and can apply them more naturally and with less strain.

There is more to improving than merely shooting, obviously. It is a matter of pressuring yourself to do better, then absorbing everything you have learned and acclimating to the new performance. This doesn't come by lamebrain blasting away at targets but by a concentrated effort to do things right followed by a rest to give your brain and body a chance to adjust and rebuild. At least that's the way sports psychologists tell us to do it, and it seems to work.

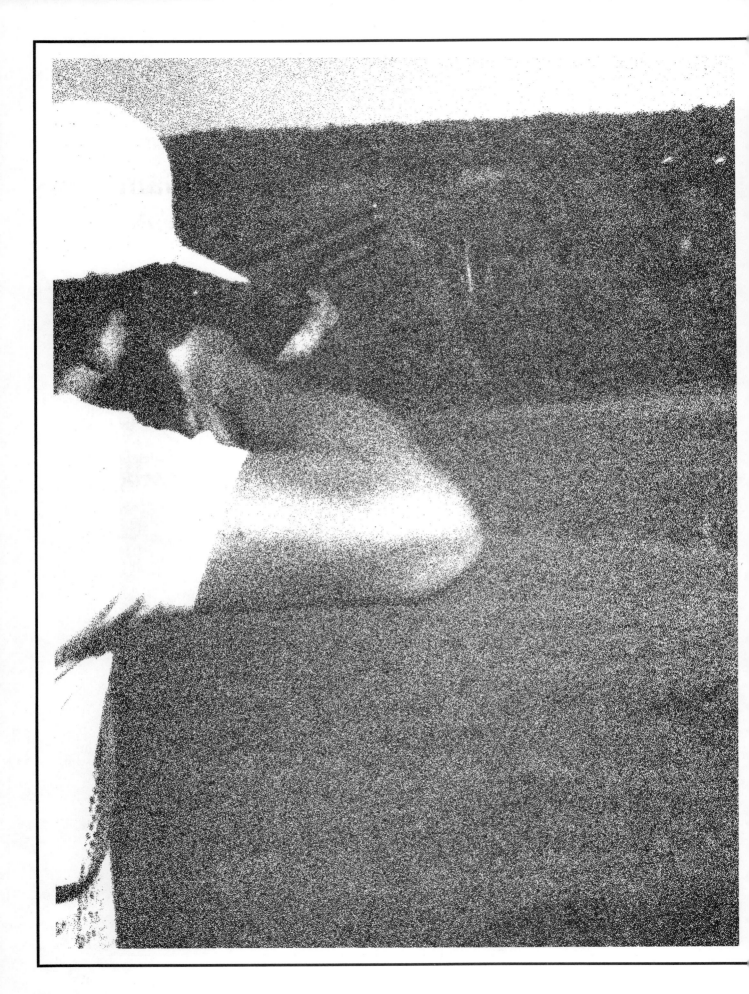

The Ultimate Shotgun Game — F.I.T.A.S.C.

Sporting Clays originated in England and, as it evolved, it became a game of doubles. There are seldom, if ever, single targets in British Sporting, as it is predicated upon pairs of targets — simultaneous, report or following — at each stand, and a major tournament of 100 targets means five pairs at ten stands. As a means of identifying this format, we can rightly use the term "British" Sporting Clays.

There is another version of Sporting Clays known as F.I.T.A.S.C. (pronounced "Fit´-ask"). In effect, F.I.T.A.S.C. is the international form of Sporting Clays; the initials stand for the Paris-based governing body, *Federation Internationale de Tir Aux Armes Sportives de Chasse*. As those with a little high school French behind them will

British Sporting Clays is based on doubles at all stations, and it is a lot of fun. This shooter is swinging on a simultaneous pair.

The game of F.I.T.A.S.C. can include doubles at each station, and a pair of bouncing rabbits can be part of the package.

realize immediately, F.I.T.A.S.C. is slanted toward the hunt (*de chasse*).

"Big deal," you say, "British Sporting Clays is also supposed to emulate field shooting." Yes, but as observed above, British Sporting is a game of doubles, and not all hunting involves two birds in the air. Moreover, field shooting doesn't present repeated patterns the way British Sporting Clays does.

F.I.T.A.S.C. is considerably different from British Sporting, as it is much more realistic when it comes to emulating the shots you get afield. The goal of F.I.T.A.S.C. is never to give the same shot twice, which is the reverse of the repeated pairs standard in British Sporting Clays. Moreover, F.I.T.A.S.C. includes singles as well as doubles, and you can take two shots at every single, just as you can in hunting.

HOW IT IS DONE

How can all these numerous target variations be thrown? Multiple traps are used on each stand, as opposed to the single trap machine normally used in British Sporting Clays. On a F.I.T.A.S.C. stand, you might find as many as four or five different trap machines around you, each throwing a different distance and angle.

When you do get a repeated angle in F.I.T.A.S.C., it is normally with a different-sized target, thus giving you a different sight picture. You may get three single targets off the same trap on a F.I.T.A.S.C. stand, but one will be a standard-sized clay, another a midi or mini and the third a rocket or battue. That may not impress you if you have never shot the gamut of F.I.T.A.S.C. clays, but believe me, a mini coming off a trap arm looks nothing like a standard clay or battue. These seemingly minor variations can throw you like you wouldn't believe!

There are doubles in F.I.T.A.S.C., but they are not handled like those of British Sporting Clays. Rather than being repetitive, the pairs in F.I.T.A.S.C. are always different, even from the same stand. The target sizes are mixed up, too. One pair on a F.I.T.A.S.C. stand might be a mini coming in and a standard target crossing, while the next pair from the same stand might be a midi quartering with a battue passing crazily downhill.

The rules of F.I.T.A.S.C. permit each club to use its imagination when setting up its course according to the terrain available. The main stipulation is that the ". . .layout must be equipped with a sufficient number of traps so competitors will shoot under conditions resembling game shooting — partridge, pheasant, ducks and rabbits; in front, low and high; battue, crossing and quartering; on fields or in woods; the targets may be hidden or not by trees and bushes." Although this same concept applies in British Sporting Clays, F.I.T.A.S.C. carries it out more realistically using singles and a myriad of variables per stand. Some shooters can "groove" a British Sporting layout because of the repeated pairs, but that

is virtually impossible on a F.I.T.A.S.C. course where the traps are all over the place and each target is different.

Other important F.I.T.A.S.C. rules also bring it closer to the field. For instance, there can be up to a three-second variable delay in the target's release after you have announced "Ready." (By international rules, "Pull" is not used to signal target release.) You must stand with your feet inside the stand, and your gun must be held below the top of your shoulder. As of 1991, the rules concerning gun position for F.I.T.A.S.C. were changed to prevent shooters from "creeping" their gun progressively higher. The rule was formerly written so the gun's heel had to be at armpit level or lower, but many shooters kept bringing their gun higher and higher into an almost shouldered position. The new rule demands that guns be held so the heel is "under the nipple line." This has been standardized at a point 25 centimeters below the center of the top of your shoulder. F.I.T.A.S.C. shooters must have a permanent marker running horizontally at that spot as a visible checkpoint; bright thread or a stripe running through that area will do. The rule also states the gun must be touching your body *below* that point and, apparently, cannot be held out front as some people used to do.

Field shooting isn't always pairs; much bird hunting involves singles of every angle. That's where F.I.T.A.S.C. is great, as it attempts to give shooters a myriad of different angles with no shot duplicating another. There are plenty of singles in F.I.T.A.S.C., too; all of which can be given both barrels!

BASIC GUNS AND LOADS

Guns for F.I.T.A.S.C. can be no larger than 12 gauge, and 1¼-ounce (36-gram) shot charges are the maximum allowable. Charges must be lead shot with diameters between 2mm and 2.5mm, which means 7½'s to 9's. No shot-scattering (spreader) devices can be employed. A 3¼-drams equivalent load with 1¼ ounces of shot is the maximum a sensible shooter will use, and many F.I.T.A.S.C. stands can easily be taken with trap loads of 1⅛ ounces (32 grams) of 7½'s or 8's; Remington's Duplex® charge of mixed 7½'s and 8's is excellent.

Although American Sporting Clays' shooters have made a fuss over choke tube changing — like golfers who change clubs for each shot — *F.I.T.A.S.C. rules deny any choke switching.* The rule states, "Any changing of gun (or any part of the gun which functions normally, adjustable chokes included) is forbidden throughout the duration of a layout. Any breaking of this rule will automatically lead to the disqualification of the competitor." The key word here is "layout," which can mean a "parcours" or a series of traps, *not* the whole course; a layout or parcours can be a certain number of stands.

Which guns and chokes work best for F.I.T.A.S.C.? In general, the leading shooters stick with Improved Cylinder (IC) or quarter choke. This may sound wrong to inexperienced shooters who think 35-yard targets look awfully small, but experience has taught these shooters that IC can pick up practically any target that is properly pointed and swung. The results may not be as explosive as on trap fields where full-choked guns smokeball clays, but a broken target is a broken target in F.I.T.A.S.C. Hunters, of course, do tighten chokes to put a clean-killing concentration of pellets on game, but clay targets don't bleed and crawl away crippled. I once read how a British shooter broke a string of successive targets over 70 yards using just a 20-gauge skeet gun — so much for wild choke tube changing!

The guns for F.I.T.A.S.C. pretty much parallel those for British Sporting Clays. Two shots are needed, and autoloaders and over & unders (O&U's) dominate. The O&U's are the most popular, although I personally do not understand why; it is much easier to recover from the recoil of a gas-operated autoloader than it is from that of a stackbarrel. I have a feeling shooters will eventually gravitate to semiautos. American F.I.T.A.S.C. National Champion Dan Carlisle used a 28"-barreled Beretta Model A-303 to win that title, and British expert A.J. "Smoker" Smith has been experimenting with a Beretta A-303 with a 32" barrel; other serious shooters have placed high with Remington Models 1100 and 11-87.

BARREL LENGTH

Barrel lengths for Sporting Clays and F.I.T.A.S.C. have made for interesting discussion. There can be no question longer barrels of 30" to 32" provide more weight forward for smooth swings and positive follow-throughs, but my own observation is that such lengths aren't suited to everyone, nor are they suited to all courses.

The British and Europeans tend to emphasize stands which give longer, more-open shots reflecting their background of shooting driven game. Stateside, however, our layouts more often hinge upon the shorter shots of Yankee uplanding. An overseas shooter can well apply longer barrels for open-country swinging, but the same 30" to 32" barrels might be a detriment in the U.S. on those quick, close-in chances.

While I don't recommend 26" barrels on O&U's or side-by-sides (SxS's) for either Sporting Clays or F.I.T.A.S.C., I do believe many, if not most, American shooters can do nicely with 28"-barreled O&U's or SxS's, and 30" barrels are about maximum for stateside courses.

On autoloaders, a 26" barrel can work because the receiver gives additional length; however, the 28" barrel on Beretta's Model A-303 Sporting Clays Gun is just about right because the A-303 is lighter than its stateside competitors, the Remington 1100's and 11-87's. That is why shooters like "Smoker" Smith and others can experiment with barrels of 30" to 32" on the A-303.

THE SHOOTING

Now that we have covered the basics of F.I.T.A.S.C., let's shoot a mythical stand. There are three traps: About 20 yards to your left is a ground-level trap we'll call trap "A"; trap "B" sits on a hill, maybe 30 yards to your right; trap "C" is behind solid protection, about 50 yards in front of the stand, throwing targets directly back at your gun. It's a ten-shot stand, and the sequence could go something like this.

The first shot is a single from trap A going left to right, quartering across brush; if you don't get it inside 35 yards, it'll be behind a pine tree. It's humming because it's a high-speed mini. You load two shells, pivot to your starting position or hold point and say "Ready!" Within three seconds, the mini is darting to the pine. It takes a bit to get it out of peripheral vision and by then it's well on its way behind the pine. Your first shot is pokey and behind, but you have another in the second barrel and that bird's no different than a ruffed grouse diving for the swamp. You don't generate enough gun speed, and like br'er grouse, the target gets away. Oh well, this isn't skeet or trap — one miss isn't all that bad!

The second target is a midi from the hill — a diver, going fast. You reload, pivot to the hold point and again say "Ready." This time the trapper lets go right away, and the midi is zinging at a steep angle like a chukar coming off an Idaho canyon wall. You point it out, swing and shoot

and see two white streaks as your wads flash over the top of the clay. Looks like your lead was right but your elevation wasn't. "Gotta depress more the next time," you think while you reload for trap C.

Now your nerves have calmed a bit and you're getting used to the format. With the chambers reloaded, you position yourself for the incomer from trap C. It turns out to be a high floater, a standard-sized target you shatter with a smooth, upward swing. Now the pressure is off; you've scored!

It's back to trap A, which is now loaded with a standard-sized clay. It flies the same course as the mini you already missed, but this time the bigger mark is easier to see and you pick it up and catch it with your second pattern. Confidence builds; you reload and pivot back to trap B.

This time B throws a single battue. At first you don't see the razor-edged mark and your eyes get behind, then the battue begins to bank and its circular profile appears. It's sinking fast, and because of its sharp edge, it

Open field shots? Sure — coming at you, going away and crossing all over the place at varying speeds and in several different target sizes. That's F.I.T.A.S.C. — the ultimate shotgun game for hunters.

is cutting air like crazy. Your first shot is well behind and your second is snapped in haste before the bird disappears into the bushes. Oh, well. . .the guy ahead of you whiffed it, too!

Now there's one more single. It's a climbing incomer from trap C, and it's a mini. At first your eyes must work to find it, but then it pops up as a mere dot against the sky. It looks to be 200 yards out, but it isn't. You make a good swing and blow it apart! Minis virtually explode with any kind of multiple-pellet hit, and there is some satisfaction in this hit. So much for the singles.

In some F.I.T.A.S.C. events, shooters take their singles then step back and wait to get their doubles only after everyone has run the single birds. In fact, the rules stipulate that single shooting must take place first in major tournaments; in practice shooting, you may stay in the stand and complete your run, however, because it is not official. I think it is more fun to extend the round by splitting the singles and doubles on each stand as per the tournament rules.

As you stand aside and watch others try their singles, you realize you didn't do all that bad. The others miss plenty of them, too, and you begin to wonder about all those hunters who bragged about getting geese with 80-yard shots or not having any problem with ruffed grouse. It's fun when the guy who says, "I never miss pheasant," steps up to a stand and doesn't so much as chip a clay. It merely shows that most hunters still have a lot to learn about swinging a shotgun, and I only hope they will get interested and try to improve rather than give up in disgust or fear of embarrassment.

Now you are back in the stand for your doubles. These will not be the same kind of doubles you see in most Sporting Clays' rounds. Each target will be different, normally not launched from the same trap. The puller will explain all this before the doubles' shooting begins, so it won't be a surprise to anyone.

The first pair comes from traps C and B. On your call, trap C pitches a mini skyward, and on report there is a diver from B, which is a speedy midi. You get the climbing mini with no sweat, but the slanting midi stabs down from the hill too fast and your shot string

goes a tad behind and considerably over it.

The next pair is a criss-crosser. Trap A slings a midi quartering to the right, headed toward that danged pine tree, while hilltop trap B angles a standard-sized clay into the bushes. This time you're ready, and you chop the midi going left. Your eyes pick up the standard-sized clay from the high trap and you remember to depress your gun and swing below the diving bird — it blows apart. What a great feeling — you just got a pair in F.I.T.A.S.C.!

If you feel you have been drained and challenged by all this, enjoy it. This one stand in F.I.T.A.S.C. has given you a lot of different angles and challenges, more than in Sporting Clays, and each shot has looked very different. Indeed, if any shotgun sport is *the* bird hunter's sport, it is F.I.T.A.S.C., not British Sporting Clays, because of the myriad angles and singles.

THE PROBLEMS WITH F.I.T.A.S.C.

If F.I.T.A.S.C. has a problem, it is that the game is so labor-intensive, which means it is expensive to run. In British Sporting Clays, the work can be done by one trapper and one puller, but multiple-trap F.I.T.A.S.C. requires more labor. One alternative is an automatic trap-machine setup, but that requires a substantial investment of $15,000 to $40,000.

To lower the cost of F.I.T.A.S.C. operations, Sporting Clays' clubs can shorten the courses and concentrate the labor and investment on a few stands. Shooters who are new to Sporting may think they are being gypped at first, but the overall fun of F.I.T.A.S.C. will change their attitudes in a hurry.

Moreover, because so many different shots can be worked into a F.I.T.A.S.C. stand, there is the possibility to weave more shooting into less land area. Depending upon the lay of the land on any field, one F.I.T.A.S.C. stand can actually have 2 to 3 stations on it. A mere 10 to 15-yard move in any direction can change the entire complexion of the field. It's entirely possible to get 25 to 30 shots at one set of three traps, and that's a pretty good workout with the ol' scattergun!

Although it may not appear a F.I.T.A.S.C. course has enough stands to be challenging, each stand can actually encompass 2 to 3 stations. Moving these stands by 10 to 15 yards can alter them due to the layout of the land, too. It's possible to get 25 to 30 shots at one set of three traps!

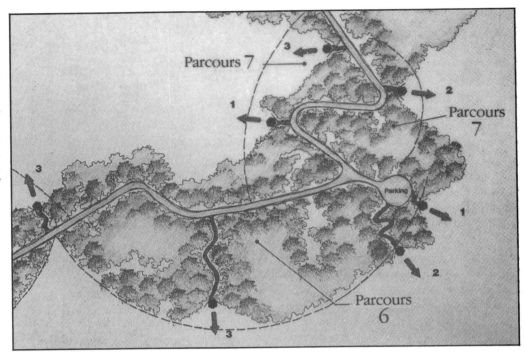

Rather than just following the practices of British Sporting Clays, club operators can begin to introduce shooters to F.I.T.A.S.C. by throwing each target angle as a single before throwing the routine doubles of British Sporting. It is a lot more challenging and realistic that way.

THE ULTIMATE

F.I.T.A.S.C. is the ultimate shotgun game. Hunters don't always get doubles, nor are they restricted to one shot per bird afield. Game usually flush as singles, and hunters can use two loads. Likewise, each shot on game tends to be different, not a repeat of the one before.

International Sporting Clays, alias F.I.T.A.S.C., mixes up the shots and, therefore, demands the most skill of any shotgun game. The unfortunate thing is many shot-gunners walk away from tough challenges. Those who stick it out fall in love with F.I.T.A.S.C. — there is nothing closer to the vagaries of actual field shooting.

In the United States, the U.S. Sporting Clays Association (USSCA) is the sole affiliate of the Paris-based F.I.T.A.S.C. organization. Some F.I.T.A.S.C. tournaments are held each year stateside under international rules, and the USSCA's annual National Championship is now being shot according to the F.I.T.A.S.C. format. Shooters and gun club managers who are interested in learning more about F.I.T.A.S.C. can contact the USSCA for further information. Their address is 50 Briar Hollow, Suite 490 East, Houston, Texas 77027; phone (713) 622-8043.

If you haven't tried F.I.T.A.S.C. yet, do it now. I guarantee you will fall in love and won't want to go back to repeated targets and grooved shots!

12

Swinging And Timing Shotguns Of Different Weights

Watching a game bird or clay target keep flying when you *know* you were leading it is one of the most frustrating situations in shotgunning. You feel the gun moving, you see daylight between the muzzle and the bird and still — nothing — not a feather, not a tiny chip! About then, many people begin to wonder about that old bugaboo, the "blown pattern," and complain, "There must be something wrong — I *know* I was ahead of that bird!"

Rather than a failure of the pattern, however, the cause of such misses frequently rests with the subtleties of shotgun swinging and timing. Mere gun movement doesn't constitute a true swing, merely seeing daylight doesn't automatically mean the lead is right and merely pulling the trigger isn't invariably perfect timing. In a true swing and well-timed trigger pull, the overall move must coordinate with the target's speed. Move the gun too slowly on a fast-crossing bird, and the pattern will streak behind the mark even if some daylight was showing between the target and muzzle. Move too fast on a slow-rising, close-in flush, and the shot string will whistle ahead of the bird despite the appearance of what looked like a good lead. It is this rhythm, this coordination of your movement with the target, that you learn so well on the skeet field.

Adding to swing speed and trigger timing are the additional factors of gun weight and, to a degree, gun length. Despite the casual approach some hunters take to shotguns and shotgunning, saying a gun is a gun and if you can shoot one, you can shoot them all is incorrect. There are definitely differences among shotguns. Each weight class tends to have its own dynamics, and those dynamics become especially important as you go to the extremes of weight and length. Switching from one weight class to another can upset timing, influence swing and frustrate or enhance follow-through.

LIGHTWEIGHT GUNS

Several years ago, I was sitting at the skeet club with some friends when a pretty good skeet and trapshooter came over with his spankin' new upland gun. It was a 28-gauge over & under (O&U), slick as the proverbial whistle and trim as a movie starlet. The 26″ barrels and English-style grip gave it a racy look that smacked of speed. "I'm really gonna get on those ruffed grouse with this little beauty," he beamed.

He signed up for a round of skeet and within 15 minutes was ready to sell the little critter! He missed the first two high-house targets, chipped away on the doubles and picked up only one target out of the next four from Station Two. He whiffed both targets at Station Three and barely chipped the tail of High Four before shooting a mile behind Low Four. The rest of the round followed suit; he missed plenty. Obviously, this was a serious comedown for a man who could turn out scores of 23x25 rather nonchalantly with a heavier 12-gauge autoloader or O&U.

What happened? It's simple — the light weight of the 28 gauge threw him for a loop. You simply cannot handle a 6-pound smallbore the same way you handle an 8¼-pound 12 bore. The 12 gauge's greater weight tends to dampen aggressive hand/arm action, but a spirited smallbore applies no such discipline to your hands and arms. The featherweight smoothbore jumps along with your hands, going faster to and through the

Swinging a 10-pound Remington SP-10 is different than...

target than the heftier 12 gauge. If you let hand/arm action take place as it does with the bigger 12, the little featherweight will be to and through the target in a wink, well before you can react with a coordinated, well-timed trigger pull.

That's what happened to our friend on skeet with his new 28 gauge; he used the moves he had grooved with a much heavier gun and his hands bossed the 28 into a fast start while his trigger timing was delayed as he sought the feel or picture he had grooved with the 12. By the time he got around to pulling that 28's trigger, he had either slashed the gun well ahead of the target or come to an abrupt stop because the light 28 didn't have enough momentum to carry him into a positive follow-through.

...handling a 6-pound upland double with stubby 25" barrels.

The light guns often given to youngsters and beginners may hinder their development as shooters. Such guns can be whippy, and it might be better to give these shooters somewhat heavier guns to assist smoothness and a positive follow-through.

IMPROVING WITH FEATHERLIGHTS

There are two ways to handle feathery shotguns. One is to speed up your timing to harmonize with the gun's explosive start when you apply the aggressive hand/arm action you might use with a heavier gun. This usually requires more practice than most hunters want to put into their shooting, but without a knowledge of how your lightweight shotgun moves, you will see many missed shots that may puzzle you.

The second way to improve with a feathery bird gun is to minimize hand/arm action and move the gun mainly with body pivot. This practically eliminates mistakes caused by excessive hand/arm action, which can throw the gun away from your master eye and upset alignment. The best grip on a smallbore is next to no grip at all; a hunter's reaction to a bird should be with his body, not only with his thrusting hands. Taking the aggressiveness out of your hands and arms can bring a lighter shotgun back into rhythm for a complete pivot rather than just a hand snap. In the old days of skeet when .410's were still

scaled-down guns of relatively light weight, such as the Model 42 Winchester and Model 11-48 Remington, tournament champions put lead shot or slugs into the buttstock and tubular magazine to provide enough inertia to resist jumpy hand/arm movement. Even then, the saying among skeeters was that the .410 shouldn't be gripped but should simply be cupped by the hands to reduce any tendency toward overcontrol. A bird hunter with his .410 or 28 gauge unweighted, however, needs to alter his technique if he wants to master the lithe guns on game.

AVOID THE SUSTAINED LEAD

I have long believed the sustained lead is anathema in smallbore shooting unless, of course, it is being used in skeet with a 12-gauge O&U hosting full-length smallbore tubes that provide extreme weight up front. Lightweight guns — which includes many 12, 16 and 20-gauge doubles and trimmed-down repeaters — have a tendency to die at the end of the stroke due to a lack of momentum. The only way a sustained lead will work with light guns is if you apply perfect technique and continue your pivot for a complete follow-through. If, like many other mere mortals, you leave just a tad out of your pivot with a small-bore, your lead will be lost quickly; what looked like the right lead one instant is suddenly gone, leaving you to wonder what happened. The swing-through method is generally better with light guns because it is usually accelerating when the trigger is pulled, which tends to insure a better follow-through.

The real tragedy of lightweight smallbores is when hunters try to be too fast with them. An explosive thrust ruins accurate pointing and carries the gun well ahead of your body pivot. After all, good shotgun shooting requires pivoting, not hand shooting, hand snapping, hand poking, hand thrusting and certainly not hand aiming. You need a gun swinging in rhythm with a pivoting body to successfully apply trim, elegant and racy featherweights and shorter doubles, so you must think total technique rather than just a lightning-like start.

THE HEAVY GUNS

When you go to the opposite extreme — long, heavy shotguns — you find other techniques that can help or hinder your scoring. Unlike lightweight, short-barreled bird guns that fairly jump after the target, longer, heavier models roll more slowly into their swing. To get the most from such guns, you must acknowledge this trait and fashion your technique to use it advantageously.

In recent years, the 10-gauge Magnum has come on strong among goose hunters. The 10-gauge Magnum is a 10½ to 11-pound gun in most instances, and I once owned a trio of 10-bore side-by-sides (SxS's) that topped 11 pounds by at least ¼ pound. Some attempts have been made to improve the handling qualities of the Mag 10 with 26″ barrels, but even this leaves the overall gun heftier than most field-grade 12's. I have seen it happen time and again. Hunters take to the blind with their new artillery all enthused about their bulky shot charges and then miss shot after shot because they are still swinging the same and using the same sight picture they did with their lighter, faster-swinging 12's.

The key to hitting with an extremely heavy shotgun is understanding that it takes longer to get that inertia rolling than it does to snap up an ultra-light smallbore; consequently, your trigger pull must be a tad later to harmonize with the gradual development of forward allowance. If you use the same rapid trigger timing on a 10 gauge or heavier 12 that you do on a 5½-pound 28 gauge, you will almost invariably shoot behind the moving target because the more-ponderous gun needs more time to stretch ahead of the target. It is quite possible to see daylight between a heavy shotgun's barrel and the target and still miss behind the bird, as the daylight does not invariably represent gun speed. A hunter who

Special clay-target guns, such as this 34″-barreled trap model, have swing characteristics unlike those of shorter field guns.

brings his 8-pound 12 gauge ahead of the target can see forward allowance and think everything is right although the gun might not yet be moving half as fast as the bird. With a heavier gun, therefore, you must feel the swing dynamic taking place to be sure the gun is moving briskly instead of merely lagging along.

Your grip on a heavier shotgun can be tighter than on a lighter gun without exerting an overcontrol condition. However, most experts feel it is wrong to clench a shotgun of any sort, as clenching tightens your hand and arm muscles and that, in turn, tightens your shoulder muscles, which mitigates against smoothness and a fluid pivot. Perhaps a better way to describe the grip on a heavy shotgun would be "firm."

This method for handling a heavy gun doesn't only apply to 10-gauge waterfowl guns, of course; the 30″-barreled 12 gauge is still apparent in the uplands, and some auto-loaders are still rather ponderous although totally applicable to upland work. I often feel the short-barrel syndrome has been overdone, and I would sooner use a 28″ or 30″ barrel on open-country game birds, like windy-day sharptail and spooky pheasant, than a stumpy lightweight. My own feeling has always been that the shooting qualities of the shotgun should come before its carrying qualities.

AN UPLAND COMPROMISE

An ideal open-country upland shotgun may very well be one that is based upon a compact receiver and has some length to it for smoothness if it is a break-action gun, or one with an alloy receiver if it is a repeater. This is sort of a compromise between length and weight. An example might be the Model 303 Beretta autoloader, which has an alloy receiver and can still be handled easily with a 28″ barrel. The M/303, in fact, is gaining a reputation as an outstanding Sporting Clays' gun because of those features, which provide some responsiveness without any semblance of whippiness.

At one time, the Ithaca M/37 slide-actions

fit the same category, and I remember hunting one season back in the early 1960s with a Deluxe Grade M/37 with a 30″ barrel — a tandem that was steady yet reasonably dynamic. The Model 37 Ithaca is back on the racks after some seasons of financial difficulty, but it is now known as the *Model 87*. It should still serve the same purposes it always has, though — taking the drudgery out of the carrying part while still making good wing shooting possible without whippiness.

The point is, weight extremes in shotguns call for different techniques. You must be flexible enough to blend your timing with the acceleration qualities of the given gun weight. With a rather short and feathery gun, every-thing is done briskly — there can be no dawdling on trigger pull while you look for and admire your forward allowance — the shot must go *right now* on a featherweight that jumps after targets or the pattern will either flash ahead of the bird or the gun will die for lack of momentum. With a heavier smoothbore, trigger timing must be altered to let the gun build up momentum before the shot is tapped off.

Of course, there are casual shooters who don't believe switching guns and gun weights makes any difference. Just try a round of skeet with an 8-pound 12 gauge and another with a 5½-pound .410 or 28 gauge, even a 5½-pound 20, and you will understand the difference quickly. Most shooters don't miss skeet targets with a .410 because of pattern diameter, they miss because a bona fide .410 is so easily whipped and overcontrolled they don't take it through a perfectly smooth swing into a posi-tive follow-through; nor do they miss far-flushing sharptail with a 30″-barreled, full-choked 12 because the patterns were too weak. They often miss because they shoot too fast and don't let the longer guns roll into their swing speed to accelerate through the birds.

Timing and swing speed are indeed subtle-ties in the art of wing-gunning. Rhythm and coordination are essential and must be applied with a knowledge of the gun's weight and dynamics. You must accomplish a complete swing and follow-through without upsetting your timing, regardless of the gun's weight.

13

Learning To Visualize
The Long Shots

One of the funniest things in wing shooting is hearing a once-a-year hunter tell how he bagged a goose at an extremely long range by giving it only a foot or two of lead. A tale I heard recently at my gun club is a case in point. A hunter was bursting with pride as he told us about his goose. "The goose must have been 75 yards high, maybe more. I gave him a foot of lead on my first shot and missed, then I got way out in front by about two feet and got him. Now, that was a long shot, let me tell you!" His smile ran from ear to ear, so I didn't bother to burst his bubble.

It is physically impossible to hit a flying target at 75 yards with just a 2-foot lead with

Be it a dove, duck, goose or high driven pheasant, you must learn to visualize the leads your individual swing speed and reactions (timing) require. Wing shooting cannot be done on a purely mathematical basis by measuring off a precise lead; there must be some knowledge of what the correct swing feels and looks like before you can become consistent. Anybody can get lucky once in awhile, but for consistent success you need to visualize the proper lead.

modern shotshells. In fact, a target at only 50 to 60 yards needs considerably more forward allowance.

If you consider the scientific and mathematical facts of shotgunning, you encounter a factor commonly called *air resistance*, which is perhaps better called *air drag*. It's the same thing that works against airplanes and cars to slow them down, and it is why cars are being designed with improved aerodynamic styling. Air drag reduces the mileage-per-gallon of cars, and streamlined bodies help cars slip through air molecules more efficiently. Like automobiles, shot pellets aren't exactly good aerodynamic forms; consequently, they are rather quickly slowed by air drag. Deformed pellets are even worse performers.

According to newly revised exterior ballistics (see Chapter 18), for example, a steel #4 pellet with a published velocity of 1,365 f.p.s. is down around 572 f.p.s. when it reaches 50 yards. That's not only a considerable velocity loss but also helps explain why you can't hit a flying goose at 50 yards with an honest 1-foot lead; it simply takes the pellets so long to cover 50 yards the bird will have moved well out of the pattern's area by the time the shot string arrives. A goose, duck, dove or driven pheasant flying at about 45 m.p.h. is covering about 66 feet per second, and it takes the above-mentioned steel #4 0.1775-second to fly 50 yards. While the pellets are going from muzzle to target, the bird travels roughly 11 to 11½ feet. A hunter trying for a hit on such a bird, then, must somehow manage to set off an 11 to 12-foot lead, and aiming a foot off the bird's bill won't do it.

Even with steel BB's, which overcome air resistance better than steel 4's, the forward allowance is still considerable. Steel BB's with published velocities of 1,350 f.p.s. take about 0.2120-second to cover 60 yards, in which time they also fall to a velocity of about 586 f.p.s. If the high goose is still doing 45 m.p.h., it will move about 14 feet. Even if we generously provide a 3-foot pattern circle, the bird is still at least 10 feet ahead of the shot string of any hunter who merely measures off a foot or two of lead.

LUCK VIA MOMENTUM

How do hunters score when they don't use enough lead? Well, those who do hit a high bird probably do so despite themselves. After missing the first shot made with a slow-swinging gun that was practically aimed with a short lead, they get excited and move the gun forward to catch up to the still-flying bird and shoot with what *seems to be* a mere 2-foot lead. The gun has now taken on momentum, however, and depending upon the hunter's actions, may virtually swing *by itself* into a proper lead. The hunter is oblivious to the gun's overthrow generated by his panicky dash to throw in a second shot. In his mind, it was a 2-foot lead, whereas in reality the gun took over and made him look good — gun momentum accounting for the vast majority of the lead.

There is a big difference between hitting a high bird occasionally by luck when the gun develops its own momentum and scoring consistently because you know how it's done properly and what a long-range swing feels like. You also have to get used to visualizing much longer forward allowances than skeet or trap require. The 3½ to 4-foot leads used on skeet Stations Three, Four and Five are nothing compared with the 10 to 15-foot forward allowances needed on truly high birds. Many hunters have difficulty with this type of shooting because there is such a long gap between the target, upon which they should be sharply focused, and their gun's muzzle, which works well into their peripheral vision. Until you become comfortable with a swing that sweeps far into your peripheral vision, you probably won't become a good long-range shotgunner.

There is an educational philosophy that says anything can be a learning experience and you can learn from failure as well as success. When it comes to wing shooting, however, I'm not so sure failure can teach us anything except that whatever we did on a particular missed shot was wrong. There are a zillion things you can do wrong when a bird passes high overhead or flushes wildly on the prairie, and assessing all those negatives won't necessarily bring you to a positive answer.

Skeet and trapshooting are not as helpful for learning hunting techniques as Sporting Clays. Skeet is too close-range and the angles in trap tend to be very shallow.

To learn how to handle high and long shots, you need a reference point to determine where your shot charge went so you can make corrections. Only by a quirk of luck, I learned what the lengthy forward allowance must be.

One morning, years ago before anyone ever heard of steel shot, mallards came from behind and I didn't see them until some hunters on my right opened fire. The flock split in all directions, climbing as they went. A drake was heading directly over me with a hen in tow by about 15 feet. They were lofty birds, but with the prevailing light of the morning and my inexperience they still appeared to be in good range. I slapped about a 4-foot lead on the drake and triggered my load of lead 2's. As I followed through, the hen crumbled practically out of my field of vision. I had been concentrating so hard on the drake, at first I thought somebody else had shot the hen, but I called and nobody answered. It was my hen — I had missed the drake by at least 15 feet!

That shot formed a basis for my long-range

wing shooting. I had never in my young life visualized that much forward allowance. In fact, I was ready to write it off as a fluke until shortly thereafter I had a similar experience on a goose hunt.

The morning had been snowy, and the geese didn't fly until nearly midday. Then they came off the marsh in massive waves, and from my blind on a farm well inland I could hear them long before I could see the vanguard. The first birds to come within range of my gun were a flight of five in a perfect vee passing high and to my left. As always, they appeared close and huge. I swung my pump gun through the leader, opened daylight and let go as my swing continued briskly. I actually thought I was giving that bird too much forward allowance, but instead of the leader folding, the last bird on my side of the vee fell out. I'd missed the correct lead on the point bird by at least two goose lengths and the distance between them, which I calculate was a minimum of 5 to 6 feet but perhaps was

8 to 10 feet!

If it hadn't been for my patterns scoring on those trailing birds, I never would have had a reference point for visualizing long-range leads. The shots would simply have sailed a mile behind the birds and been lost against the sky; it's difficult to see your own shot string's streak or turbulence because of recoil and muzzle jump.

I'm sure a lot of other hunters have had similar experiences of knocking down a bird that's well behind the one being shot at, so it wasn't a fluke. It was a matter of air drag slowing my shot strings drastically in flight. You have to s-t-r-e-t-c-h your leads much farther than most typical hunters ever visualize.

PRACTICING LONG LEADS

It is quite possible Sporting Clays, with its high tower shots, could eventually teach hunters about long-range shooting. Unfortunately, many ardent hunters simply won't practice and certainly won't shoot Sporting Clays. Skeet and trap won't teach you how long-range leads look, because skeet is a close-range game with a nominal range of 20 to 25 yards for the farthest shots and trapshooting involves such shallow angles the apparent leads are terribly short. No shotgunner will ever learn to visualize and get the feel of a fast-swinging, 15-foot lead by shooting 16-yard trap or handicap.

Skeet can do a hunter some good if he backs off Stations Three, Four and Five by 10 to 20 yards to make them crossing shots of 30 to 40 strides. Otherwise, skeet mainly teaches you pivot and body rhythm but not actual long-range leads. I know a doctor who takes his duck hunting much more seriously than his skeet shooting. Despite the fact he won some skeet events, he gave up skeet because he felt it hurt his duck shooting; he said he was becoming too mechanical on short leads and was not developing the timing and visual aspects of more-distant shooting.

We used to play a game called "Long-Range Skeet" at our club. The gunners stood 10 yards behind Stations Three, Four and Five

with lowered guns and the puller could throw whichever target he chose, the high or low house. The forward allowances over just those 30 yards were enough to confuse many shooters completely. Those who used their normal 2 to 4-foot skeet leads missed practically every target. Indeed, air drag's impact on the pellets magnifies markedly as the range increases, and the required mathematical leads often seem to be out of proportion to the meager added distances. Just 10 yards more range necessitates considerably more lead at these shotgun ranges.

COMPARATIVE LEAD DATA

To illustrate the slowing effect of air drag on pellets, let's check the downrange values of certain steel and lead pellets using the revised exterior ballistics published by Ed Lowry. As our target, we will use the crossing mark at a perfect 90° angle moving at 45 m.p.h. Above, I observed that a steel #4 with a published (3-foot, coil) velocity of 1,365 f.p.s. needs 0.1775-second to cover 50 yards, so the forward allowance on our theoretical target would be about 11½ feet. If we extend that range to 60 yards, we find it takes the pellets about 0.2338-second to cover the distance. By then the pellet's velocity is down to just 496 f.p.s., compared to 572 f.p.s. at 50 yards, and the forward allowance increases to about 15½ feet. That's a loss of about 75 f.p.s. over just 10 yards and necessitates 4 feet more lead!

I don't recommend steel 4's for long-range wing-gunning, and this example explains why. Air drag simply slows the lighter pellets faster than it slows heavier ones, so steel 4's run out of gas around 35 to 40 yards.

Even steel BB's feel the effects of air drag as they stretch out. At 40 yards, a steel BB launched at a published velocity (3-foot, coil) of 1,350 f.p.s. is still doing 747 f.p.s. and requires a lead of roughly 8 feet on a target doing 45 m.p.h. By 50 yards, however, that steel BB is down to about 659 f.p.s. and needs a lead of 10½ to 11 feet. When you get to 60 yards, which I feel is reaching the limit for steel BB's on geese, the retained velocity is just 586 f.p.s. and a 14-foot lead is needed. In just that 20-yard span, the steel **BB** has been slowed so much by air drag 8 more feet of forward allowance is needed.

The same thing happens with lead shot beyond 40 yards. A favorite old shotshell is the 3¾-drams equivalent, 1¼-ounce, 12-gauge duck load which has a published velocity (3-foot, coil) of 1,330 f.p.s. When this load contains unbuffered lead 4's, that velocity is down to 734 f.p.s. at 40 yards, 648 f.p.s. at 50 yards and 577 f.p.s. at 60 yards. In terms of forward allowance at 40 yards, it means about 8 feet, but 10 yards farther out the forward allowance is 11 feet. At a full 60 yards, the lead must reach out to a mite over 14 feet. This means an addition of at least 6 feet of forward allowance is needed between 40 and 60 yards despite the relatively high published velocity. Hunters who have difficulty setting off 4 feet of lead on skeet's full-deflection shots from Low Three and High Five cannot imagine an extension to 14 feet of lead.

The longer shots in Sporting Clays can also befuddle shooters who are used to the shorter leads of skeet and trap, as the lighter lead pellets slow down drastically even within 40 yards. For example, a #7½ lead pellet with a published velocity (3-foot, coil) of 1,200 f.p.s. requires a forward allowance of 4.3 feet on a 50-m.p.h. crossing target at 20-yard skeet range; slow that target down to 45 m.p.h., and the 20-yard lead becomes 3.8 feet. On a 40-yard crossing or tower shot in Sporting Clays, however, the mathematical forward allowance grows surprisingly. For a 50-m.p.h. target, it becomes a lengthy 10.3 feet, and for the slower 45-m.p.h. target it is 9.4 feet.

That's more than double skeet's 20-yard lead and is close to the same lead needed at 50 yards with steel BB's. Air resistance gets tough as distances lengthen, and much depends upon the pellet's ability to overcome air drag. Casual shooters are amazed when they first observe the extreme distances between their muzzle and the target on longer shots.

VISUALIZING LONG LEADS

One of the main problems hunters and budding Sporting Clays' shooters have with long-range targets is wanting to "aim" the shot, thinking accuracy is more important than swing speed. They dawdle, perhaps squinting down the barrel, and swing rather slowly while measuring off a meager foot or so of lead. This just won't do. Your shotgun must be swung briskly and accuracy derived from eye/hand coordination rather than any alignment of receiver and bead.

How do you accomplish this? You must generally accept that you will not be seeing your gun in direct juxtaposition to the target, at least not as a sharply seen object. In keeping with the tenets of classic wing-shooting theory, your eyes should be focused on the target's leading edge while your gun is seen as a fuzzy blur, if at all. What this means, of course, is your gun will always be in your peripheral vision as it swings far out ahead of the target by 6 to 16 feet. If your gun is clearly seen, you're doing it wrong.

How can you become comfortable with this sort of optical situation? You can't always rely on getting lucky the way I did when those trailing birds fell and gave me a picture on which to build, but you can create a measured situation to give you an idea of what such long leads look like over a gun barrel when your eyes are focused on the target. This can be accomplished by measuring off 40, 50 and 60 yards and driving in stakes at each of those distances. The stakes can be topped by the target in question, such as a mounted mallard or clay target, or left plain. Always remember a target looks larger on the horizontal plane than on the vertical; aside from that, though, this setup can be a good teacher once you drive in a second set of stakes to represent the approximate forward allowance for each range.

Let's say you are interested in learning the mathematical leads needed with steel BB's for long-range mallard shooting. At 40 yards, drive in a second stake 8½ feet from the first (target) stake; at 50 yards, drive one in 11 feet from the target; and at 60 yards, carry it out to 14 or 15 feet. Once these are measured off, go back to the firing point and study the visual effect when your gun is pointed at the extreme forward-allowance stake while your eyes are focused sharply on the target. This

You probably will not master good long-range shotgunning techniques until you acquire a swing that sweeps far into your peripheral vision. You have to stretch your leads a lot farther than you think.

will acquaint you with the gap that should exist between the target and your gun when the charge is triggered. Above all, it should give you an idea of how the visual aspect develops when the fuzzily seen gun is swung well away from your center of focus and extends into your peripheral vision. This is important because it helps you feel more comfortable working without sharp visual contact with your gun.

Do not, however, burn these sight pictures into your mind with the idea of bringing them into play later for precise leads. Precision is anathema to a wing shot's thinking and actions. Your swing must be dynamic and general; any attempt at aiming a definite 14-foot lead will result in disaster. Wing shooting is, after all, a game of movement and action; it is dynamic, not static like rifle and handgun shooting. Forward allowances must be generated by your swing speed, which is covered in more detail in Chapter 12.

14

Cures For Head Lifting

Head lifting may very well be disaster *numero uno* in shotgunning. In essence, it's like using a rifle with the rear sight set to the uppermost adjustment, which causes the bore to pitch upward and send the bullet high. As has often been written, your eye serves as the rear sight on a shotgun. If your eye is in a lofty position, your hands, in carrying out natural eye/hand coordination, can tilt the smoothbore upward and send the shot string high. At least, that is the theory.

My own observation is that head lifting doesn't invariably mean high shooting. The theory above is based upon the assumption that natural eye/hand coordination always occurs; I'm not inclined to agree with that assumption. Not every shooter has natural coordination and not everyone applies it perfectly. After watching more than a few shooters make head-lifting errors, I have come to believe patterns sometimes fly low and behind the target because the shooter's hands didn't automatically work to the eye and left the bore axis low and generally dragging after the mark rather than swinging through it aggressively.

Head lifting, therefore, can produce low pattern placement as well as high pattern placement, depending upon how well your hands coordinate with your eyes. Regardless of whether the shot string flies high or low, however, the important point is an out-of-position eye is tantamount to disaster. The best way to wring the most from your natural

eye/hand coordination is to get your head down on the comb of a well-fitted stock and keep it there throughout the entire swing.

That's easier said than done, of course, so along with the traditional advice for curing head lifting, I have added a few thoughts on the subject that have not been emphasized in this context before but which I believe will help minimize head lifting.

TRADITIONAL ADVICE

When discussing head lifting, most writers harp on stock fit and self-discipline. These are legitimate aspects, of course.

If your stock doesn't fit your anatomy and you can't get your head down comfortably, there is a tendency to lift it. Sometimes this is a matter of not being able to see sharply over the receiver and rib; sometimes it is a matter of muscle tension pulling your head away from an unnatural position. Having a well-fitted stock is indeed a prerequisite for super wing shooting.

There must also be some discipline involved. You must fight off the temptation to peek at the target throughout the pressure, excitement and anxiety of competition. The hunter who wants to see his pheasant fold and the clay-target marksman who wants to see the target break for his first 25-straight will miss if they are so eager to see it they lift off the comb before completing an entire swing, shoot

Why shouldn't you lift your head? This shooter did and missed this skeet target. Head lifting or just plain failing to get your head in the right position is the cause of many misses. This fellow illustrates the problem beautifully.

and follow-through sequence. Shooting may be a sport, but in its finest sense it also involves work. Keeping your head down can be surprisingly difficult and requires as much discipline and muscle memory as any other part of your overall swing.

NEW IDEAS

I have noticed a head-high position is sometimes due to a failure to get the gun up properly. Your head has a tendency to shift about when there isn't snug eye-to-comb contact, but the tendency to lift is lessened when the stock is brought up solidly and your eye feels comfortable.

I often see shooters go through a series of head-lifting errors when they work their first rounds of Sporting Clays because their hands don't bring the gun to the proper location

when they are confronted with birds in the air. They exacerbate the situation further by peeking and/or failing to stretch their necks to find the comb. Hunters make the same errors afield, and as a result, we find there are a lot of misses in hunting and Sporting Clays. Trapshooters and American skeetmen can

This is more like it — head down all the way through your swing and follow-through. It takes discipline, of course, but gun fit and gripping features are factors, too.

premount their guns before the target is thrown, and we find very high scores and comparatively few occurrences of head lifting in those games. If you can get your shotgun solidly and properly mounted, then, there is less chance for head-lifting mistakes to occur.

TRIGGER GRIPS

This is where two vital factors enter the picture. One is your gun's grip design; the other is your trigger-hand effort.

The grip's size and geometry provide lifting leverage while your hand makes a positive mount to the eye. If the grip doesn't provide leverage for easy lifting or your trigger hand doesn't carry out its function, your hands will leave the comb variously low relative to your cheekbone. In many instances, it isn't that you don't know better. Sometimes a head-high position *isn't* caused by lifting at all but by a failure to make a good mount. Your gun should come to your eye, *not* vice versa!

A shotgun's grip should provide the leverage needed to elevate your gun. I think shooters plagued by head lifting haven't delved deeply enough into the subtleties of grip design, which were often discussed by the great British gunmaker Robert Churchill. Churchill was somewhat less than totally a British traditionalist when it came to barrel length; his 25"-barreled double, the controversial XXV gun, sparked heated debate in the U.K. for years. Churchill's doubles, however, did retain the trimness of the famous British Game Guns, including the straight-hand grip, albeit modified, as Churchill questioned the effectiveness of the "English" grip fashioned by many of his contemporaries.

In his book *Game Shooting*, Churchill argued, "The tendency of many modern guns has been towards a grip which is too straight for practical mounting. The line is graceful and looks well in illustration, but it is a handicap in use." In other words, Churchill found the angle of the English-style grips produced by his fellow gunmakers didn't provide the right geometry for ease and perfection in mounting. The underline was too high and made shooters flex their elbows unnaturally to bring the gun to their eye.

To alleviate this condition, Churchill made

". . .very material alterations to the grip. The tang of the action and trigger plate were curved down so the hand moves naturally parallel to the line of sight without enforcing a strained position to the right [trigger] arm." Churchill's modifications to the straight grip were subtle; a person who doesn't know about them may not recognize them, but a sophisticated collector or shotgun buff should understand the design nuances.

A more radical approach to the trigger-hand grip was taken by American trap and live-bird shooter Fred Etchen Sr., whose search for a solid grip led to what we now know as the "Etchen grip." The Etchen grip is a tightly curved version of the full-pistol grip that is carried to such an extreme the grip's toe practically curves forward. This geometry bunches your hand and provides positive gripping contact for the lower fingers. It is pictured on the next page and in Etchen's book *Commonsense Shotgun Shooting*, which was also reprinted as a soft-cover book called *How To Be An Expert At Shotgun Shooting*. Both books are still around as collectors' items and are well worth finding.

I was told by Etchen's son, Fred "Rudy" Etchen Jr., the original Etchen grip came about when his father felt uncomfortable with the straight grip on his slide-action shotgun. He decided he needed more trigger-hand purchase and added mounting leverage. All he could find at the time was a big bottle cork, so he attached this to the straight grip via the simple expedient of a long nail and some tape. The line of the straight grip angled the cork forward, but Etchen found he liked it.

The idea was soon translated into a custom stock with a very tightly curved geometry that brought the little finger firmly in contact with the grip for lifting assistance. One problem with many grips had been that the lower fingers did not touch the grip tightly enough to be of any help in lifting. Besides helping to elevate the gun and keep it snug under the cheekbone, the Etchen grip is believed to mitigate against flinching, which is a whole other topic.

The point is, your shotgun's grip should be shaped and sized so you can elevate your gun easily all the way to your eye. There should be no need for unnatural hunching or scrunching, all of which invite head lifting.

THE "LAZY" HAND

Improper eye-to-comb contact can also be caused by a "lazy" hand that simply hasn't been trained to come all the way up. I have seen many hunters and beginning clay-target shooters, especially beginning Sporting Clays' shooters, display this laziness.

If you watch closely, you will see many shooters mount their gun terribly low, often just above the armpit, out on the deltoid or even on the biceps. A low-mounted gun and faulty trigger-hand elevation undoubtedly stem from a lack of knowledge about how a shotgun should be mounted. Among experts, the gun is always brought to the face, never vice versa. Most typical shotgunners, however, don't study expert practices and tend to mount their shotguns as they would a rifle, meaning they bring it to some shouldering point and then lower their head to the comb — wrong!

A shotgunner who handles his gun properly will always bring the gun to his face — always. The first point of contact should be the comb to the cheekbone directly under your eye so there is immediate eye-muzzle-target alignment. This method is often called the "thrust out" system and is described in Churchill's book *Game Shooting*, which is recommended reading for every wing shooter.

Although gun fit and discipline play a big part in proper wing-gunning technique, it is my opinion head lifting is frequently caused by poor mounting. Your trigger hand and grip's size and style play roles that are more important than formerly thought; their failure

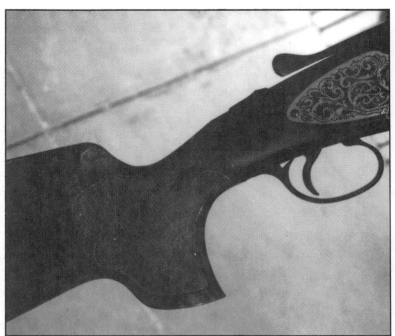

An Etchen grip, as worked onto this Remington 90-T Trap Gun, provides good lifting leverage from the lower fingers and also is said to help reduce flinching.

to assist in getting the gun in place can lead to head lifting.

The most important thing you can do to prevent head lifting is practice your mounting move. This can be done on a skeet field or with a Trius trap at home. Like any athlete learning a new technique, you must force yourself to make the right moves to overcome a lazy hand and bring your gun up aggressively.

Attention should be given to the grip when a new gun is purchased. As Churchill indicated, there are some designs which, although racy and appealing, don't have the necessary qualities for optimum mounting ease and repeated perfection. I believe a secure mount with the correct eye-to-comb contact will result in considerably less head lifting.

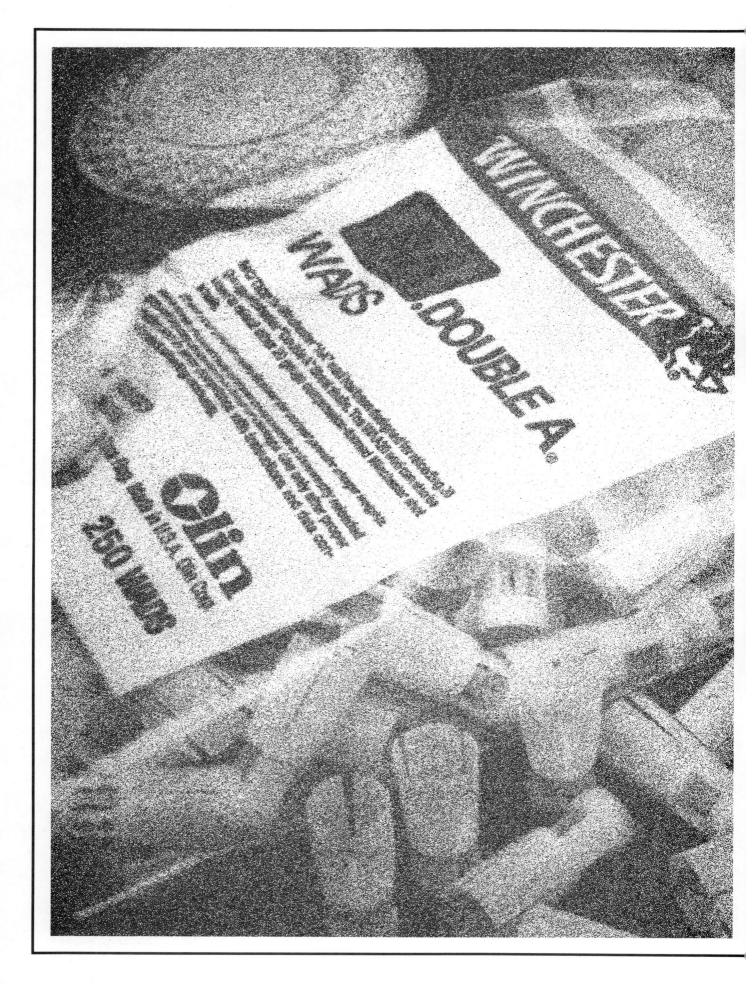

15

Updating That Good Ol' 16 Gauge

I have to admit the 12 is my favorite gauge because of its versatility and effectiveness, but if I had to make a second choice, it would be the 16. Yes, that's right, the 16 gauge! Luckily, I don't have to make that choice, because nobody is going to yank the 12 gauge off the market. Although I thoroughly enjoy hunting with a 16 and have been using one more and more for upland hunting these past few years, there is a problem with getting the right ammunition and finding new guns in that gauge. The scene has brightened somewhat, however, in recent years.

Browning lifted my spirits when they introduced the 16-gauge Citori over & under (O&U) and reintroduced their nicely scaled Sweet Sixteen autoloader, but after a few years they broke my heart by dropping the Citori abruptly. Frankly, I never thought Browning treated the 16-gauge Citori properly. It had a low comb like the other field-grade Citori Lightnings, and Browning didn't upgrade the 16 until the very last year. A straight-gripped 16 with a slightly elevated comb line might well have been what enthusiastic uplanders wanted, but alas, Browning didn't see it that way. Modern marketing decisions often run contrary to the feelings of gun buffs.

Browning did leave the Sweet Sixteen in their line, and some hunters have gravitated to it, as well they should. It is a well-designed

semiauto that points well. It is very fast in the uplands with a 26″ barrel, especially on ruffed grouse and woodcock, and with a 28″ barrel in place, it swings quite smoothly on ringnecks and waterfowl.

16-GAUGE IMPORTS

The 16 gauge's cause has been taken up by a few of the smaller importers who bring Spanish and Italian doubles to U.S. shores. The Spanish are the primary source of 16-gauge side-by-sides (SxS's) at reasonable prices and, happily, some of the Spanish gunmakers have improved their quality.

One importer who has recognized a market for spirited 16-gauge SxS's is Bill Hanus, whose current product is called The Birdgun II. Incorporating some of the points I described in *The Double Shotgun*, Bill designed his fowling gun around the basic action employed by Ugartechea, a Spanish gunmaker.

The Bill Hanus Birdguns have 26″ barrels bored Skeet 1 and Skeet 2, the forend is a semi-beavertail and the stock is straight-gripped with ¼″ of cast-off. What pleases me is the frames are proportioned to the gauge; I hate it when gunmakers slam out 16's on 12-gauge action bodies or receivers. At 6¼ to 6½

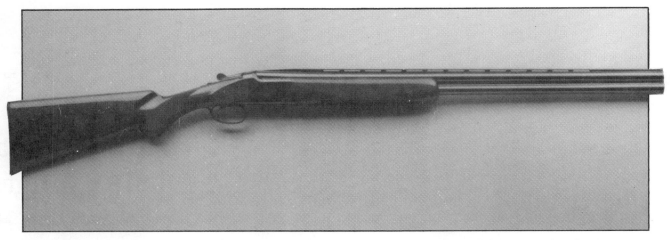

Browning's announcement of a 16-gauge Citori over & under in the late 1980s was a shot in the arm to the nearly forgotten 16-gauge market, but alas, sales didn't excite Browning and it was dropped abruptly from the 1990 line. Too bad, I don't believe Browning ever really gave it a chance.

pounds, the Hanus Birdgun is a neat and trim 16. It is available from Bill Hanus or from Precision Sports, Inc., P.O. Box 708, Cortland, New York 13045.

At the start of this year, I received news that Bernardelli is also shipping 16-gauge SxS's to these shores, where they will be handled by Magnum Research, Inc., 7110 University Avenue N.E., Minneapolis, Minnesota 55432. The Bernardelli Model 3E, a boxlock otherwise known as the Gamecock Deluxe, can be ordered with an oil finish or high gloss and with a double or single trigger. Although it is a boxlock, this Bernardelli sports a false sideplate that is case-colored in the traditional European fashion. The one I handled was a heckuva nice gun.

One of the truly deluxe, while still afford-able, 16-gauge SxS's to come out of Europe is the Arrieta from Eibar, Spain. Arrieta has emulated the British Game Guns for years, and the workmanship that goes into them seems to be among the best applied in Eibar. The guns have excellent balance and hand-to-hand relationships. They are being handled by Jack Jansma of Wingshooting Adventures, 4320 Kalamazoo Avenue S.E., Grand Rapids, Michigan 49508 and range in price from $2,400 to $3,500, but optional equipment can be added. They are true sidelocks, and the workmanship inside appears quite good for this price. Stock dimensions, barrel lengths and chokes are made to order, and the wait is

not forever and a day as it is with the British.

The fact that all these European 16's are SxS's shouldn't dampen your enthusiasm. The SxS is at its peak of efficiency in the uplands, and so is the 16 gauge!

The 16 isn't dead and gone just because Yankee gunmakers seem to have discriminated against it. These imports and the American used-gun market can satisfy hunters who prefer the 16 gauge.

USED 16's

The 16 wasn't always down and out in the U.S., of course. Some great ones were made in the past and occasionally appear on dealers' shelves or at gun shows. If you want a 16, opportunities abound in the secondhand or trading market.

One of the best 16-gauge upland auto-loaders I ever carried was a Remington Model 11-48 with a 26″ barrel and Poly-Choke. The M/11-48 was a properly scaled 16, and it had trim, streamlined geometry. The same was true of the M/11-48's companion, which in the late 1940s was the Remington Model 31 pump gun. With the lightweight receiver (designated by an appended "L"), the Model 31L was an easy-carrying, fast-pointing pump gun, and its action was, in my opinion, faster and slicker than that of the vaunted Model 12.

Unfortunately, when Remington went to

The 16 isn't a dead issue; many importers are bringing in side-by-sides from Italy and Spain. Here the author pockets a pheasant taken with the Hanus Birdgun in 16 gauge with Skeet 1/Skeet 2 chokes — an ideal upland combo.

the Model 1100 autoloader, it no longer scaled the 16's receiver to match the gauge; the 16-bore M/1100 had a 12-gauge receiver — as did the original 20-gauge M/1100's, for that matter — and who wants to lug a 12 gauge to shoot 16-gauge shells?

Finding a like-new, 16-gauge Model 11-48 or 31L at a gun show or used-gun shop would be great for anyone who is addicted to this bore.

Marlin also made a 16-gauge O&U which, again in my opinion, was a good-handling smoothbore. Its lines may not have been classic, especially through the trigger guard and receiver area, but it pointed nicely and had a lively muzzle area that responded

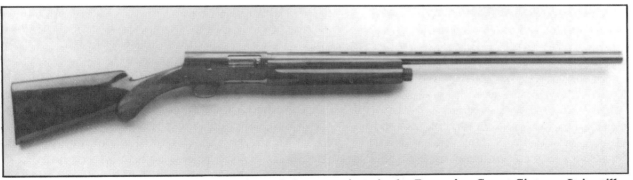

One of the 16's still available in properly scaled proportions is the Browning Sweet Sixteen. It is still quite a gun.

readily but was not whippy. I could think of a lot worse gun for upland hunting than a Marlin Model 90 O&U!

There were some American SxS's made in 16 gauge, but I always found them less than perfect. They were either too heavy through the barrels or had crooked stocks — some had a combination of the two problems. I once owned two L.C. Smiths in 16 gauge that had some spirit through the barrels; however, in typical Yankee fashion, they had combs considerably lower than the British doubles and certainly too low to fit my anatomy. This was also true of many Philadelphia Foxes, Lefevers, Parkers, various old Ithacas and other mail-order 16's of yesteryear.

About the best-fitting American 16-gauge doubles were the Winchester Models 24 and 21. These were given higher combs, and their pointing qualities blended more with our modern lean-into-it style of shotgunning. Other SxS's were designed for the more upright stance that prevailed around the turn of the century.

Although traders ask a lot for the Model 24 these days, it really isn't worth much; it was a sheer knockabout gun back in the 1930s and 1940s, which was its heyday, and it was made cheaply to fit the price demands of a nation suffering from a severe depression. However, the Model 24 had excellent gripping qualities and a full comb; it may well have been the first American SxS to achieve a good fit. The Model 21 improved in quality as it evolved, and both guns are easy to get on the trading market these days if you have $3,500 or so in your jeans. I've said before that a skeet-grade Model 21 in 16 gauge is a great American upland gun and I still believe that, but you have to pay the price.

The original Browning Sweet Sixteens were also excellent field guns with quality workmanship. They were correctly scaled to match the 16-gauge cartridge, and with a 26″ barrel and Improved Cylinder choke, were beautiful in the uplands. Again, original Belgian-made guns are priced at collector levels, and you will be forced to write an even bigger check than if you were buying the current Japanese-made version of the same gun.

STEEL SHOT AND THE 16

If anything has undermined the 16 as an all-around shotgun, it is the advent of steel shot. The 16 simply does not have adequate capacity for heavy loads of steel shot. There are currently only two commercial steel-shot loads for the 16 — one made by Federal and one by Winchester.

The Federal round has about $^{15}/_{16}$-ounce of shot, while the Winchester offering has about ¾-ounce. These light loads are not necessarily detrimental because there are more steel pellets to the ounce than there are with lead pellets; hence, the lighter 16-gauge steel loads can supply some pretty good density.

The capacity limitations of the 16-gauge hull also have a bearing on the shot sizes you can load, and this is the problem. The commercial 16's, for example, are commonly loaded with only #2 and #4 shot, neither of which is a truly effective long-range pellet. The steel #2 barely has the energy of a lead #4 around 40 yards, and the energy tapers off quickly in the face of air resistance. That is why the 16 does not have a robust loading for geese or high ducks.

Why not load steel 1's or BB's into the ol' 16 gauge? Primarily because it is almost impossible to get a full ¾-ounce charge of those bigger pellets into the hull. There is so much air space between bulky 1's and BB's that the charge automatically becomes lighter and, in turn, sacrifices density. The density sacrifice is too great for effectiveness on geese and high ducks, and why promote crippling? A hunter is foolish to blast away with insufficient pattern energy — I cringe every time I see empty 20-gauge, standard-length hulls lying around a goose blind!

In my opinion, the 16 gauge won't regain its all-around status until there is a 3″ 16-gauge Magnum case able to accept heavier loads of steel 1's and BB's. I will be amazed if such a hull appears, however, because its immediate commercial appeal would be minor and it would take years for a company to regain its research and development monies.

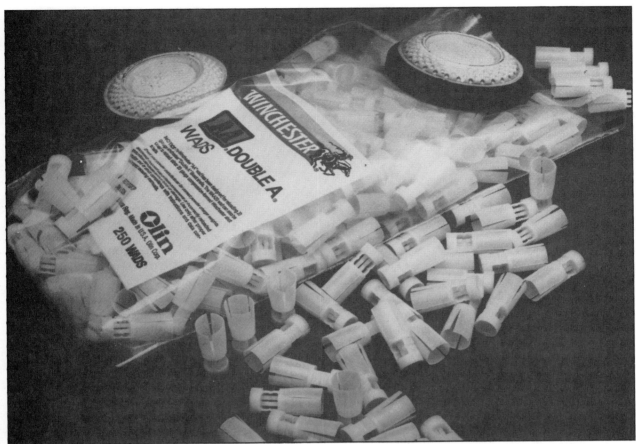

A spurt of interest in the 16 gauge prompted Winchester to include a 16-gauge wad in its line — the light blue WAA16 — for reloading 1 and 1⅛-ounce shot charges.

NEW LEAD-LOAD CONCEPTS

The 16 was almost forgotten by commercial ammo makers during the 1970s and 1980s, but at the tag-end of the '80s a few changes came along, thanks mainly to the introduction of the Browning 16-gauge Citori and the reintroduction of their Sweet Sixteen. For a time, these stimulated the market.

Winchester was the first to improve its 16-gauge loadings after decades of using the Mark V concept, which is a cupped cardboard overpowder wad topped by a fiber filler and polyethylene shot wrapper. In the late 1980s, Winchester took the next step and came up with a Double-A type wad for their 16-gauge field loads. Moreover, they brought out a Double-X Magnum for the 16 using 1¼ ounces of copper-plated shot and a plastic buffer to enhance patterning; Federal has an identical load in its Premium line. These buffered Magnums are the first important new 16-gauge loads in a long time, and they pattern superbly for long-range shots in the uplands or for turkey hunting.

RELOADING COMPONENTS

For many years, hunters who wanted special fodder for their 16's were forced to handload. The problem is there was a shortage of 16-gauge components — after Remington dropped its R-16 wad, we had no 1-ounce wad. From the stack of correspondence I had, however, there still appeared to be a big demand for such a wad.

Eventually, into this gap came a pair of plastic cushions: the Gualandi-28 from ACTIV Industries, Inc. and the new Winchester WAA16 wad, both of which can handle 16-gauge 1 ouncers very nicely within their parameters. These have pretty well handled the 16's all-around chores with lead shot, going from ⅞ to 1⅛-ounce loads. For basic upland hunting, I am not sure you ever need more than 1⅛ ounces in the 16.

Several new shotshell powders have also come along to enliven 16-gauge reloading. The powders are Solo 1250 and Solo 1500 from the relatively new Scot Powder Company and Super Field Ball Powder from Winchester. Here are a few recipes.

Winchester AA hull
Winchester 209 primer
20.0/Solo 1250
Gualandi-28 wad
1 ounce lead shot
Pressure: 9,200 l.u.p.
Velocity: 1,165 f.p.s.

A good powder for 1¼-ounce, 16-gauge Magnum reloads is Scot Powder Company's Solo 1500, a clean-burning disc-type propellant.

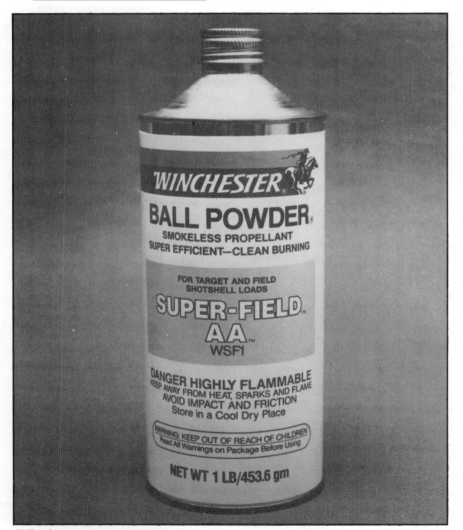

Winchester Super Field Ball Powder is a very efficient propellant in modern 16-gauge plastic hulls with loads of 1 and 1⅛ ounces.

Remington SP hull
Remington 209P primer
21.0/Solo 1250
Gualandi-28 wad
1 ounce lead shot
Pressure: 10,900 l.u.p.
Velocity: 1,220 f.p.s.

Winchester AA-type hull
Winchester 209 primer
29.0/Solo 1500
Remington SP-16 wad
1⅛ ounces lead shot
Pressure: 10,900 l.u.p.
Velocity: 1,260 f.p.s.

ACTIV all-plastic hull
Winchester 209 primer
28.0/Solo 1500
Remington SP-16 wad
1¼ ounces lead shot
Pressure: 10,800 l.u.p.
Velocity: 1,220 f.p.s.

Winchester AA-type hull
Winchester 209 primer
20.0/Super Field Ball Powder
Winchester WAA16 wad
1 ounce lead shot
Pressure: 8,400 p.s.i.
Velocity: 1,165 f.p.s.

Winchester AA-type hull
CCI 209 primer
20.5/Super Field Ball Powder
Winchester WAA16 wad
1⅛ ounces lead shot
Pressure: 10,800 p.s.i.
Velocity: 1,185 f.p.s.

These are some very effective field loads for the 16, and the recipes using 20.0 to 20.5 grains of Super Field Ball Powder make excellent target loads for those who take their 16's to skeet or Sporting Clays' layouts.

IT AIN'T ALL BAD NEWS!

For those who like the 16 gauge, then, things ain't all bad. There are excellent guns available for hunting — new doubles from importers and some American leftovers that can be found at gun shows or secondhand shops. The important thing is there have been some substantial improvements in the field of ammunition; both factory loads and reloads can be jazzed up with new powders and wads.

The versatility that was once the 16's is still there, and the ammo for it is actually getting better. I would still like to own a 16 gauge that has a 3″ chamber and barrels that can withstand steel loads; of course, I'd need the hulls for it, too. Oh, well, we can dream, can't we?

16

A New Look At Brush-Busting Bird Guns

The term "brush-busting" may seem out of place when tied to shotguns, especially upland game guns. It has traditionally been used to describe deer rifles that use blunt-nosed bullets to better their travel through timber and thickets on their way to a trophy stag. Rounds like the old .45-70, .35 Remington, .444 Marlin and .35 Whelen are good examples, but a brush-busting bird gun — what's that all about?

Upland guns have historically been teamed with open chokes — Cylinder bore, Improved Cylinder (IC) or Skeet — in relatively short barrels to handle flushes which are, theoretically at least, close-in and among heavy cover. The idea has always been to get the broadest possible hitting area and spread the pellets out so some will find openings in the clutter and slip through to the bird. Early writers on the subject of ruffed grouse hunting sometimes advocated using 9's to fill the air with pellets in hopes of finding tunnels through the branches and twigs. It sounded good and left a lasting impression on those who hunted in heavy cover. Light, fast, short guns with open patterns of fine shot are supposedly ideal. . .but I wonder.

TIGHTER CHOKES AND BIGGER LOADS

Several things happened to make me skeptical. Could the reverse actually be true? Could a tighter pattern and heavier loads be more effective in the brush? Observations I have made since the 1940s indicate snug shot strings and more pellet energy may do a better job in the brush than scattered light loads because birds hit by tighter, heavier patterns are easier retrieves.

The idea began during my college years when I broke my left elbow in an early football game. With a hunting season staring me in the face, I learned I was to spend four weeks with my left arm at a 90° angle immobilized in a cast! At the time, I hunted every weekend and afternoons when I didn't have classes. I had a 1939 Hudson with a leaky radiator, and in the trunk of that car was my 20-gauge Remington Model 31-L with a Poly-Choke, boxes of different loads and jugs of water. I'd had other parts of my anatomy in a sling, figuratively speaking, but it never obstructed my wing shooting. Who could crank a pump gun with his arm in a sling? But, I wanted to go hunting!

The solution to my dilemma came while I was hanging around the local hardware store looking at new guns. I found I could handle the then-new Remington Model 11-48 with only one hand. I had made a few extra dollars from a pretty good summer job, so I bought the 11-48 and took home some change from a $100 bill.

The only drawback was the 20-gauge M/11-48 had a full-choked barrel and there wasn't time to have it fitted with a Poly-Choke. I took it hunting anyway, and one of my most memorable shots that season was a rooster pheasant on opening day, a one-hand effort that required just one shot!

After I shed my cast, I kept using the M/11-48 because by then I had warmed up to it, Full (F) choke and all. I started taking it into the grouse covers around my home, which at that time held a surprising number of birds. The cover was a mixture of mature pines, tamaracks, alders, birches, ash, willows, scrub oaks and the like. The birds were normally screened by something, and in the past I'd had cripples and feathered-but-lost birds with the open-choke setting on my Poly. With the full-choked M/11-48, however, there were very few cripples and floppers, especially when I used 1-ounce charges of 6's. I grew to hate 8's because of the way I had to chase down birds, and 7½'s were a bit dicey. The 6's slammed through and produced positive retrieves, and interestingly enough, I didn't feel disadvantaged with the Full choke; it's the swing that counts, not a few extra inches of pattern width. Those

experiences with Full choke in grouse thickets stayed with me, but after college I started using all sorts of guns and drew no firm conclusions.

I never did much grouse hunting with a dog. I saw too many wild flushes ruin a good day in the coverts when dogs bumped birds. There are very few great grouse dogs, and the few I tried were untalented, so I gave up and went after br'er partridge alone and liked it. A pair of partridge taken walk-up style is more

A tighter choke helped make positive retrieves on grouse in tangly cover like that in the background. Put the emphasis on your swing, not added pattern distribution.

satisfying to me than a limit taken over a dog.

Dog fanciers will moan and groan at that, I know. So be it. I know hunters who regularly leave their dogs home when they go after grouse because an unruly canine can louse up a hunt something awful. A grouse dog is either great or terrible. But I digress. . .the point is, for a dogless hunter the hit should be a clean kill in midair or at least a solid, anchoring one. In my experience, this wasn't invariably the case with traditional open chokes and frilly 8's and 9's.

One of the first expensive guns I bought was a Browning Superposed bored IC/M. When I patterned it, I found the Modified (M) barrel was quite tight, but I didn't have it regulated. I also found during the course of two grouse seasons that Modified wiped up very neatly whenever I needed it for a second shot. The bird would be well out, as walked-up birds usually angle away from the shooter and would normally have some screening, but that Modified barrel hammered through and stopped a number of them.

My most impressive long-range, through-the-brush hits came one afternoon when I found only 6's in my vest pocket, leftovers from a pheasant hunt I forgot to replace with #7½ trap loads. Again, I did not draw a definite conclusion.

Then came a series of years I spent hunting with smallbores — 20's, 28's, .410's — with the doubles bored IC/M and the repeaters ranging from Skeet to Modified. Again, I experienced some cripples and runners in the brush, and my cleanest results came from heavy charges of 6's in each respective gauge.

After spending time with the little guns, I counted my coins and came up with enough to buy a Merkel. Although marked for Modified and Full patterns, the Merkel had extremely tight bores

In brushy areas, heavier shot and tighter patterns may penetrate growth better than lighter loads that scatter all over.

This type of pattern might seem too tight for ruffed grouse, but for a second shot taken farther out through a thicket, it can bust its way through for cleaner kills than a wider pattern. For brush-busting work, 6's are preferred over the 8's used here just for the purpose of illustration.

and long, tapering chokes that really delivered full-choke averages from the lower tube and Extra-Full (XF) densities from the upper one. I developed a spreader-type reload that gave approximately Improved-Cylinder patterns from the lower barrel but generally chambered a normal load in the upper barrel to give me what amounted to IC/XF. That might sound like a weird combination for ruffed grouse, but it was the best partridge gun I ever used. With 1⅛-ounce loads of 6's in the upper chamber, that follow-up barrel slammed shot strings through all sorts of growth to fold birds dramatically. I have since had the Merkel revamped with a Briley choke in the lower tube and both barrels bored somewhat to relieve the European tightness (it originally had a 0.722″ main bore). The top barrel is still dynamite in the brush and can batter 16-yard trap clays mercilessly.

In hunting, shots that were mere cripples with the open-choked guns and fine shot were clean kills with the Merkel's top barrel and either 6's or copper-plated 7½'s. By then, the conclusion had seeped into my laggardly brain: Tight patterns and heavier shot bust through brush far better than light loads that scatter all over and need to find holes in the cover to do their thing.

When I began field-testing some of the newer smallbores with screw-in chokes, I experimented with an uncommon (for the U.S.) choke combination. The lower barrels were either Skeet or IC tubes, while the top barrels were Full chokes. While I employed 7½'s in the open chokes, I tended to favor 6's in the Full barrel. I like it better that way, meaning IC/F; the second shots can use the density and concentrated shot string. A compact shot string has more of a battering-ram effect, while a wide-open pattern can be picked off by twigs and branches, even heavy leaf growth. Personally, I think the 28-gauge double is more effective with IC/F than IC/M.

EASE OF HITTING

A lot of patterning has shown me there is a paltry difference in the effective hitting area of a Modified or Full choke once the range reaches 30+ yards. In fact, the main difference between Modified and Full isn't width but rather the number of pellets. Modified invariably puts fewer shot in the core than Full choke; therefore, it is less likely to pound through cover. To affect a clean kill, your swing is more important than a few more inches of pattern diameter, as I've discussed in my book *Shotgunning Trends In Transition*. Suffice it to say, the difference between hitting with Modified or Full choke beyond 30 yards is mainly mental, not physical.

What cinched the idea of the correctness of tighter chokes for second shots in brushy environs for me was an experience on a Sporting Clays' course. I was in a mixed-up squad going through a practice round, and one of the shooters was a rank beginner with a side-by-side (SxS) bored M/F. That's not the best selection for Sporting, but he was primarily a hunter having fun with his field gun, which is what Sporting Clays is supposed to be all about. The rest of us had open-choked guns, generally IC, with 8's.

The beginner didn't do badly; he could swing his gun rather well. We came to the last stand, which was a flushing-quail test along an old stone fence grown up with weeds and some tall brush plus, as I recall, a few Hawthorne apple trees. If you didn't move briskly on this pair of clays, they got behind the heavy brush. A lot of people tagged the first target in the open but fired on the second only after it had ducked behind the brush. I didn't see one hunter using an open-choked gun break that clay when it got behind that screen, not even a chip!

The beginner stepped up with his tightly choked gun. He was a tad slow and the second bird easily got behind the fence, but he let fly anyway and the bird blew apart. I don't mean it was chipped; it blew apart! He obviously got multiple pellets on it. Then he did it again and again. That full-choked pattern tore through the thick growth along that fence and pounded the target. What more proof did I need?

It may have taken me a few decades to come to this "radical" conclusion, but for hammering second and third follow-up shots into cover I have come to believe the old boys were wrong — wide-open patterns and dinky pellets are not optimum. It takes power to ram through thick brambles with authority, and that calls for snug shot strings that concentrate their pellets into smaller areas and force their way through. Living with the hope that a few 8's or 9's will find voids to get through the clutter is a mistake; you have to make your own luck with accurate pointing, swinging and hammering. A tight Modified pattern or basic Full choke can be great for the second barrel in the bushes!

With single-barreled repeaters, the answer for all-around performance may be tightening up by a degree of choke, such as going from IC to Modified when the potential for longer shots presents itself. This can easily be accomplished with screw-in choke devices or a Poly-Choke.

Brush-busting isn't only for deer hunters anymore. Make sure you are equipped to bust through the brush with your bird gun!

17

A Critical Look At The "Fine Shot" School Of Pellet Selection

When I was just an impressionable kid, outdoor magazines were running articles enthusiastically endorsing the so-called "fine shot" school of pellet selection. Essentially, this school of thought argued that multiple hits with smaller pellet sizes — 8's, 9's and especially 7½'s — produced cleaner kills than fewer hits with larger shot sizes which, nevertheless, penetrated deeper.

The theory was that multiple hits intensified the "shock effect" and did more immediate damage to the bird's neurological system than the heavier pellets could do to the vital organs. It was believed the shock to the bird's system was not just a total of the number of hits, but rather a square of the number of hits! In other words, a bird hit by five 7½'s, fine-shot advocates believed, was actually impacted with the sensation of being struck by 25 such pellets. They further believed the resulting shock overpowered the bird's nervous system and either killed it or at least anchored it for an easy retrieve.

The fine-shot concept received a lot of attention and many hunters accepted it. One outcome was the eventual discontinuation of #7 shot, because the fine-shot school of pellet selection boomed 7½'s. They pointed out there were about 350 7½'s to the ounce, while 7's

counted only about 300, and that gave the potential for greater pattern density to the 7½'s, according to them. More-populous patterns put more shot on each bird intercepted, according to theory, and the extra shocking power put down birds and held them.

As an impressionable kid I bought the idea. At the time, it was all new to me and reflected modern thinking as opposed to the old notions that pivoted around 30″ barrels, full-choked guns and heavy loads of 2's and 4's. During my last year in high school and my first years of college, I sent box after box of 8's and 7½'s through my 20 gauges, one of which was a Remington Model 31 pump and the other a Remington Model 11-48 Sportsman autoloader. When I sneaked out my father's Winchester Model 42 .410, I also stoked it with 7½'s for those vaunted multiple hits.

As those hunting seasons came and went, I began to mature and make my own observations and analyses. All of this was possible because there were a lot of game birds practically in my backyard back in the late 1940s and early 1950s, and whenever I didn't have afternoon classes I went hunting. Saturdays and Sundays during school were also taken up by bird hunting, and after school ended

I spent a couple months following the beagles my father and uncle ran. So you see, my involvement with the fine-shot school's way of thinking was neither brief nor wanting for test shots.

BECOMING CRITICAL

After about my third season, I began to wonder about the fine-shot theory of multiple hits. It simply wasn't working for me. Birds that gave up a lot of feathers to 7½'s and 8's, and showed obvious multiple hits when I plucked them, often hadn't held after they had been dropped. I mostly hunted without a retriever then, and it gradually dawned on me I was running down birds too often. Where was the electric-like shocking power of the multiple hits from fine shot?!

I have written before that my disgust with the light shot sizes caused me to switch to 6's for ruffed grouse, and I started hand-loading initially to make my own 1-ounce, 20-gauge upland loads with #7 shot. It was back in the early 1950s that I laid my first clusters of 6's on ruffed grouse, and since then I can't remember losing a grouse folded with 6's.

I can, however, still remember the day I hit a grouse so hard with 8's above Watercress Creek it looked like an exploding pillow and then the bird popped right up and ran off before I could throw a second shot! I also recall a sunny afternoon in west-central Wisconsin's sand country when my 9's felled a pair of bobwhite that I never saw again. Then there were the times when 7½'s brought down pheasant but let them get up and streak toward heavy cover. That I got most of these birds is something I

attribute more to my time on my high school and college sprint teams than to the shocking power of fine shot.

My professors taught me to be a critical scientific thinker, and it all began to come together for me relative to fine shot. By the time I graduated from college, I had lost faith in the fine-shot theory because multiple hits with smaller pellets simply didn't produce the clean kills claimed for the supposed shocking power from sprinklings of the lesser shot sizes.

The author never regrets using 6's on grouse. They are the most-positive pellet on thicket-dwelling birds and produce anchoring hits that hold birds where they fall.

EXPERIENCE IS
THE BEST TEACHER

I came to my own conclusions about pellet sizes for hunting. For cottontails and squirrels, I pick lead 5's because they balance pattern density with penetrating energy, and the animals I hit, be it from a .410 or 12 gauge, stay where they fall. Those 5's also get the call for ducks, close-range geese inside 40 yards and certain pheasant hunts. I always believed 5's were underrated, and they still are for the larger species of upland game, like ringnecks, sharptail and sage grouse.

If the larger birds are close in, 6's are my choice, as the 7½'s touted by the fine-shot school let too many roosters bounce back up and run. I think geese need BB's or 2's.

Our bobwhite hunting wasn't all that great and I had to drive many miles for it, but I found 7½'s held them better than 8's or 9's. Hungarian partridge tend to flush wildly, and 6's are my basic pellet in tightly choked guns. Ruffed grouse season sees me stocking up on 7½'s for a lot of shooting, with some of my reloads made with #7 shot for backup or charges of 6's if the birds are skittish and flush farther out. Finally, 7½'s have become my

For furred game, such as squirrels and rabbits, the lead #5 is an exceptional choice, balancing density with adequate penetration.

After sprinting after too many ringnecks knocked down but not anchored by 7½'s, the author gravitated to lead 5's for ringnecks and has never found reason to question that decision.

favorite load for woodcock.

What pellets don't I like? After years of observation, I find I am no fan of lead 8's or 4's. On rearend hits on birds of any size with strong backbones, neither 8's nor 7½'s penetrate enough for serious impact. This past bird season, I bagged a pheasant that was hit at a distance of about 30 to 35 yards by a 1-ounce load of 8's in a promotion load, and although the bird picked up five pellet hits, it ran and eluded hunters for over a half-hour. When I cleaned it, I found three pellets had merely struck the broad, flat bone on the lower half of the bird's back and ranged along it, never penetrating to the vitals; the other two pellets hit the left leg and drew fuzz in for perhaps ½" to ¾". Where was the shocking impact in that case?

I OUGHTA KNOW HOW IT FEELS!

I wonder about the accuracy of the fine-shot school's theory that the impact upon a bird's nervous system is the square of the number of hits, not merely the total number of hits. I also question if all pellet hits register the same impulse on a bird's brain. I question the fine-shot school's theory because I didn't get the professed "shock" when I was hit by a high-velocity load of steel 4's a couple seasons back! That first-hand experience made me rethink the whole theory behind the multiple-strike argument of the fine-shot school. It now seems to me all pellet hits are *not* equal in intensity; hence, the total impact on a bird is probably *not* the square of the number of hits.

On a very dreary opening day of duck season, a mallard happened to fly low between another hunter and myself, and the other hunter let go a blast with a 12-gauge, 1⅛-ounce load of steel 4's. I was about 45 yards away from him, maybe 50, with light cover between us. In fact, most of the protective cover was no higher than my hips! I also saw the mallard but was following it with my eyes, waiting for it to rise and clear the other hunter. I heard a shot string snapping around me, but I was so intent on the bird I didn't notice anything more than a minor twitch in my left thigh. In fact, I folded that mallard as

it rose behind me after the other hunter had emptied his gun. Only after I lowered my gun did the pain in my leg hit me!

An ultra-sharp pain stabbed through my left thigh and felt as if someone were running a 6" hat pin through my leg. Intense though it was, it only lasted a brief instant. When I felt my leg, I discovered a pellet buried hemispherically and pinched it out like you would pop a pimple. Within a short time, the pain was gone and only a little soreness lingered. I noticed no other pain and hunted until the closing minutes of the day. By the way, the other hunter did apologize to me over the weeds.

Now for the part of the story that bolsters my argument that the fine-shot school can't rely upon all pellets in a multiple hit to carry the same nerve-shattering impact. After the hunt, we stopped for a pizza, and about then my left forearm began to itch. I rolled up my sleeve to find another pellet wound. The pellet was gone, but the wound was there along with some torn tissue that indicated a deflection, and what little blood colored the surface wasn't enough to trickle. I had been hit twice but only felt one impact. . .or so I thought until I got home.

When I took off my hunting shirt at home, I found a patch of blood on my t-shirt's left shoulder. Stripping off the t-shirt, I found a third wound, this time another hemispheric hole with a lot of bluish coloring around it. I hadn't even felt this shot! At a range of about 45 to 50 yards, then, I had probably picked up three pellets from the pattern's fringe and never even felt two of them!

From this personal experience, I garnered information that upset the fine-shot school's theory. Either all the pellets of a multiple hit do not register with the same impact upon the nervous system or the nervous system responds more to hits which impact with higher energy. Why else could I, like a pheasant that eludes hunters for a half-hour or more despite five hits, keep hunting without knowing I had two more wounds?! Could it be that portion of the nervous system which feels the most pain overpowers the remainder of the system? I dunno, but my own experience of receiving three pellet hits and only feeling one caused me to cock a skeptical eyebrow at the

When lead shot was king, the author's favorite duck pellet was the #5. Now it is the steel BB because of its penetrating power.

fine-shot school's theory that the impact on a bird's nervous system is the square of the number of hits. Now more than ever, I believe you need more to kill a game bird cleanly than just a sprinkling of fine shot.

MULTIPLE HITS
BUT HEAVIER SHOT

There is no doubt in my mind that multiple hits are important for making clean kills afield. Relying upon the so-called "golden BB" is ridiculous because you can't always get lucky and get a head/neck hit with heavy shot. You can, however, select pellet sizes which, when teamed with the right degree of choke for the game and range, will give good pattern density and added penetrating power.

I have a hunch that's why, after sorting through the shot sizes, I have come to enjoy lead 5's for ducks and the larger species of upland game when the latter birds are taken over longer ranges. The 5's split the difference between the patterning density of 6's and the energy of 4's, thereby giving multiple hits and ample penetration for greater shocking power.

The same is true for 7½'s, 6's or straight 7's on ruffed grouse; they give multiple hits but penetrate deeper to generate more shock and more tissue destruction. I have long hunted ruffed grouse without a dog, and I can't remember ever losing a bird hit by 6's. Sorry, but I can't say the same for 8's or 9's, sizes which are espoused by members of the fine-shot school.

All this doesn't mean the smaller shot sizes are totally useless, of course. It is a matter of range and, in many respects, the target's angle. I have killed numerous pheasant with 8's on hunting preserves while working with a close-ranging dog. At 20 yards, 8's can deck a pheasant, but always remember, just 20 strides.

Many of those hunting-preserve shots were crossing angles with the bird's head/neck region openly exposed. On several occasions, I had a quick long shot with 8's and needed the dog; the pellets simply didn't dig deeply enough because they lost energy to air resistance. For quail at short range, woodcock and even overhead doves, 8's will work. The point is, to handle longer ranges that occur even under the most-controlled situation, heavier pellets are better because they retain more energy in the face of air resistance and can penetrate deeper, causing more shock.

The angle of the bird is also important. Outgoing shots are difficult because pellets must fight through rump fuzz and the broad, flat bone that covers the rear segment of the bird's body. I have seen more than a few ruffed grouse lost with 8's on outgoing hits; ditto for 7½'s, but never with 6's. One of the worst situations I have ever seen happened in Canada when an absolute novice at hunting told me he was using 9's on sharptail because, "They're only little upland birds and you want multiple hits." He crippled birds all over Manitoba!

The theory of multiple hits is a good one, but those hits must be made by substantial pellets, not gentle little ones that can't break through bone and muscle to do real damage! For upland gunning at reasonable ranges, 5's, 6's and 7's are more-positive performers than 8's and 9's. The 7½ is often marginal; when it is used, you would do well to select copper-plated or 12-gauge trap loads because trap loads have hard, high-antimony 7½'s that don't deform as readily as the 7½'s found in bargain-basement loads.

STEEL-SHOT LOADS

I have done a certain amount of hunting with steel shot on upland birds and, although this may be greeted by the Bronx cheer from some of you, I find correctly selected steel more efficient than lead. Steel shot cuts sharper than lead and doesn't get balled up with feather fuzz; consequently, steel actually seems to deliver more shocking power than lead because the pellets cut through with more retained energy.

The #5 steel pellet, for example, has about the energy of a lead #7, according to the ballistics tables, when ranges get to 30 to 45 yards. On upland game, the 5's have impressed me with their put-down power on smaller game birds, including ruffed grouse at most legitimate ranges and pheasant inside 35 to 40 yards.

Pheasant at moderate ranges will fold and hold for steel 4's, which have the energy of lead 6's, but to be very honest, I prefer steel 3's for all-around pheasant hunting, with 2's in the second barrel if the birds are known to jump well out. Indeed, if there is an overrated steel pellet, it is the #4, a size most unknowing hunters buy because they always used lead 4's in the past and can't break the habit or don't know anything about downrange ballistics.

The point is, for multiple hits *and* shocking power, I think steel shot will come into its own as a cleaner-killing load than the smaller sizes of lead which have been boomed by the fine-shot school.

As a conclusion, I can only repeat that the idea of multiple hits is good, but pellet energy must also be there to register adequate shocking power. Carried to its extreme, the fine-shot school is like sprinkling salt on a bird's tail, and I for one question whether all pellets impact with the same energy to cause a multiplication of the impact energy. I've got the scars to prove it is not so!

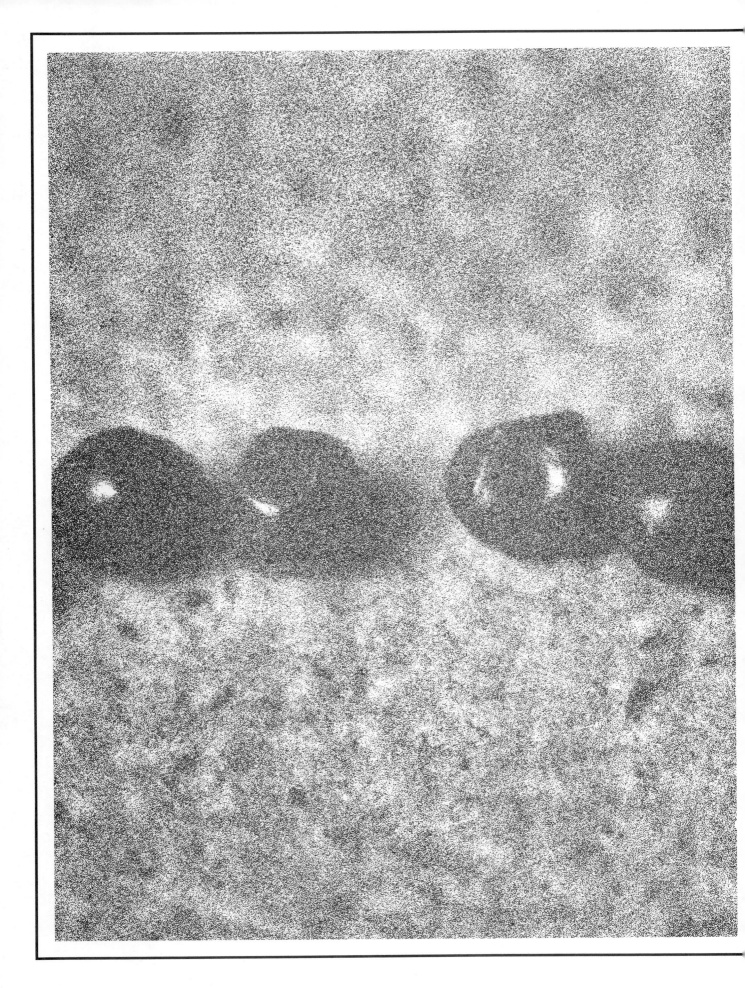

18

Waterfowl Loads And The "New" Ballistics

The first high-performance shotshell to capture the public's attention was the so-called "high-velocity" duck load, a 12-gauge round that also became known to many hunters as the "high-brass" load. It used a 3¾-drams equivalent charge of progressive-burning powder to move 1¼ ounces of lead shot to an advertised velocity of 1,330 f.p.s., which was well ahead of the former 1¼-ounce 12-gauge load's published speed of something like 1,220 f.p.s. Remington called this load the Nitro Express, Winchester termed it the Super-X and Federal listed it as the Hi-Power.

Call it what you may, the point is, for decades if not generations, we have equated the 3¾-drams equivalent, 1¼-ounce, 12-gauge load with a velocity of 1,330 f.p.s. Check catalogs and ballistics tables as late as 1989, perhaps even 1990, and that is still the published speed.

What the general public doesn't consider is *where* that published velocity is measured. To many shooters, that published figure and the published figures for all other shotshells are considered the "muzzle velocity" — which they aren't! Although some books, magazine articles and even catalogs may call it a muzzle velocity, it is really a chronograph reading taken 3 feet ahead of the muzzle.

Your initial reaction to the difference between muzzle velocity and a velocity read 3 feet out may be "No big deal! What can go wrong in just 3 feet?" Well, according to the results of some new research, a lot can happen in that seemingly paltry distance.

THE NEW BALLISTICS

Work done by Ed Lowry of Winchester and summarized in the December 1989 issue of *American Rifleman* magazine shows there can be a velocity loss of 50 to 100 f.p.s. during the first yard of free flight. For example, the new shotshell ballistics table worked out by Ed Lowry indicates a shot charge which reaches 1,330 f.p.s. for a 3-foot chronograph reading needs an actual muzzle velocity of 1,394 f.p.s. with BB's and 1,447 f.p.s. with 7½'s to retain 1,330 f.p.s. at 3 feet!

The same situation affects steel shot, of course. I like to use steel BB's which have a published velocity of at least 1,350 f.p.s., but to get a load to that speed 3 feet from the muzzle, manufacturers must load enough powder to give the load an actual muzzle velocity of 1,459 f.p.s. That means the lead 7½'s mentioned above and the steel BB's lose about 100 f.p.s. in those first few feet outside the muzzle.

There are some steel loads which host heavier shot charges and have published velocities around 1,275 f.p.s. The 12-gauge, 1⅜-ounce, 3″ Magnum loads are a case in point, as are 1¼-ounce, standard-length 12-gauge loads. To get a chronograph reading of 1,275 f.p.s. on a 3-foot instrumental setup, these loads need an actual muzzle velocity of about 1,375 f.p.s. if they are stuffed with steel BB's or 1,415 f.p.s. if they move steel 4's. In the case of steel 4's, the actual muzzle velocity is about 140 f.p.s. higher than the published 3-foot speed, indicating how rapidly steel 4's are slowed by air resistance.

The point of all this, of course, is to clarify the terminology. The load velocities you read in ammo listings should *not* be confused with actual muzzle velocities. There are really two different terms used regarding the early free-flight velocities of shot charges: 1) actual muzzle velocity and 2) normally published figures, which are 3-foot instrumental chronograph readings also sometimes called "starting velocities." Shooters should learn to differentiate between these terms.

DOWNRANGE BALLISTICS

Another segment of the Lowry research uncovered evidence that the old downrange (exterior ballistics) data for unbuffered lead shot was wrong. Using advanced electronic gear to measure downrange pellet velocities, Lowry learned lead shot lost its velocity quicker than former ballistics tables indicated. The reason is lead shot loaded without a buffer deforms markedly under the pressures of firing setback and squeezing through the narrow forcing cone and choke taper of the barrel. A sphere isn't a very aerodynamic shape, anyway, and when it is deformed it becomes a horrible one that slows down quickly.

According to the old exterior ballistics tables, for instance, a lead #4 pellet with a 3-foot instrumental velocity of 1,330 f.p.s. got to 40 yards in a flight time of 0.1187-second retaining 815 f.p.s. of its original velocity and carrying an energy of 4.78 foot-pounds. What Lowry learned just recently, however, is lead 4's with a 3-foot instrumental velocity of 1,330 f.p.s. actually took 0.1234-second to

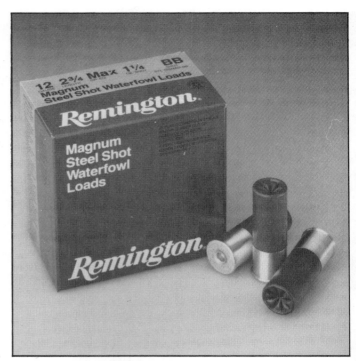

If we learn anything about pellet and velocity selection from Lowry's work, it is that going to steel shot two to three sizes larger than your normal lead will give you the same approximate energies. This is why some manufacturers now indicate on their boxes what the loads are best suited for.

travel that far and retained only 734 f.p.s. and 3.87 foot-pounds of energy. In other words, the old unbuffered lead 4's weren't as great as we thought!

STEEL SHOT

That leads us to the clincher of this chapter. As Lowry observed in his open-minded observations, steel shot showed up quite well against the old lead favorites. Why? Because steel shot doesn't deform! It remains aerodynamically more efficient than the deformation-prone lead. If you select a steel pellet that is a tad heavier so you have weight to overcome the air resistance, you will find steel closes in on the performance of lead.

The new rule of thumb for picking steel is to go at least two sizes larger than your former lead shot. If we compare lead 4's with steel 2's using Lowry's new tables, we find steel 2's, with a 3-foot velocity of

Deformed pellets (above) spoil patterns. Steel shot (below) is aerodynamically more efficient than lead because it does not deform. It doesn't take much imagination to guess how these deformed lead pellets would fly through the air.

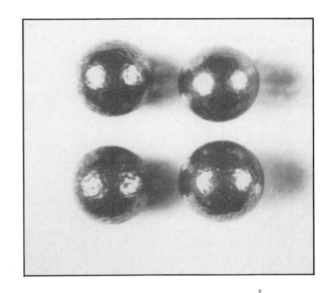

1,365 f.p.s., generate a 40-yard energy of 3.84 foot-pounds, retain 703 f.p.s. and cover the distance in 0.1245-second. Those are very equivalent figures.

On the other hand, steel 2's loaded to a 3-foot instrumental velocity of just 1,275 f.p.s. take 0.1308-second to get to the 40-yard point, retain a velocity of 676 f.p.s. and have a lower energy level of 3.55 foot-pounds.

If we learn anything about practical pellet and velocity selection from Lowry's work, it is that going to steel shot two to three sizes larger than your normal lead will deliver the same approximate energies *only* if higher steel-shot load velocities are employed. Drop the steel loads' velocities in favor of heavier shot charges, and the comparative figures are no longer as impressive for steel. So, sharp water-fowlers should learn the respective velocities of various loads and opt for the fastest ones.

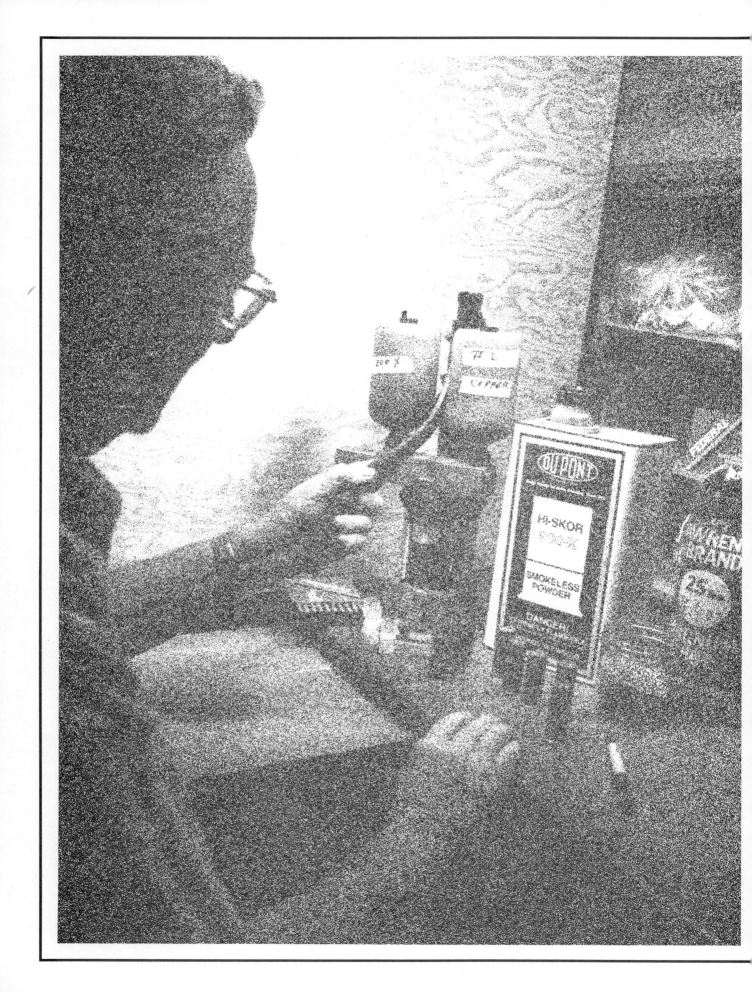

19

A Serious Look At Powder Charging

When I got my first chronograph many years ago, I took it to my local club and offered to clock everyone's ammunition. That is when I first became impressed by the typical handloader's failure to grasp the importance of scaling powder charges.

It all started with a young man at my club who was just getting into trapshooting. He had been at it perhaps only two seasons and was having problems with both his Model 870 Remington and his flinchy trigger finger. The 870 was still relatively new, but he already had put an oversized locking block in it. Despite the new block, however, his hulls were showing evidence of excessive headspace. He was also becoming a flincher, and his scores weren't climbing.

With that as a background, he handed me his 870 and reloads (I insisted on doing the shooting so no one would blast my chronograph's screen!). I hunkered down, lined up over the Oehler's skyscreens and let go.

That trap gun hit me so hard I thought I was benchresting a .458 Winchester Magnum! Glancing over at the chronograph, I saw the velocity had recorded at more than 1,300 f.p.s., which is about 100 f.p.s. beyond ATA maximum and kicks like the devil!

I quickly asked the shooter how much powder he was using. "I dunno," came the answer, "I bought the press secondhand, and they just told me to use Red Dot, so I do. Why?"

After I explained that his loads were running well over ATA maximum and I'd nearly been jolted off the bench by the recoil, he said his press' powder bushing was an MEC No. 39, which is made to drop about 23.0 grains of Red Dot.

That was the basic skeet loading in the 1950s when MEC first began making presses and all reloading was done with paper hulls and card/filler wad stacks. Even then it was a hefty, hard-kicking load, and many shooters dropped off to the No. 37 bushing which was intended for about 21.0 grains of Red Dot, the suggested trap charge at the time. Now here we were, about two decades later, and he was still dropping the heavy skeet charge into pressure-building Winchester hulls using Winchester WAA12 wads and Federal's potent F209 battery cup primer!

I have no idea what chamber pressures he was getting, but 1990 Hercules literature lists 17.5 grains of Red Dot for a close-to-maximum working pressure of 10,600 p.s.i. using the AA hull, Federal 209 primer and Winchester WAA12 wad. Is there any wonder his gun developed excess headspace, he flinched and I nearly got knocked off my seat?

GET SMART — GET SCIENTIFIC!

Unfortunately, many enthusiastic shooters jump helter-skelter into reloading just like that beginner did, applying no scientific thinking and never checking charge weights or reloading manuals. Their goal is to get inexpensive ammo quickly, and they assume both they and the equipment are infallible. They begin cranking out rounds without any regard for ballistics, fundamentals, accuracy, safety or gun/load performance.

The fact is, handloading can be dangerous and counterproductive to gun performance. Although gunpowder is known as a *propellant*, which means it burns progressively and *pushes* the ejecta rather than expending all its energy at once to explode like dynamite, it can still burst a gun and cause injury to the shooter when improperly used.

In addition, not all reloads pattern the same. Guns and loads are very individualistic. A reload that patterns beautifully in your friend's gun may not do so in your gun. The different vibrational patterns imparted to a shotgun

barrel by various chamber pressures, along with the flow characteristics of the load and the impact of gas pressures on the pellets (setback), determine how a load patterns from a given gun.

There are reloading components with gas-sealing properties meant to build high pressures quickly, while other components

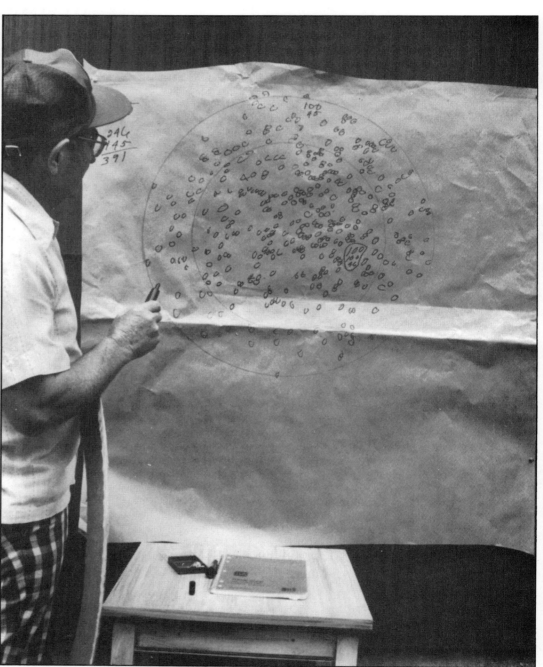

Patterning is important — not all reloads pattern the same. A reload that patterns great in your gun may not do so in your friend's.

have low-pressure qualities. Switching primers and/or wads can cause as much as a 2,000 to 3000-p.s.i. change in a reload! That change may not blow up your shotgun, but it can certainly reduce pattern density and/or cause uncomfortable recoil.

GET A SCALE!

One of the first things a reloader must understand is the ejecta (shot charge and wad) is forced out of the shotgun barrel by constantly expanding powder gases. When gunpowder burns it breaks down into atoms, and some of these atoms have an affinity for each other so they group together into molecules. A scientific definition of gas is molecules in constant, random and ever-expanding action.

The gases need expansion room, which means the ejecta must move forward to provide this room. If the additional space isn't available almost immediately upon early ignition, the hyperactive gas molecules will hammer against their surroundings and break them down, which can mean a burst. In a gasoline engine, the piston assembly drives downward in its power stroke to make room for the expanding gases; in a shotgun, it is the wad/shot mass that must move ahead. The powder charges in a shotshell must jibe in burning rate and charge weight with the weight of the shot charge and with the gas-sealing and pressure-building properties of the other components.

There is only one way to know exactly how much gunpowder is being dropped into your charge — scale it! Indeed, the first thing a beginning reloader should buy is a handloader-type scale, not a reloading press or other fancy doodads. Powder bushings are not to be trusted! Manufacturers' listings that declare bushing No. XYZ drops 21.7 grains of Purple Dot Powder are merely approximations. Many bushings do not come within a grain of the weight listed for them in advertisements. I have had powder bushings that threw 1½ to 2 grains light, and I had others that went about a grain overboard.

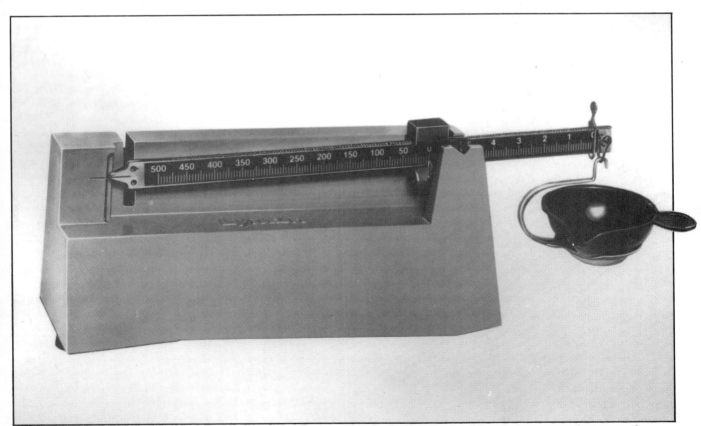

Scale it for safety's sake! Buy a handloader scale to double check your bushings' accuracy; they vary from lot to lot and are not always to be trusted.

Each bushing should also be checked with each new lot of powder, because gunpowders are not universally consistent. Nothing is perfect except scientific theory, and this especially applies to powder bushings and handloader-type powders. Also, do not trust secondhand bushings. Many of these have been manipulated by their previous owners to give the correct charge. Made of light aluminum or plastic, bushings are often whittled out for greater capacity. I know because I have done that to a number of bushings I found threw light charges. Moreover, I have reduced the interior capacity of some bushings by applying coats of nail polish, so be sure to check all used bushings by scaling before depending on them.

HOW TO CHECK A BUSHING

It would seem the easiest way to check a bushing would be to fill the powder hopper and weigh the charges as they are dropped — not so! Merely sliding the charging bar back

Handloading can be dangerous and can ruin your gun's performance if not properly done. It must be undertaken scientifically, taking accuracy, ballistics, safety and gun/load performance into account.

and forth tends to drop charges lighter than those metered out during the actual reloading process. When a press is in actual operation, there are heavy vibrations that influence the way the powder packs into the bushing's cavity. On a single-stage reloading press where one empty at a time is taken through the stages from start to finish, there will be more vibrations per reload than on a progressive press where each crank of the operating handle produces a finished load. The point is, the vibrations of a single-stage reloader can pack more powder into the bushing than the vibes of a progressive machine generally will, but both machines are affected by vibration. To make a scientific check of each powder bushing's charge weight, the press must be operated in normal fashion to reproduce the typical vibrations felt during the production of actual loads.

To do this, set up the machine and run a few reloads through it to get everything flowing. Let the vibrations settle the powder, then begin scaling each powder charge as it drops during the normal operating sequence. This will tell you how the bushing is operating in the flow of things.

Expect some variations, but don't let $\frac{1}{10}$ to $\frac{2}{10}$-grain variations upset you. Variations of that amount are typical in the use of charging bars with powder bushings.

Also be aware that powder charges can vary depending upon the amount of powder in the hopper. A full hopper will often throw differently than one that is just ¼ or ½ full. My most consistent charges come from a hopper that is from ⅓ to ⅔ full, but yours may operate differently.

Powder bushings are important to the overall load, but they cannot be trusted implicitly! To know exactly what your charge weights are, ignore the published data and scale them yourself. If that beginning trap-shooter had done just that, I would have been spared a vicious kick in the face from his strained 870!

20

The Way To Shoot Woodcock

My neighbor's name was Eugene, and in the autumn of 1948 he parlayed the proceeds from a pair of after-school jobs into a Stevens .22-410 over & under. About that same time, we discovered woodcock flights were dropping into a low spot perhaps a 10-minute walk from our homes, their attention apparently captured by the soil that was kept soft by spring tricklings from a hillside. We knew the place well, having spent hundreds of hours there with air rifles or just horsing around.

The woodcock had come as a surprise, as we'd never seen more than a single bird there in the past. Now, suddenly we were flushing them in flocks. When Eugene got his .22-410 stackbarrel and a box of 3″ 6's, we headed out to that low spot.

Now, Eugene was a far better buddy than he ever was a shooter. He loved to tramp around the hills, but he lacked athletic talent and wouldn't spend any time learning the fundamentals. His high school track career had lasted for about one workout, during which he had become violently entangled in a hurdle. Although he once reported for football in high school, he missed half the workout because he couldn't figure out which pads went where.

When the first woodcock flared from practically under his foot, Eugene took forever to get the gun cocked and mounted. The bird was just a disappearing dot between distant trees when he finally let go with that .410 and did little more than hasten the autumnal process of leaf shedding. "I couldn't get my sights on him," Eugene complained, referring to the open sights on the Stevens .22 barrel. So, we moved along.

The woodcock flight was in thick and heavy and the next three birds rose directly in front of Eugene. His flurries of action were replays of the first bird. A bird would flush, there would be an appreciable time lag, then "*bang*!" Leaves would drift down, the bird would keep going and Eugene would blame the sights.

I wasn't getting any action, but Eugene continued to get plenty. As we neared an edge, he stepped right into the middle of three resting birds, all of which climbed steeply before him. Befuddled, he took longer than ever to launch a load into the airspace where none of the trio happened to be. He was dejected, of course. So was I — he was practically walking on birds, but I couldn't get a flush. . .until we turned toward the hillside, that is.

Suddenly, there was a russety form hurtling over me, angling to my left and topping the yellow-crowned birches. It tilted slightly as if to angle downward and plane away, and the next thing I knew there was a soft recoil bump against me and the bird was falling. "You got it!" shouted Eugene.

"Yeah," I replied with a certain nonchalance and more than a mild outbreak of teenage braggadocio, "That's the way to shoot a woodcock!" Eugene heard me, but I'm not sure he understood what I was driving at.

FORGET THE ROMANCE

Although my reply was smart-alecky and a tad sarcastic, that indeed is the way to shoot woodcock — right now, on the rise, with no aiming or dawdling for a precise hold or measured lead. Taken with crisp timing, woodcock are too close to demand much forward allowance and the speed of the swing does it all. Indeed, the essence of woodcock shooting is eye/hand coordination paired with a trigger pull that lets go as the muzzle catches the target. With an open pattern and a spirited gun, it's one of the easiest shots in the uplands.

The fact is most books and magazine articles tend to be overly romantic about woodcock shooting, and such writings can quickly convince gullible hunters that woodcock simply cannot be had and the shooting of them is akin to a comic opera. The woodcock is given rave notices for being so tricky, dexterous and evasive, but the real humor lies in the writings, as woodcock are actually very easy targets. They hold well for pointers, flush close-in and are not swift flyers. If you select the right equipment and learn to use eye/hand coordination, you should bag a good percentage of the birds you flush. Misses on woodcock frequently stem more from poor shooting technique than from any willful swivel-hipping by the long-billed bird.

I bagged my first woodcock in the 1940s with a 20-gauge Remington Model 31-L and a 1-ounce load of 7½'s; the gun's 26″ barrel hosted a Poly-Choke set at the Cylinder notch. Some readers will react strongly to that, as the purist in them will argue that woodcocking should be done only with a neat

side-by-side (SxS).

I must immediately point out that doubles had not yet taken on a nostalgic or classic aura in the 1940s. A long-barreled pump gun symbolized shotgunning throughout much of the mid-20th century, and there was no stigma attached to slide-actions. The idea that SxS's are *the* gun for game-bird shooting hadn't yet developed stateside. If anything impressed the kids in my rural neighborhood back then, it was a 30″-barreled, full-choked pump gun that

The dynamic side-by-side, this one a 16-gauge, is excellent for the point-and-shoot, instinctive technique that works so effectively on woodcock.

could "shoot like a rifle."

The fact is, I was being a bit racy using a shorter-barreled 20 with an open choke, but then I was still a teenage gun nut who wasn't bound by convention. Thanks to its alloy receiver (the "L" in the Model 31's designation means lightweight), the little 20-gauge pump gun scaled something like 5½ pounds and handled with reasonably effective spirit for this specialty.

THE WOODCOCK GUN

If I had taken measurements on all the shots I have made on woodcock since the 1940s, added them together and divided to find an average, I might have found my typical shot was between 12 and 17 yards. Seldom would they have been beyond the 17-yard mark and barely ever past 20 yards. In some respects, the high-house target from Station Four in skeet is a long-range shot comparable to what you encounter in woodcock covers. Sometimes the cover is too dense for anything but a close-in poke-and-hope shot, but woodcock usually give you more than ample time to make a good point while they are still inside 15 strides.

This doesn't mean the rest of skeet shooting isn't good practice for woodcock hunters, of course. The gun handling in a round of skeet shot with a low-gun starting position can help you refine your coordination and trigger timing.

In a lifetime of hunting, I have not been able to pinpoint any particular gauge as optimum for woodcock. I have taken woodcock with everything from a skeet-bored .410 to a full-choked 12, and that includes a spicy little 24-gauge Neumann (Belgian) double for which I reloaded for awhile. Gauge doesn't seem to make much difference on woodcock; the important thing is how the gun handles.

Although a light gun springs into action rapidly, it can also have some undesirable whippy qualities. Personally, I favor 12 and 16-gauge upland guns for woodcock simply because they have good gripping proportions and are heavier than the lesser gauges so they instill a bit of discipline for controlled smoothness.

If I could design an optimum woodcock gun, it would probably be a 16-gauge SxS with 25″ to 26″ barrels or a lightweight 16-gauge autoloader. In any case, the 16 has enough bulk for good gripping and enough weight for discipline without being laggardly. Put a 25″ to 26″ Skeet barrel in place, and a 16-gauge semiauto would do just fine I'm sure. I have always thought the Remington Model 1100 20-gauge Lightweight would be a great upland repeater if it was redesigned to 16-gauge dimensions. Browning's Sweet Sixteen with a 26″ Invector-equipped barrel would be good, too.

A lot of upland guns have been sold with barrels bored Improved Cylinder (IC) and Modified, but this isn't a great combo for woodcock. Far better would be a tandem of Cylinder and IC. Few shots ever approach 20 yards, so there is no need for a Modified choke on a woodcocking gun unless, perhaps, it is a .410.

A truly good double is a precious item these days, and not every hunter can lay down the required coin to get one. The answer seems to be one of the ultra-short-barreled repeaters now in vogue. Some of these have overall lengths akin to those of doubles with 25″ to 26″ tubes, and they move with haste.

I like a 25″ to 26″-barreled double better than a stumpy repeater because 26″ doubles burn powder more thoroughly than 21″ to 22″-barreled repeaters. Even trap loads give a nasty gas blast in some ultra-short barrels that verges on riot-gun quality. If you have tough ears, though, a gun like the Remington Special Field can be just great in woodcock covers; it will make the swale ring but will also get you to the target in time.

WOODCOCK TECHNIQUE

Woodcock are elusive targets only if you allow yourself to be mesmerized by their hijinks and try to make a perfect aim on them. I recently met a hunter who was doing so poorly on woodcock he had a gunsmith punch a middle bead into the rib of his 12-gauge double so he could "bead up," which is taking a giant step in the wrong direction. What he probably should have done instead was take a hammer and knock off the front bead to eliminate any temptation to look sharply at the gun. Anyone who is conscious of a sighting radius or tracks a woodcock in flight is doomed. That's not the right technique.

Woodcock shooting is a classic example of the use of eye/hand coordination. There is not sufficient time or distance to line up the beads, take a squinty-eyed aim down the rib or get the front sight squarely positioned with the matted receiver top of a repeater. A good woodcock shot does nothing more than point his hand to where his eyes are looking — even a toddler can point out his favorite candy without lining up his forearm and finger by consciously peering down his arm!

Successful woodcock shooting pivots on focusing sharply on the bird and retaining that optical connection perfectly regardless of how the bird carries on. The gun's upper features should be practically ignored and are seen only in peripheral vision, if at all. Alignment is established by the hands working to the eye, and the trigger is pulled instantly as the gun catches the target. There must be no hesitation, no attempt to draw a fine bead and no bother with setting off an exact lead. Tracking a woodcock is like tracing a pretzel — the line never seems to go straight, so a woodcock hunter simply cannot anticipate ever seeing his gun perfectly aligned and leading a woodcock.

When you focus sharply on a timberdoodle and pay no attention whatsoever to the background, your surroundings or gun, the bird is practically frozen in flight and becomes an obvious point of reference for optimum eye/hand coordination. Let the gun-pointing instincts you learned on skeet's Station Eight do their thing without any hitches caused by human apprehension, hesitation or second-guessing. Just look, point and let go — trust your natural coordination, gun momentum and pattern to do the rest.

Now, that's the way to shoot a woodcock!

Don't aim at a woodcock. Don't try to line up the barrel or beads. Just watch him rise and let eye/hand coordination take over as you focus sharply on the bird. Woodcock are usually so close your pattern can take advantage of many chances as your gun swings by.

21

Varminting With A Shotgun

Although you may tend to think of bull-barreled rifles when you hear talk of varminting, it is surprising how much pest sniping can be done by shotgunners looking for some action beyond the normal game-bird seasons. In some respects, varminting with a shotgun is considerably more sporting than varminting with a long-range rifle because the hunter must get much closer to his target. When you are talking about skittish targets, like foxes, crows or the coyotes that live in the heavily populated fringes of our cities, you are dealing with spooky, savvy quarry indeed! The spread of a shotgun pattern might make the shot a little easier in the final instant, but getting to make that shot can take a lot of hunting skill.

With the continued expansion of housing into the countryside, the future may find us doing more varminting. For those who like the challenge of hunting better than the rapid-fire trigger pulling of skeet and trap, smoothbore varminting may be just the summer activity.

As I look back through the decades, I believe I have spent more shotgun shells on varmints than on ducks and geese, perhaps on all game bunched together! As a kid, I had great shotgun country just a 10-minute walk from my home, and nobody cared if I walked down the street in midsummer with an uncased shotgun and my pockets bulging with shells. My targets were the starlings and crows that hung around the local rendering plant.

The air may not have been the freshest around that plant, as the smoke and scattered remains lent a distinctive odor to the morning breezes, but those smelly remains were what brought the starlings from all the neighboring farms. I had plenty of opportunity for smoothbore varminting back then.

If I learned anything about wing shooting as a kid, it was because of those starlings. They would buzz the smelly remains scattered on the hill behind the rendering plant, and I would blast at them from the deep shadows of a tree line. The guys in the plant didn't care if I shot away all the earnings from my part-time job, as long as I shot high overhead. Even pellets falling on the plant's roof didn't bother them. They didn't much care for it when I leveled on a low flyer and sent a shot string glancing along the ground, though, so I stuck with high-angle birds and had a ball.

Some people may not call the starling a varmint, but I do. I spend a lot of time in the country, and time and again I have seen starlings raid the nests of songbirds. They are a devilish pack and show what can happen when a bird is imported without consideration for the native environment. If there are low populations of beautiful songbirds in your area, watch the starlings and grackles carefully when they make raids in the spring. Bird lovers who think the bird world is one harmonious hive of song and fellowship are dead wrong! There are muggers and hit men among our feathered friends, and I have never regretted folding any starling.

Crows are varmints. However, an

international treaty protects many migratory birds these days, and crow hunting as a pure sport is subject to a myriad of state and national regulations. The crow has somehow gone from being a black bandit to a good guy.

Most states do have some relaxations of the stringent international rules, however, and there are times when crows can be hunted. In general, the hunter must be able to prove the crows were doing damage. Most farmers can give permission for hunters to go after crows around their fields in many states, and a lot of game wardens simply turn their back on crow sniping to protect the nesting waterfowl and game birds that crows often decimate. The crow is an efficient raider of duck nests, and I constantly wonder how well-meaning conservationists can protect a bird that decimates duck eggs. In my book, the crow is a killer.

Crows are also smart. They are very street savvy. You may call them in once, but after that you'll have a problem.

VARMINT GUNS AND LOADS

Practically any shotgun will serve on starlings. I like the 20-gauge with 1 ounce of 9's or 7½'s. Somehow 8's have never appealed to me.

Some of the most fun I ever had on starlings came with a single-shot .410 bolt-action Mossberg my father used to use on cottontails. At the time, I was reloading paper-cased .410's with a ½-ounce charge of 9's, and once I learned to time the swing of that willowy .410 I made some surprisingly hard, long hits. That little gun's full-choked

A shotgun can be pure poison on foxes with a tight pattern of heavy pellets.

barrel held some tight patterns.

Crows can be a different matter, however. They can present very long shots. When I was a kid, the 20-gauge pump and its 1-ounce load of 6's gave me sound performances, and I am not certain you need much more than 6's for any crow hunting except sheer skyblasting shots. Number 5's may actually be all you need, and the 1⅜-ounce short Magnum in 12-gauge persuasion is a positive performer with 5's aboard for long-range crow work.

When I became interested in the 10-gauge Magnum, I felt I needed plenty of practice to get the feel of it. It is an iron monster and starts slowly, not like my old 6-pound, 20-gauge pump. Sensing the need for some off-season wing shooting, I worked up some reduced 10-gauge loads and took that beast crow hunting. One of my reloads used 1⅝ ounces of 5's and didn't recoil very much in the 11¼-pound, 10-bore double. Those reloads were quite effective on passing crows.

I knew a flyway the crows used every afternoon when they returned to the roost, so I got in some excellent practice on overhead birds. Eventually I learned what I needed to do to score reasonably well with that big 10, thanks to varminting with my smoothbore.

If a farmer near me feels he's having trouble with crows, I unselfishly lend my assistance. Full chokes are in order, and my Remington SP-10 gets a call to action.

The last time I saved a farmer's crops, I used steel 3's rather than my old reduced-load concept, and they worked out just fine. My 1¾-ounce charges of Remington steel 3's conserved the farmer's young greens and probably a few duck nests besides.

There are a lot of areas in this country where fox and coyote are hunted with shotguns. Generally, serious hunters use buckshot. In past seasons, I took foxes with everything from a grouse load of 8's to a pheasant load of hard 5's.

On a sunny opening morning of a grouse season, I was walking the edge of a thorn apple thicket when a red fox jumped no more than 10 yards ahead of me. He must have been

The jack rabbit is overlooked as a shotgun target in many regions.

sleeping in the grass. I snapped a quick shot and felt I had been on, but the fox didn't flinch. Anyway, what can you do with 8's on foxes, right? I kept zigzagging through the thorn apple thicket hoping to flush a grouse despite the fox's run and my shot, and about 100 yards later I came upon the fox, stretched out and stone dead. The 8's had penetrated his hide at that close range and peppered his lungs, but I don't recommend 8's for foxes.

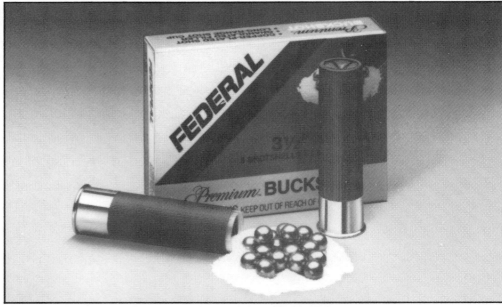

Federal introduced this buckshot load for the 3½″ 12-gauge Magnum. It can be great for coyote hunting.

Number 4 buckshot is pretty good on foxes, but many hunters opt for #00. It all depends upon your local hunting conditions. What I have seen in open farming country doesn't speak well for #00, as a fox can often carry a single #00 pellet if it doesn't hit a vital spot. The ideal gun is a snug-patterning one.

Quite a few summers ago I noticed heavy fox movement around one of my pet grouse covers. Feeling I didn't need any competition for those grouse, I began staking out a fence-row that ran past a wooded hillside since the fence showed plenty of fox traffic signs. My gun was a standard 12 with Magnum loads of #4 buckshot, a combo that had showed me on paper it could hold rather uniform patterns of 80 percent at 40 yards. It took a week of waiting each evening, but finally the red fox came loping along, scenting here and there and headed for the thicket. The #4 buck caught him in mid-stride and stretched him out. It was an rewarding hunt that required plenty of patience.

My state has since tightened the season on foxes, and they are now primarily winter hunting. Shotgunners who live in states with looser laws should give summer fox hunting a try.

Which chokes work best with buckshot? Intermittent patterning sessions with various chokes and buckshot loads indicate Modified choke is best for buckshot. If Full choke is used, it seems to do better with buffered buckshot rounds than with unbuffered loads, the obvious reason being that buffered payloads suffer less pellet deformation and the buffering agent lets the pellets shift about within their mass for a more-fluid flow through the full-choke constriction.

If I were to pick only one choke for buckshot, it would be Modified. It seems to apply a controlling pinch to the shot charge without clamping down on it destructively as a Full choke does. Popular myths aside, I have never seen buckshot loads pattern as tightly from a Cylinder, Skeet or Improved Cylinder choke as they do from a Modified. Buffered rounds and Modified choke are, in my experience, the optimum combination for buckshot usage.

I have some friends who hunt coyotes with shotguns, and they say the 10 gauge is simply the best because it lobs more buckshot than the other bores. If you find yourself with a 3½″ 12-gauge Magnum, you should know Federal Cartridge Corporation has a #00-buckshot load for it stuffed with 18 big balls of #00.

For some reason, most magazines show

pictures of hunters using rifles to hunt jack rabbits. It may be somewhat more sporting to plink at them with a .22 in either rimfire or centerfire persuasion, but I have a hunch the rifle dominates the picture because only riflemen seem to get into this sport.

The jack can be top shooting with a shotgun, as it is the real "rabbit" target of Sporting Clays. I have seen very few jacks that didn't jump from a nearby clump of sage, bunch or cheat grass well within full-choke shotgun range. If a rancher really wants to control a jack rabbit population, a shotgun will suffice nicely!

From what I have seen, the jack is a tough ol' critter and should be hit hard. A full-choke pattern of 5's or 4's is suggested in heavy cover and basically close-in work. If the range is extended, I would pick some 2's for their

energy, but before 2's are used, the gun should be checked for pattern. There's no use using a heavy pellet if the pattern doesn't give adequate density. A snug pattern of 4's is favored over a thin pattern of 2's.

From starlings to coyotes, the shotgun can be used successfully for varminting. This may become more and more important as our population expands and more rural housing developments spring up. We certainly don't need rifle bullets zipping over ranch-style homes or apartments and giving shooters a bad name.

As a rule of thumb, tight patterns are in order for shotgun varminting, as are heavy loads for all but the smallest, closest targets. If you are an active hunter, don't let the close of the small-game and waterfowl seasons stop you — take up varminting with your shotgun!

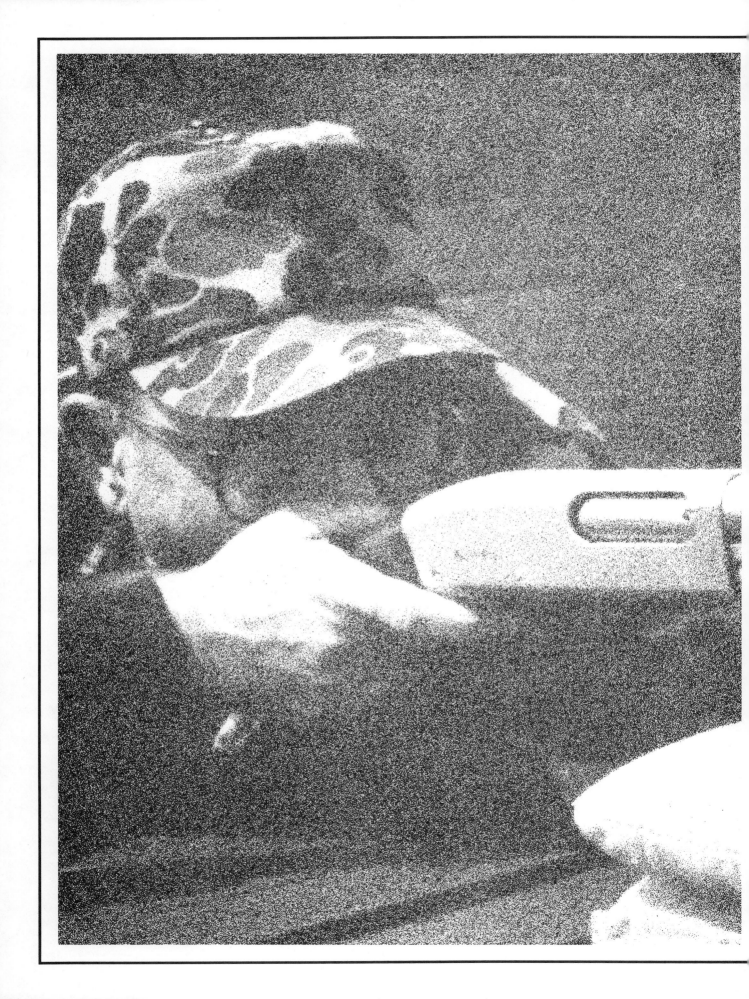

22

Slug Stuff I: The Basics Of Slug Gun Accuracy

When I was growing up in the 1930s and 1940s, there was no deer hunting in the southeastern corner of Wisconsin, and few of the midwestern states below Wisconsin, Minnesota and Michigan had deer herds. There may have been occasional sightings in Illinois, Iowa, Indiana and Ohio, but those states didn't have much action, either. If a sportsman wanted to hunt whitetail prior to the late 1950s, he had to pack up and head for the northern counties of Minnesota, Michigan and Wisconsin. That was rifle country then, home of the .30-30 and .35 Remington.

Anyone who took his deer hunting seriously had a rifle, for in those days the shotgun slug had a terrible reputation. "You never know where a shotgun slug is going," hunters used to say, and they firmly believed it.

This rap against the shotgun's rifled slugs was often unjustified, however. In part, their terrible reputation was a carryover from the performance of the rifled slug's predecessor, the lead-ball loading. The lead ball was indeed a wild flyer; it could be nothing else. The ball would deform under setback pressure and come out of the muzzle spinning, and the spin could vary from shot to shot depending upon how the ball contacted the bore and choke at exit. It wasn't fair to equate the slug with the lead ball because the two were entirely different.

THE "ROCK IN A SOCK" CONCEPT

The rifled slug was designed to overcome the wild ways of lead-ball loads. It was given a preponderance of weight up front so it would fly like a sock with a rock in its toe. Moreover, the slug was given a spiraled rifling "skirt" to reduce bore friction. My earliest shooting with basic rifled shotgun slugs found the accuracy wasn't as punk as armchair experts made it sound. Certain combinations of guns and slugs would print amazingly tight groups for me.

The problem many hunters have, of course, is they never shoot critically or try to understand the scientific side of slug performance. They listen to hand-me-down advice and merely accept it and pass it along. Those of us who actually shoot slugs on pattern paper began to learn a few things that exploded the carryover myths.

THE TWO ESSENTIALS

Early deer hunters did not understand the two essentials of slug accuracy, namely, the

A slug gun with open sights can perform on deer if you find the right slug load for it, adjust the sights and hold steady like a good rifleman. The author hammered this two-shot group with Remington 1-ounce slugs through a Mossberg M/500 at 50 yards.

impact of barrel vibrations and the importance of slug/muzzle fit. Just understanding the influence of barrel vibrations on point-of-impact would have helped these early hunters do much better with slugs.

THE VIBRATION FACTOR

Although a shotgun barrel looks rigid, it actually vibrates under the hammering of the powder-gas molecules. This vibrating also takes place in rifle barrels, which is why rifles will send bullets of one weight to one point on a target and throw those of another weight to a different point. In fact, riflemen know that just changing the powder charge under the same bullets can often cause a change in the point-of-impact at 100 yards. This is one reason serious riflemen use the heavier "bull" barrels; they handle heat better so they don't become as whippy or erratic as they heat up and don't have the same extreme vibrations

that skinny hunting barrels do.

After you do some careful accuracy work with shotguns, you begin to see that a barrel will not invariably place group centers with slugs to the same place where it plants the centers of patterns with fine shot. Slug loads churn up different barrel vibrations, and the muzzle is therefore in a different position when slugs exit than when shot charges exit, so the point of downrange impact will inevitably be altered.

Some years ago, I met a man who was thoroughly disgusted after the opening weekend of deer hunting. He had seen a nice deer crossing a pasture and got in several open shots, but everything he fired missed, seemingly by feet if not yards. He was cursing rifled slugs and saying, "With my ol' .35 Remington I'd have been right on him, but since we have to shoot slugs in this area, a guy doesn't have a chance."

I invited him out to the rifle range, and he

gladly accepted. It seems he had never fired a sighting shot through his autoloader and had taken its down-the-rib accuracy for granted. "I line up the front bead with the groove in the receiver top," he said, "just like sighting a rifle."

The first thing we did was set up a patterning sheet and let go with a field load of 6's. It splashed dead center. "See," he said, "just like I told you — right on. Those slugs are crazy!"

Then we set up another patterning sheet with a definite aiming point in the middle, and I had him fire carefully aimed slugs as he had apparently done on that deer. Each slug came in at least 10″ to 12″ low at a point six-o'clock to the aiming point, which was definitely enough to undershoot a deer. He

The surprised hunter hauled out a different brand of slugs and fired another three-shot group. This one came up perhaps ½-foot low, but it also shifted about 4″ to the right. In general, though, its accuracy was okay, as it punched out another 4″ cluster.

"It isn't the slugs," I told him. "They're making pretty good groups. What's missing is an adjustable sight to compensate for the different vibrations."

He had a gunsmith install an adjustable receiver (peep) sight, and when it was adjusted properly, his autoloader tore up the bull's-eye. His repeater was actually quite accurate with slugs, grouping at least three different brands into 3½″ to 4″ over 50 yards. What was absent was a method to get the gun's muzzle to point

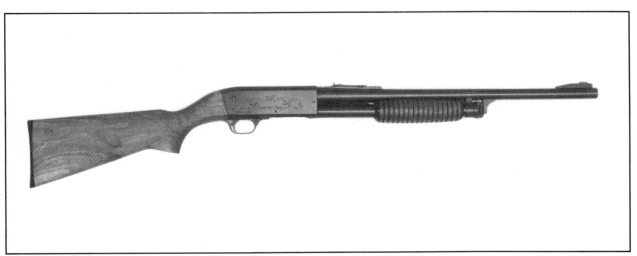

One of the first bona fide slug-style shotguns was this Ithaca Model 37 Deerslayer.

couldn't believe it. "But I'm holding dead on the bull's-eye!" he protested.

What he didn't understand, of course, was his gun was vibrating differently with the slugs and was throwing them low — the slugs weren't going crazy. I had him settle down and shoot a serious three-shot group at 50 yards, and his trio of Remington 1 ouncers gave a 4″ cluster, which wasn't bad for those crude sights and his 60-year-old eyeballs!

It is group size that determines slug accuracy, not point-of-impact. All experts in shooting accept the existence of vibrations, including naval gunners working with massive 16″ battleship guns, and vibrations are factored into their firing equations.

at the bull's-eye when it was vibrating with slugs rumbling through it.

There are hundreds, perhaps thousands, of whitetail still running because some hunter missed when his barrel vibrated and he didn't have the right sight. The hunter assumed his ol' duck or cottontail collector would automatically shoot straight with any and all ammo, but it won't. The groups can be quite small, but you have to test-fire to learn the exact point-of-impact caused by changes in the vibrational patterns.

SLUG/CHOKE FIT

The second essential in slug-gun accuracy

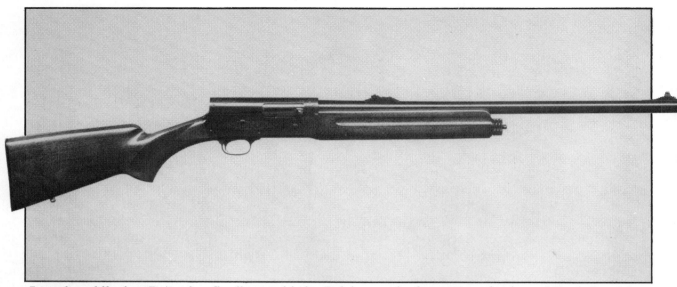

It took awhile, but Browning finally provided a Belgian-made slug gun — the Auto-5 Buck Special.

is the fit of the slug to the muzzle diameter at exit. The theory behind all slug accuracy is that the slug should bear *evenly* against all surfaces of the choke at exit to help center the slug.

If the slug and choke are a sloppy fit, the potential for small groups declines. You can visualize what happens. A slug that is smaller than the muzzle diameter doesn't bear evenly on all sides of the muzzle/choke at exit, so it can strike any side of the muzzle and glance in the opposite direction. If a slug hits the choke wall at three-o'clock, for example, it will angle toward nine-o'clock on the target; if a second slug comes along and glances off the choke at nine-o'clock, it will deflect toward the three-o'clock point on the target. The two shots can be a foot apart, as can a slug that glances from the bottom of the choke and goes up and one that glances off the top of the choke and slants downward.

Through the years, I have had good luck with Modified (M) chokes because they seem to have a smaller opening that impinges on all sides of an exiting slug without deforming it the way a tight Full choke might. Today many writers advise hunters to use an Improved Cylinder (IC) choke with most slugs, but I still see better groupings with a light Modified choke around 16 points of constriction in the

12 gauge.

Some shooters try to determine accuracy by the way their slugs fit the muzzle when checked by hand. This won't work because slugs widen when they are rammed forward by the accelerating energies of powder gases. Since the pellets are made of rather soft lead, the pressure from the rear expands the skirt of the hollow-based projectiles and increases their girth. The best way to find which slug is the most accurate from your shotgun is to test it from a solid rest at serious range conditions. Just shooting at a soda can balanced on a cedar fence post will tell you absolutely nothing; you must use the slugs in actual shots because of the widening.

The Ithaca Deerslayer is about the only shotgun that seems to take slug-to-bore fit into serious consideration. It is made with a lightly undersized bore to enhance circumferential bearing on the slug, and I have found it to be quite accurate with the 1-ounce rifled slugs from Winchester and Remington. Now known as the Ithaca Model 87, rather than the Model 37, it is a very sound smoothbore for slugs. Ithaca also makes a Deerslayer II model which was the first production-grade shotgun to have a factory-rifled barrel. Ithaca has its head on pretty straight when it comes to slug shooting!

Different brands and weights of slugs can shoot to considerably different points-of-impact from the same sight setting. Wise hunters will spend some time at the benchrest holding carefully over a sandbag rest to determine their combo's best accuracy and point-of-impact.

THE DOUBLES' DILEMMA

In the past, I continually heard that double-barreled shotguns performed terribly with slugs, and my own shooting indicates side-by-sides (SxS's) are indeed very dicey with slugs. Not only are SxS's prone to vibration because there is virtually nothing to support them below the barrels, but they are also angled to superimpose their fine-shot patterns at 40 yards, meaning slugs can crisscross.

In my experience, though, over & unders (O&U's) can be extremely accurate with slugs. This doesn't mean they will automatically handle rifled slugs famously, but some I have tested were unbelievably accurate, especially from the lower barrels. I had a Remington field-grade Model 3200 that could beat out 4″ three-shot groups at 50 yards while I did nothing more than sight down the rib over a sandbag rest. I also had a Beretta BL-4 that tore a ragged hole at 50 yards when I sighted down the rib and used the bottom barrel; the upper barrel shot tight groups, too, but jumped several inches as I have had happen with a number of other Berettas. The first Browning Superposed I ever owned was bored IC/M and

grouped dead center, with very few flyers ever popping from the basic 3½″ to 4½″ groups.

Why would O&U's give such acceptable groups with slugs while SxS's flop? The main reason is the O&U's are very rigid and, therefore, less inclined to vibrate wildly, erratically or independently. Setting one barrel atop the other stiffens the barrel assembly and dampens the up-down vibrations. I wouldn't, however, pay big bucks for an O&U if I were only looking for a slug gun, as a less-expensive repeater with adjustable sights is totally adequate. If I already owned an O&U and hunted deer only once a year in my home county on opening weekend, I'd certainly give my stackbarrel a test at the rifle range.

Side-by-sides, then, are dubious and dicey with shotgun slugs, and you are lucky if you have one that pitches slugs directly to the point of aim when it is aimed like a rifle. The flexibility and alignment of SxS tubes negate the potential for good groupings and dead-on impacts. The O&U is another ballgame, however, and some are extremely good with slugs. The main difficulty with O&U's is getting advanced sights on them without going to a

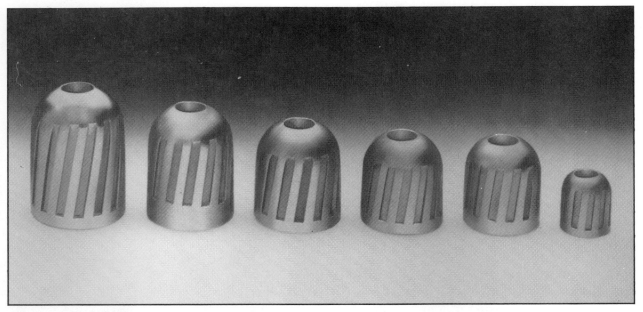

There are a lot of rifled shotgun slugs around, and Federal Cartridge Corporation has some in each gauge, beginning with the massive 10 gauge on the left to the punk .410 on the extreme right — only the 28 gauge is missing. However, the .410 slug really has no legitimate place in big-game hunting.

grotesque assembly. Sighting down the rib with a bold-bead front sight doesn't work very well on game afield because the hunter, like the wing shot, often lifts his head and loses precise alignment. The rib/bead sighting unit is coarse enough on its own, but with an added head lift it almost insures misses or crippling hits.

THE SIGHT-EQUIPPED DEER GUN

Many deer taken by slugs are inside 50 yards, and smoothbores that can print 4″ groups at that distance are certainly up to the chore, provided you can do your part. Realizing the crude rib/bead sighting devices on shotguns are anything but effective with slugs, manufacturers began supplying slug or "deer" barrels with adjustable sights on them. The open-field sight may hardly be optimum, but it's far better than a bold bead on the muzzle.

Many hunters still lift their head when using open-field sights and many mistakenly believe the guns are sighted in precisely just as they come from the factory. That is not necessarily so. Like rifles, slug guns will vibrate differently whenever you switch from one brand of slugs to another, and if you employ a different load than the factory used to make its initial sight adjustments, the gun's point-of-impact could be considerably different.

As an experiment, I took a slug gun equipped with an open sight just as it came from the box and set up at 50 yards to fire groups with a half-dozen different slug loads. Not one group punched into the bull's-eye — the closest centered about 3″ to the left and a tad low, and one brand hit roughly 10″ low and left. After four brands of slugs had gone to the left from that barrel, I assumed they would all go that way, but that was not the case. The fifth brand of slugs centered 4″ to the right. So, don't depend on smoothbores to shoot dead-on with rifled slugs.

Even guns with sights will vary their points-of-impact. Indeed, slug and deer guns come with adjustable sights for one good reason — so you can adjust them according to the vibrational characteristics of each individual loading!

Modern rifled slugs are not wild and crazy. Even when shot from smoothbore barrels, they can be accurate enough to bag deer reliably at ranges beyond 50 strides. You just have to do some testing so you will know where the barrel's vibrations are sending your slugs.

23

Slug Stuff II: The Slug Gun Goes Modern

I hunted throughout the 1940s in my home county in southeastern Wisconsin without ever seeing a deer or deer track, but they began to appear in the 1950s. The first deer I ever saw was a real thrill.

I was grouse hunting in a hilly section of eastern Wisconsin and between two thickets there was a long, relatively open hillside with scattered jack and white pines. The young trees had been planted as a state project to bring back a forest on land that had failed to support farming and is now part of an Ice Age Forest. I had bagged a grouse in the first covert and, with my 20 gauge in hand, set out across the hillside. On my way to the second covert, I walked past a couple jack pines that were quite wide on the bottom. I paid no special attention to them, as I had walked past them practically every weekend of the bird season for the past three years. Suddenly I heard a snort and ruckus under the pines and out came a pretty six-point headed downhill into a swamp.

I had heard about deer sightings, but this was my first experience with one. Before that season was over, I saw several more. It appeared the whitetail were not only back, but they were having a population explosion. By the 1960s, I was hunting deer in places where, just a decade earlier, they hadn't seen a deer for over 50 years!

The deer herds spread quickly. Illinois, Indiana, Ohio, Iowa — states that hadn't seen deer since the white man began farming the land — were covered with whitetail. The food was good, of course, and the whitetail flourished. They were healthy and possessed strong racks. Hunters no longer had to pack their .30-30's or .35 Remingtons and trek off to the northwoods for a week in a cabin; they could sleep at home, leave early and be deer hunting on a nearby farm by sunup.

AN EXPLOSION OF HUNTERS AND PRODUCTS

Not only did the deer herds explode in the 1960s, so did the crowd of deer hunters. In my home state of Wisconsin, for example, the army of deer hunters has grown to about 675,000 and has reached such proportions it is not very much fun for people who like a quality hunt.

This amazing expansion spurred the development of many new products to help hunters improve their chances with shotgun slugs. Most of the new hunting areas are rather heavily populated by people as well as deer and are not safe rifle country, so shotguns with slugs are mandated, although most places also permit muzzleloaders.

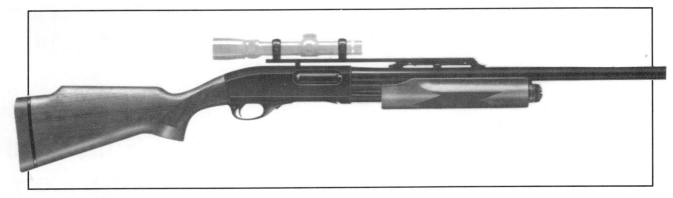

One of the best advances in slug-gun design was the introduction of the cantilevered mount, which brings the scope back to the shooter so it is within proper eye-relief distance while also keeping the scope aligned with the bore axis.

Inexperienced hunters missed and missed with unsophisticated slug guns, and the demand went up for something better. The typical hunter didn't really understand slug accuracy, so he decried it and lamented the lack of superior equipment. The cries and lamentations were heard, and there has been a steady stream of sophisticated slug-shooting products come onto the market. Open-sight equipped deer guns or slug barrels were first, but even those have paled in light of more-recent products.

NEW SLUG LOADS

The advertised weights of shotgun slugs have varied over time. Once the 1-ounce, 12-gauge slug was standard, then for a few years the industry tried ⅞-ounce slugs; now we are back to the standard 1-ounce, 12-gauge rifled slug, although some manufacturers have gone heavier with 1¼-ounce, 12-gauge slugs and 1 and 1¼ ouncers in the 12's 3″ Magnum case.

The standard 12-gauge slug has a rotund trajectory, and it was hoped the 3″ Magnum version with its higher velocity would flatten

Sabot slugs were already around in the early 1970s but didn't catch on until rifled barrels came along in the 1980s. These are Smith & Wesson sabots from the author's collection which were made around 1974 when S&W operated the old Alcan Company.

Remington introduced a Turkey barrel for the Model SP-10 autoloader, and the presence of open sights enables you to adjust for accuracy with shotgun slugs as well. Federal makes a 10-gauge Magnum slug.

the trajectory for better hitting over long ranges. Although we often think of the slug gun as a short-range gun for brush and swamps, a lot of shots at open-country white-tail are longer chances; hunters hate to pass up these shots, so they demanded a higher-velocity 12-gauge slug.

Remington Arms Company is the foremost producer of high-speed slugs, turning out a 1-ounce slug that does about 1,760 f.p.s. at the muzzle. Federal Cartridge Corporation, on the other hand, uses its 3″ load to put more energy into a 1¼-ounce slug for about 1,600 f.p.s.

To date, however, the 3″ slug loads have not been very successful. I range-tested each of them in several sight-equipped smoothbores, including a couple with scopes, and the groups were extremely wide. The Remington and Winchester 12-gauge, standard-length slug loads with 1-ounce rifled slugs outshot them both badly. In one such test, I put a 3X-9X

variable scope on a Remington Model 11-87 Deer Gun with a cantilevered mount and, at 100 yards, the Winchester 1 ouncers gave about 4″ groups, while the Remington 1 ouncers were about 1″ wider. In either case, these beat the 3″ loads easily. The 3″ rounds gave very wide groups that might well have missed a deer's vital heart/lung area at 100 strides.

It is quite possible 3″ slug loads will group better in other guns, as each gun/load combo is a physical law unto itself, but I have yet to find a smoothbore that will do well with them. I tested seriously because I would like to take advantage of the flatter-shooting slugs, but to date I have not been satisfied with the results, which I am sure are due to erratic barrel vibrations generated by the high pressures of the 3″ slug loads. As things stand, I would sooner take the better accuracy found in the Winchester and Remington 1-ounce, 12-gauge slug loads than exchange that accuracy for a few

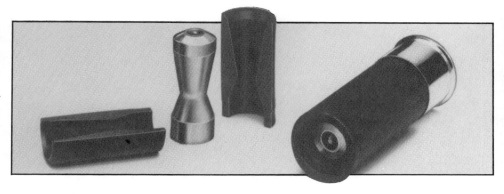

Federal Cartridge Corporation's new Hydra-Shok® sabot-slug load has a .50-caliber diameter and a hollow point for expansion, something lacking in older sabots, but it was too new at this writing for any first-hand field testing.

more feet per second in velocity. My apologies to the industry, but more is not always better — at least not yet for 3″ 12-gauge slug loads.

The comeback of the 10-gauge for goose hunting with steel shot, along with some hunters' desire for optimum slug energy, prompted Federal Cartridge Corporation to bring out a whopping 10-gauge slug load using a 1¾-ounce rifled slug at 1,280 f.p.s. Remington is now making a 22″ Turkey barrel for the Model SP-10 autoloader that wears open sights that should accommodate rifled slugs as well.

Not many serious deer hunters use anything smaller than the 1-ounce, 12-gauge slug, but rifled slugs are available in 16 gauge (⁴⁄₅-ounce), 20 gauge (¾-ounce) and even .410 bore (¹⁄₅-ounce). I know of instances where the 16 and 20-gauge slugs did clean jobs on deer, but the punk .410 slug has no place in big-game hunting in my opinion. I have also heard of instances where 20-gauge slugs have wounded and lost deer; unless they are placed precisely into the heart/lung area or make a head shot, 20-gauge slugs can leave an animal on its feet to run a long distance. Some people equate the slim barrel of a 20 gauge with rifle-like qualities, but the reverse is closer to the truth — the 20-gauge slug gun lacks positive clean-killing power on anything but a perfect hit.

THE SABOT

Although the sabot slug has only recently become popular, it has been around for quite some time. I used some in 1973 and 1974 when the Remington Model 3200 first came out, but it took considerable time for the sabot concept to catch on, and even now I question its qualities despite what seems to be an excellent

potential for accuracy in fully rifled shotgun barrels. Accuracy is one thing; knockdown power and clean-killing effectiveness is another, and my correspondence indicates sabot slugs are not reliable in the latter role.

Essentially, sabot slugs get their name from the word "sabotage." They are solid slugs designed something like aerial bombs, with a long body tapering to a tail and encased in two plastic enclosures that fit perfectly around the slug. These plastic halves are cylindrical to fit the shotshell case and, when fired, they keep the slug centered in the bore. On exit, the plastic "sabots" fall away while the slug, theoretically, remains true to the bore axis for accurate, head-on flight, a flat trajectory and high rates of retained energy.

Theory and practice don't always jibe, however, and when I shot some of my first sabot-slug loads in the 1970s I found some would "keyhole," meaning they came in sideways, while a few snapped in flight and separated at the base of the body/tail juncture to impact on the target in two different places. Of course, these sabot slugs were shot through smoothbore barrels which, as time has proved, aren't the best match for them. The point is, sabot slugs are rather specialized and don't invariably give optimum performances through every smoothbore and certainly don't pancake deer with every shot.

Through the years, people have taken a hard look at shotgun-slug accuracy and did some experimenting. Even though the old-timers said rifled slugs don't need rifled barrels, some experimenters began trying full-length rifled, 12-gauge shotgun barrels and proved that rifling did indeed enhance slug-gun accuracy. Hastings, P.O. Box 224, Clay Center, Kansas 67432, is the foremost supplier of such barrels, which are made in France for many popular repeaters sold stateside. Some companies like Remington are providing rifled screw-in choke tubes to impact slug accuracy. The old idea that slugs get all their accuracy from the hollow-based slug flying like a rock in a sock has been questioned.

Hastings' barrels plus sabot slugs have shown some amazing long-range potential. The Hastings barrels shoot like a dream — no criticism there — but more and more hunters have written me saying they have had discouraging hits with sabot slugs. The slugs seem to pencil on deer, giving no expansion to cause a prompt knockdown, and they have no apparent shocking power, allowing the deer to remain on its feet and running. I have a letter from one hunter who tells of having to trail a deer for three hours in the snow before he found it bedded from loss of blood. Other letters tell of hitting deer and never finding them.

Until the sabot gets better reports, I will cock a skeptical eyebrow in its direction. Sabot slugs do not seem to be the answer for improved deer hunting, as they are still potential cripplers and wounders. Federal Cartridge Corporation has announced a new sabot slug of .50-caliber with a hollow point for expansion, but how it will fare remains to be seen. Meanwhile, I believe the jury is still out regarding the overall effectiveness of the sabot-slug load. I won't recommend them for anything but accuracy shooting until I hear more hunters bragging about a lot of clean kills with them.

I would sooner use Winchester or Remington 12-gauge 1 ouncers with a scope-sighted rig, like the cantilever-equipped Model 11-87, 870 or Mossberg pump. These soft, broad, rifled slugs seem to have more impact because of their broad frontal area and do more radial tissue damage to knock deer down sooner by shock as well as penetrating damage.

THE CANTILEVERED MOUNT

Most slug guns today are repeaters with

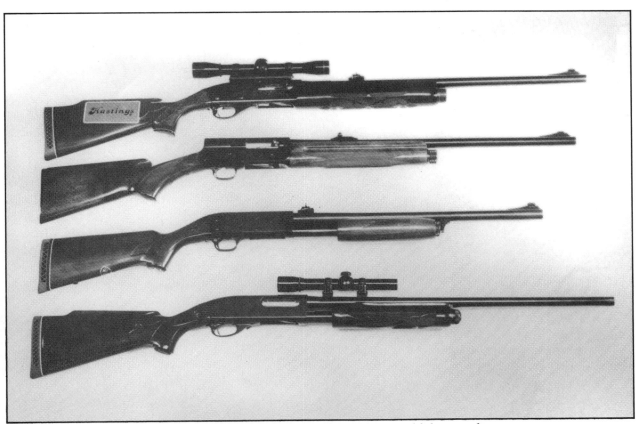

The Hastings Company has a full line of rifled shotgun barrels, which are a boon to accuracy with slugs.

removable barrels and, as such, the barrels tend to be variously wobbly when the gun is assembled. Even if the gun seems very snug when put together, there is always the likelihood the force of firing will shake it loose. This wobbliness tends to change the relationship of the barrel to any scope or other sighting device mounted on the barrel. The idea is to have the sight aligned with the bore axis, and this is not possible for every shot when the barrel jiggles about while the sighting device is solidly secured to the receiver. That's where the cantilevered mount comes in.

By definition, a cantilever is something that is anchored at one point but has a projection extending over a space that needs to be bridged for some reason. In the case of a cantilevered scope mount on a slug gun, the purpose is to have the extension bridge the gap from the barrel to the shooter's eye so the scope can be aligned with the barrel while also being brought to the correct eye-relief distance. It's as simple as that, and it works.

I used a Remington Model 11-87 Deer Gun with a cantilevered mount and high-powered scope to shoot some 3″ groups at 100 yards from a benchrest. That's mighty good; it beats some .30-30's I have tested! Once you learn the trajectory with a load that groups like that, you can hit a whitetail's vital heart/lung area at 125 yards rather easily — provided you don't get buck fever and yank off the shot! Unless your gun's barrel is welded to the receiver for stability, the cantilevered mount is the next thing to perfection. Happily for deer hunters, Remington is now making the economy-grade Model 870 Express with a cantilevered mount at affordable prices.

TRIGGERS CAN ALSO BE AT FAULT

In the 1970s I was bitten by the big-game hunting bug and did a lot of benchrest work with rifles. Shooting 1″ groups wasn't difficult because rifle triggers tend to be crisp and clean, but when I tested shotgun slugs I noticed a significant difference between shotgun triggers and rifle triggers.

Shotgun triggers are terrible for shooting groups with a firmly held gun used like a rifle. The typical trigger (fire-control) mechanism on a repeating shotgun can be described many ways: Long, heavy, sluggish, spongy, hard, creepy or gritty. The result is the same — you simply cannot hold and squeeze a shotgun trigger like you do a rifle and expect the same results. Some match rifles have 1 and 2-ounce triggers, whereas the pull of shotgun triggers can run 6 to 8 pounds, maybe more. I had one trigger pull on a foreign-made double measure at 10 pounds!

The heavy, long, spongy trigger pulls on shotguns can upset accurate shooting. When I wanted to test for optimum accuracy with a Remington Model 11-87, I replaced the factory pull trigger with a Schwab release trigger. A release trigger demands no pull, of course; you simply pull the trigger back, hold it there while you line up and then relax your trigger finger. Spring pressure releases the hammer, and there is no flinching or yanking to make that #@&*#! trigger go!

Generally speaking, double-barreled shotguns have better triggers than production-grade repeaters. I sometimes wonder if that didn't play a role in the accuracy I got with the Remington M/3200 and Beretta BL-4.

Ask any tournament rifleman, and he will tell you trigger control is the name of the game in accuracy shooting. The same is true with shotgun slugs. That's why I believe a certain percentage of the supposedly inherent inaccuracy of slug loads is actually attributable to the trigger.

Something like Timney's all-steel trigger mechanism with variable spring tension can improve the trigger-pull performance on Remington autoloaders and Model 870's. I have a Timney trigger for my M/1100, and it is reasonably sharp for enhanced slug accuracy. Think about this if you are serious about slug accuracy and deer hunting with smoothbores.

RELOADS OR STORE-BOUGHT SLUGS?

Through the years, I have received a number of letters inquiring about reloading slugs. The thought is handloading shotgunners could work up loads like a rifleman, who mainly tries to find the primer/powder/slug combination that generates the same frequency as any individual barrel. Once the load jibes with the barrel's natural vibrational characteristics, accuracy is sure to happen.

Frankly, I can't get excited about reloading slugs. There are so many brands on the market you can generally find a commercial load for your rig just by testing many different ones. Instead of buying reloading equipment, pick up every type of slug load that is available and, on a warm spring or summer day, settle down at a benchrest and punch out three-shot groups. Be patient and squeeze off each one, don't yank. Check every group after firing; let the gun cool, then try another brand. I'd say start at 50 yards, then test again at 100 with the best loads.

The ones that print the tightest groups are the best. Don't worry about point-of-impact when testing; you can always adjust the sight to match the best load once you have discovered it. When you find a slug load that gives excellent results in your barrel, hurry back to the dealer and buy a bunch. They don't deteriorate with age, and you will have loads made from the same batch of components. After all, manufacturers don't always use the same powders year after year, and you want the exact same loads that printed so closely for you.

USING THE BENCHREST

Each year our rifle club opens its gates to the public who want to sight-in their deer rifles and shotguns, and each year I see shooters get pounded by recoil because they don't know how to sit at a benchrest. Shotgun slug loads can really kick when you are scrunched down aiming over a sandbag rest, and it isn't uncommon to see a cut above a shooter's eyebrow made by a scope's eyepiece.

A rule of thumb among benchrest shooters is: The harder the recoil, the straighter you sit. Build up the rest with added sandbags, but always try to sit upright with a hard-recoiling shotgun so the broad base of the entire butt can fit against your shouldering area. Hunching down and contacting the butt with only the rounded part of your shoulder lets all the energy concentrate on one spot and allows the gun to roll around, which can upset accuracy. Sit high, place the butt flat against the hollow of your shouldering area and do the rest like a rifleman.

The old-timers were wrong. Shotgun slugs *can* deliver deer-getting accuracy if you take the time to find the right load and adjust your sight. You must also pull the trigger without yanking while your head is down on the comb, not lifted up in excitement!

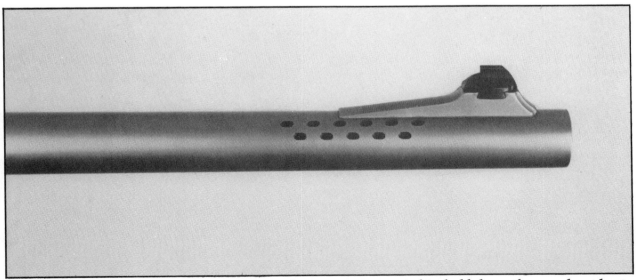

Slug loads can recoil, and it is a good idea to have your gun ported to hold down the muzzle and get back on target quickly. This is a Pro-Port porting job.

Letters, We Get Letters. . .

During the years I have been a magazine columnist, I have received hundreds of questions from readers. If I had back the money I spent on postage to answer those letters, I could buy several cases of Sporting Clays loads and have enough left over to fill my car's tank with gasoline for hunting.

A number of questions were asked repeatedly and others asked less often were, nevertheless, important to basic and advanced shotgunning. For this chapter, I selected those which found my mailbox most frequently and others I felt were important.

Q. I have a fine British double which, I am told, has a proof pressure of 8 *tons* per square inch. What does that mean in our l.u.p. values and how does it translate into working pressure? To what level can I reload shotshells for this gun, which has 2½″ chambers?

A. The British "tons" system can be changed to l.u.p. by multiplying with 2,205, in which case your double would have been proofed at 17,640 l.u.p. That's not far from the American proof-testing level around 19,000 l.u.p.

To get the maximum average working pressure of your gun, multiply the British proof pressure *as stated in l.u.p. values* by 0.55. This would give your double a working

pressure of 9,700 l.u.p., which again isn't far from the American working pressure of 10,500 l.u.p. for the 12 gauge.

As mentioned earlier in this book, it isn't possible to translate l.u.p. accurately into p.s.i.; however, as a very coarse practice, you can make a rough approximation of the p.s.i. value by adding 1,000 to the l.u.p. reading. You can reload shotshells up to the 9,500 to 9,700-l.u.p. level without stressing your gun, or about 10,500 p.s.i. if you employ the rough-approximation method.

Q. In various literature, I have come upon two uncommon terms relative to chamber pressures. One refers to "Bars," while another refers to "kilograms per square centimeter." How do they stack up against our p.s.i. system of reporting chamber pressures?

A. I do not believe the "Bar" method is employed much anymore, if at all, in firearms testing. It stems from atmospheric pressure measurements, and 1 Bar equals 14.504 p.s.i. Merely multiply the published number of Bars by 14.504 to get the pressure in p.s.i.

As far as kilograms per square centimeter are concerned, the conversion to p.s.i. is made by multiplying the number of kilograms per square centimeter by 14.223. I understand Mexico still employs this metric system with pressure barrels made to American (SAAMI) specifications.

Q. What is the difference between the British *quarter choke* and our Improved Cylinder (IC)?

A. The British began using the term "quarter choke" when it was common to hold Full choke at 0.040″; a quarter of that figure would be 0.010″. On that basis, our IC is generally a bit more open, as many I have measured run from 0.005″ to 0.007″. Sir Gerald Burrard, the great British gun writer, suggested IC is around 0.005″ or looser.

Q. I am puzzled by reports on backbored barrels. What does backboring really mean and does it affect the load's velocity? My friends tell me backboring opens the bore and lowers the velocity.

A. "Backbored" is simply another way of describing an overbored barrel. The term was coined by Seattle custom gunsmith Stan Baker, who thought the term "overbore" misled shooters into believing there was something wrong, as the word "*over*done" usually indicates a mistake.

The fact is, overboring or backboring tends to improve velocities, rather than reduce them, as long as the wads can seal the bore. In the case of modern plastic obturating wads, this seems to mean 12-gauge bores of at least 0.750″. Some wads have shown excellent results with bores as large as 0.775″, 10-bore diameter. The higher velocities stem from two factors: The wider bore provides the propelling powder gases a wider base upon which to push, thus converting more chemical energy to kinetic energy at any split instant; and the wider bore also reduces friction to varying degrees depending upon the actual bore diameter, and this means the powder gases can convert more of their energy into kinetic energy rather than wasting it on overcoming friction in a tight bore. Contrary to popular myths, backbored barrels tend to either hold or increase velocities slightly, and in my patterning they show a decided penchant for tight center densities.

Q. I would like to switch to a lightweight

28 gauge for bird hunting. How much smaller will a 28-gauge IC pattern be than a 12-gauge IC spread?

A. If we are talking about the extreme overall pellet spread, there is no appreciable difference between the larger gauges (10, 12, 16, 20 and 28). The main point is the smaller gauges tend to put fewer pellets into the fringe and outer (annular) ring of the pattern because they have lighter shot charges or may deform more pellets in their narrow bores.

Practically all of these gauges will have enough shot in their 20″-diameter cores to give clean kills afield if you can center your targets. If you can't center birds, your chances of crippling and losing birds is greater with the little guns due to their weaker outer densities. The sporting arms industry regularly patterns into a 30″-diameter pattern at 40 yards to check these gauges. Only the .410 is patterned differently; it is patterned into a 20″-diameter circle at 25 yards.

Q. Assuming the same load, is recoil greater from a long-barreled shotgun than from a short-barreled one?

A. Recoil is calculated on the total weight of the ejecta — i.e., shot charge, wads and powder charge — and the velocity with which they exit the muzzle. Theoretically, the recoil would tend to be greater from a long barrel because it would generate higher ejecta velocity; however, in actual practice it is difficult to tell the difference when the load is identical, probably because the velocity with which the powder gases leave the short barrel is higher than the muzzle velocity of the ejecta from a long barrel. Although the shorter barrel gives a lower ejecta velocity, the overall recoil sensation is quite similar.

Q. What is meant by a "progressive-burning" powder?

A. All modern smokeless powders are progressive-burning, although their burning rates vary. "Progressive" means they do not release their chemical energies all at once as dynamite does, but instead burn more gradually so their early gases can move the wad/shot mass forward and provide some added gas-expansion room before the entire powder charge ignites. Failure to provide this additional gas-expansion room can cause an extremely high chamber pressure and a burst.

In general, powders with the slowest burning rates are used with the heaviest shot charges so the initial buildup of powder gases will move the payload well ahead before the burning reaches its peak. On the other hand, fast-rate powders can be used with lighter shot charges because the payloads are easier to move ahead quickly.

Q. Why isn't there more reloading data for fast-rate powders, like Red Dot and Hi-Skor 700-X, in the 20 and 28 gauge? They would be more economical than the slow-rate powders so heavily recommended with these gauges.

A. Chamber pressures mount quicker in the narrow smallbores than they do in the larger 10 and 12 gauges; consequently, the powders used for reloading must have a slower burning rate to avoid excess pressures. A propellant like Red Dot or Hi-Skor 700-X will reach maximum recommended working pressures before reaching high velocities in the smaller gauges.

Q. Why is some lead shot called "chilled?"

A. Once upon a time, some British shot-makers caused cold or cool air to blow across the lead pellets as they dropped in a shot tower or hit the bottom of the tower. I don't know how this was done, but the process was seemingly linked to the addition of antimony to the alloy. From then on, lead pellets which had antimony contents were called "chilled" shot.

Today, the cool-air process isn't employed. In modern parlance, *chilled* shot is lead pellets with a lower level of antimony than the so-called "hard" or "magnum" shot. In general, chilled shot will have between 1 and 2 percent antimony as compared to about 3 to 6 percent antimony in hard shot.

There is another grade of lead pellet known as "soft" or "drop" shot, which has about 0.5-percent antimony. Chilled shot is an intermediate alloy in today's lead-shot grading system, since it has a bit more hardness than drop shot but is not as resistant to deformation as hard or magnum-grade pellets.

Q. What do you feel is the lightest a 12-gauge shotgun should be?

A. I believe 6 to 6¼ pounds is the bottom line, and I would prefer the 6¼-pounder. Anything lighter recoils sharply with effective loads, and even guns of 6 to 6¼ pounds can be painful if they don't fit the shooter or are used with very robust loads.

I also think such lightweight 12's should have at least 28″ barrels to help smooth the swing. Aside from the great British Game Guns, which are designed with barrels of 28″ to 30″, I feel we've carried the trend toward short, light shotguns too far.

Q. Does barrel porting reduce shotshell velocities or have an impact on patterning?

A. I have not found porting to be detrimental in either respect. I have chronographed shotgun barrels with control loads prior to and after having them ported, and the barrels gave basically the same velocities. If there were any velocity losses, they were insignificant. In a few instances, the velocities were a mite higher; in a few others, they were a mite lower, but none would have meant a thing to performance on game or clays. I have done the same thing with regard to patterning, and I have not found that porting upsets patterns, either.

Porting, in my opinion, is a desirable feature on any shotgun because it helps hold the muzzle down during recoil and thus makes it easier for the shooter to remain lined up with the target for follow-up shots.

Q. Why did the industry bring out #8½ lead shot?

A. This remains one of the great questions in shotgunning. Apparently it was thought 8½'s would serve for both skeet and 16-yard trapshooting and perhaps the industry could then drop 9's in the 12 gauge. In general, this didn't work. Skeetmen still want the more-numerous 9's and trapshooters lean toward 8's for 16-yard shooting.

I like 8½'s for skeet, but I wish the industry would make a full 3-drams equivalent, 12-gauge target load with 8½'s instead of just the 2¾-drams equivalent round. The 2¾-drams equivalent loads tend to hold rather tight core densities and could use a little more gas pressure on their tails to help them spread out.

Q. My friend says his full-choked .410 shoots like a rifle. Does that narrow bore actually hold patterns that tight?

A. People often equate the .410's slim barrel with ultra-tight patterns, but it really doesn't shoot any tighter than other guns with the same degree of choke. In fact, .410's may give patterns that are a bit more open than the other gauges for any choke because there is more pellet deformation in that narrow little chamber and bore. Too, the long shot string of a .410 lends itself to pellet deformation and added deformation seems to occur at the muzzle of a Full choke when the load is forced to swage down. I'd say your friend has an active imagination and is guesstimating patterns rather than shooting them.

Q. What is the difference between a single-based and double-based powder?

A. A single-based powder uses only nitrocellulose, which is derived from wood, or nitrocotton, which is made from cotton. A double-based powder uses either of those plus nitroglycerine.

Q. Do all shotshell primers function alike?

A. No. Some primers are known as "gas" primers and send a hot flame into the powder. Others are known as "particle" primers and shoot hot particles into the powder rather than a flame. Moreover, primers of each type can be made in different potencies. The interior ballistics of shotshells can, therefore,

be affected by the primer, and switching primers can alter chamber pressure, velocity and even pattern.

Q. I use Solo 1000 for all my trap loads and love it. I would like to use it for my hunting loads, too, but can't find any information about using it with 1½-ounce Magnums. Can you provide some data, as I would like to inventory only one powder.

A. Solo 1000 is a fast-rate powder that is *not* to be used with heavy loads. The forward resistance of a Magnum shot charge would cause Solo 1000 to reach a dangerous chamber pressure. Solo 1000 is for use *only* with lighter shot charges which its gases can push ahead quickly to create added expansion room for the developing gases.

No single shotshell powder is made to do all things. Instead of trying to find data to fit one powder, you would be better off to select a second powder for use with your heavier charges.

Q. I own a British 12-gauge double with a 2½″ chamber and would like to reload for it; however, I cannot find any data. Can you recommend some reloads?

A. There is very little information of this type stateside, as the demand is low and it is costly to do the laboratory testing. Scot Powder Company, P.O. Box 317, McArthur, Ohio 45651, has included some material in its reloading manual for both 1 and 1⅛-ounce charges using Solo 1000 and Royal Scot.

Q. I want to reload with the old-fashioned nitro card and filler wad stack but can't find any at my local dealers. Where can I still get them?

A. This type of wad is being offered by two outlets: Ballistic Products Inc., P.O. Box 408-SS, Long Lake, MN 55356; and Ljutic Industries, Inc., P.O. Box 2117-SS, Yakima, WA 98907.

Q. I recently bought a 28-gauge bird gun and would like to reload 1-ounce shot charges. There doesn't seem to be any data for this, and I wonder why the powdermakers haven't published any information. It seems the 1-ounce load would really beef up the little 28. What reloads do you recommend?

A. The industry doesn't publish 1-ounce reloading data for the 28 for a good reason — we don't have suitable powders and wads for it. None of the plastic wads fit properly and few of the powders can give effective velocities before reaching excess chamber pressures.

The only outfit I've known to list 1-ounce, 28-gauge reloads is Hodgdon, so you might try to find their current manual. In the past, Hodgdon's publications included this combination:

Winchester AA-type hull
Winchester 209 primer
21.0/HS-7
0.080" card + ⅜" filler
1 ounce lead shot
Pressure: 10,500 l.u.p.
Velocity: 1,164 f.p.s.

Care must be taken to insure firm seating of the nitro-card wad, as the hull has an inside taper that could tilt the disc. Hodgdon recommends at least a 40-pound wad-seating pressure. My suggestion is to seat the nitro card and then remove the hull from the reloading press and visually check the card to see that it is seated deeply and evenly. Then seat the filler with 40 pounds of pressure so it is press-fitted to the nitro card's top surface, which will be slightly concave.

Quite frankly, I have never understood why anyone would buy a 28 gauge to shoot 20 and 16-gauge loads. The narrow bore of the 28 tends to make the 1-ounce load relatively inefficient compared to what the 20 and 16 can do with the same charge weight. The lengthened shot string contributes to pellet deformation due to setback pressures and bore scrubbing, and I believe the 28-gauge 1-ounce load is about as imbalanced as the .410's long 3″ charge with a ¾-ounce shot load. My own feeling is the 28 handles a ⅞-ounce load with greater efficiency, and I would concentrate on it rather than the 1-ounce concept.

Q. What is meant by "efficiency" when describing load performance?

A. *Efficiency* means getting the most load energy per grain of powder. This would be calculated in terms of foot-pounds of energy at the muzzle.

SUPPLIERS

Following is a list of suppliers for products mentioned in this book. Whenever possible, I have tried to provide telephone and FAX numbers. As change is always inevitable, I cannot guarantee the complete accuracy of this list, but it was current as of the writing of this book.

Ballistic Products Inc., P.O. Box 408, 2105 Daniels Street, Long Lake, MN 55356-0408; Phone (612) 473-1550

Hastings Barrels, P.O. Box 224, Clay Center, KS 67432: Phone (913) 632-3169; FAX (913) 632-6554

Hodgdon Powder Company, P.O. Box 2932, 6231 Robinson, Shawnee Mission, KS 66201; Phone (913) 362-9455; FAX (913) 362-1307

Ljutic Industries, Inc., P.O. Box 2117, Yakima, WA 98907; Phone (509) 248-0476

Magnum Research, Inc., 7110 University Avenue N.E., Minneapolis, MN 55432; Phone (612) 574-1868; FAX (612) 574-0109

Polywad, P.O. Box 7916, Riverside Station 2, Macon, GA 31209; Phone (404) 477-0669

Precision Sports, P.O. Box 708, Kellogg Road, Cortland, NY 13045; Phone (607) 756-2851

Pro-Port, 41302 Executive Drive, Mount Clemens, MI 48045-3448; Phone (313) 469-7323; FAX (313) 469-0425

Schwab Release Triggers, 1103 E. Bigelow, Findlay, OH 45840; Phone (419) 423-2565

Scot Powder Company, P.O. Box 317, 430 Powder Plant Road, McArthur, OH 45651; Phone (614) 596-2706; FAX (614) 596-4050

Shootin' Accessories Ltd., P.O. Box 6810, Auburn, CA 95604; Phone (916) 889-2220; FAX (916) 889-9106

Shotgun Sports Magazine, P.O. Box 6810, Auburn, CA 95604; Phone (916) 889-2220; FAX (916) 889-9106

Allen Timney Gunsmith, 13524 Edgefield Street, Cerritos, CA 90701; Phone (213) 865-0181; FAX (714) 877-4713

USSCA, 50 Briar Hollow, Suite 490 East, Houston, TX 77027; Phone (713) 622-8043; FAX (713) 960-8649

Wingshooting Adventures, 4320 Kalamazoo Avenue S.E., Grand Rapids, MI 49508

NEW SNAPSHOT

STUDENTS' BOOK

Elementary

Brian Abbs • Ingrid Freebairn • Chris Barker

CW00547247

Longman

Contents

Communication	Skills	Learn to learn	Soundbite
Talk about personal details	Speaking: see 'Communication'	General advice	/ sp / Spike / st / Stella / sk / school
	Listen to someone talking about her life Read about the city of Liverpool Write notes about a city in your country		
Check on a situation	Write a description of a room Read rules for a swimming pool	Organise new vocabulary (1)	Sentence stress: It's on the floor. It's under the desk.
Revision			
Talk about routines	Read about a day in the life of a pop star Write about a typical week Listen to a telephone conversation about a problem	Test your memory	/ ps / shops / ts / starts / ks / talks
Offer food and drink with *would like*	Write a food diary Listen to a food programme Read about birthday plans	Organise new vocabulary (2)	/ tʃ / cheese, chips / dʒ/ juice, jam
Revision			
Make polite requests with *could*	Listen to a radio programme about future sporting events Read an interview with a footballer Write an interview with a sports star		/ θ / third, eighth, ninth
Ask and talk about past events	Read a ghost story Listen to a telephone conversation about exam results	Record past tense forms of regular verbs	/ t / stopped / d / climbed / ɪd / wanted
Revision			
Talk about events in the past Buy things in shops Ask for and give directions	Read about fan mania Listen to people buying things in a shop Listen to people giving directions	Learn past tense forms of irregular verbs by heart	
Describe past events	Listen to a dialogue and note the correct order of events Read about a pet snake Write an animal story	Use a dictionary (1)	/ ɔ: / horse / ɒ / fox
Revision			

Unit	Grammar	Vocabulary
11 I've lost my rucksack.	Present perfect simple Prepositions: *with, on, in*	Materials and personal possessions Clothes Physical description
12 It's the tallest tower in Britain.	Present perfect simple with *never* and *ever* Comparative and superlative of short and long adjectives Question word: *How?* + adjective	Adjectives of measurement: *fast, heavy, long, wide*
Progress check: Units 11 and 12	Revision	Revision
13 You shouldn't move it.	Verb *will/won't* for predictions and decisions Verb *should/shouldn't* for advice and obligation	Parts of the body
14 Do I have to?	Verb *have to* (present and past simple)	Household jobs Occupations
Progress check: Units 13 and 14	Revision	Revision
15 Wideangle on the world: Time to spare Culture flash 3: Rooms and possessions Project 3: My room	Consolidation of language and skills	
16 What would you like to do?	*would like/would prefer* + infinitive with *to* Verb *would rather* + infinitive without *to* The imperative for instructions and advice	Leisure activities
17 If you complain any more, ...	First conditional: *if* clause + *'ll (will) / (won't)* Adverb formation	Adjectives and adverbs
Progress check: Units 16 and 17	Revision	Revision
18 The scenes are filmed here.	The passive: present simple	Jobs in the media Types of films
19 They were sent here after prison.	The passive: past simple *much, many, a lot of*	Food and drink in a restaurant
Progress check: Units 18 and 19	Revision	Revision
20 Wideangle on the world: Nurse in a war zone Culture flash 4: Famous places in the UK Project 4: A favourite place to visit	Consolidation of language and skills	

Communication	Skills	Learn to learn	Soundbite
Ask about and describe objects Describe people	Speaking: see 'Communication' Listen to a telephone conversation about a lost bag Read a missing persons poster Write a poster	Sort into groups	/ h / have, haven't
Ask and talk about experiences Make comparisons	Listen to a dialogue and answer questions Read about RoboDog Write an e-mail about a robot	Check spelling	Sentences stress: It's the tallest tower in Britain.
Revision			
Talk about injuries Make decisions Give advice	Read and complete a questionnaire on First Aid Write a list of First Aid tips	Practise speaking	The sound / l / in final position: I'll, he'll
Talk about jobs	Read an article about helping in the house Listen to someone talking about an amusing incident	Improve your listening skills	Word stress: doctor beautician
Revision			

Communication	Skills	Learn to learn	Soundbite
Ask for and make suggestions with *shall, why don't we?, let's* Express preferences	Read What's on? advertisements Listen to a radio programme Write an invitation Read advice about how to be safe at carnivals	Use a dictionary (2)	/ aɪˈlaɪk / I like / aɪdˈlaɪk / I'd like
Apologise with a reason and respond	Write a message of apology Listen to a dialogue and choose the best answers Read about voluntary work		Intonation in conditional sentences: If you go now, you'll have lots of time.
Revision	Revision		
Remind and reassure people with *will/won't*	Listen to a cameraman talking about working in films Read about a popular film Write about a film you enjoyed	Reading in class	Fall–rise intonation: Don't worry, I won't.
Order food and drink in a restaurant	Read about reform ships Listen to someone talking about living on a sailing ship	English outside the classroom	/ ə / was (used) were (taken)
Revision			

The Liverpool Project students *(from left to right)*
Sandra Mancuso from Milan, Italy; **Gabriel Navarro** from Salamanca, Spain; **Adam Wysocki** from Krakow, Poland;
Jennifer (Spike) Hunter from Brighton, UK; **Louise Morgan** from London, UK; **Joe Phillips** from Manchester, UK

TEEN WORK

Teen Work organises projects during the summer holidays for teenagers from all over the world.

The Liverpool Project

Location	Liverpool, England
Dates	3rd–29th August
Accommodation	Hostel
The work	Community projects in Liverpool
Pay	No pay but free food and accommodation
Project leader	Mick Jordan

Map labels: SCOTLAND, Edinburgh, NORTHERN IRELAND, Belfast, Dublin, EIRE, Liverpool, WALES, Cardiff, ENGLAND, London

The Liverpool Project staff

Mick Jordan, the project leader; The Burns family: **Stella Burns**, the hostel warden, with her husband **David**, and children **Sam** and **Katie**

1

Nice to meet you.

LEARNING GOALS

Grammar
Present simple
Vocabulary
Countries and nationalities
Family members
Types of music
Communication
Talk about personal details

1 🔊 Listen and read

Mick: Hello! Nice to meet you. I'm Mick Jordan, the project leader. Now who's who? What's your name?

Spike: I'm Jennifer Hunter but everyone calls me Spike. I'm from Brighton.

Adam: My name's Adam Wysocki. I'm from Poland.

Mick: OK. Now what about the others?

(Mick checks all the students' names.)

Mick: All right, everyone. Welcome to Liverpool. The bus is over there. Let's go!

2 Comprehension

Answer T (true) or F (false).

1 All the students are from England.
2 The students are now in Liverpool.
3 Mick is one of the students.
4 Spike's real name is Jennifer.
5 Mick checks everyone's addresses.

3 🎞 Useful phrases

Listen and repeat.

- Nice to meet you.
- Everyone calls me [Spike].
- All right, everyone.
- Welcome to [Liverpool].
- Let's go!

P	O	L	A	N	D	N	B	Y
F	B	G	R	E	E	C	E	P
B	R	D	G	K	M	K	T	O
R	A	U	E	N	R	B	U	R
I	Z	I	N	U	G	D	R	T
T	I	I	T	A	L	Y	K	U
A	L	A	I	B	E	U	E	G
I	C	K	N	R	H	S	Y	A
N	S	P	A	I	N	Y	T	L

4 Vocabulary

Countries and nationalities

a) Find nine countries in the word square and write them in a list with their nationality adjectives.

Country	Nationality
1 Poland	Polish

b) Add five more countries and nationalities to your list.

5 Communication

Talking about personal details

A: What's her name?
B: It's Sandra.
A: What nationality is she?
B: She's Italian.
A: Where's she from in Italy?
B: She's from Milan.
A: What's her surname?
B: It's Mancuso.
A: How do you spell that?
B: M-A-N-C-U-S-O.

Now talk about three or four other people in the picture. Use the information on page 6 to help you.

6 Over to you

Introduce yourself and say your name, nationality and where you are from. Or imagine you are one of the students and introduce yourself.

Hello. My name's ... . I'm ... . I'm from ... .

9

7 📼 Listen and read

That evening there is a welcome party at the hostel.

Stella: Hello, everyone! I'm Stella Burns, the hostel warden, and this is my husband, David. He teaches at the university.

David: Nice to meet you. Now, where do you all come from?

Later

Spike: Hello. Sorry I'm late! I'm Spike.

Katie: Spike? That's cool! I'm Katie. Sam! Turn the music down!

Spike: Who's Sam?

Katie: My brother. He likes techno music – but Mum doesn't!

Mick: Come over here, everybody! I want to take a photo of the group!

Spike: Oh, no! I hate group photos!

8 Comprehension

Answer T (true) or F (false).

1 Stella is the hostel warden.
2 David is one of the students.
3 Stella is Katie's mother.
4 Stella likes techno music.
5 Mick wants to take a photo of Stella.

9 📼 Soundbite

The sounds / sp /, / st / and / sk /

<u>Sp</u>ike   <u>St</u>ella   <u>sch</u>ool
(Look at page 130.)

10 Memory bank

Family members

List all the family words you know.

11 Practice

Talk about the family relationship between:

• Stella • David • Katie
• Sam

Stella is David's wife.

12 Over to you

Write about the people in your family.

13 Grammar

Present simple

Positive statements	Negative statements	Questions	Short answers	
			Positive	**Negative**
I come from Spain.	I don't come from Portugal.	Do you come from Spain?	Yes, I do.	No, I ... .
He ... from Spain.	He ... come from Portugal.	Does he ... ?	Yes, he	No, he ... .

Think!

Complete the sentences above with the correct words.
Make similar sentences using *she, we* and *they*.

14 Practice

a) 📼 **Look at the information about the Teen Work students. Complete the conversation about Joe. Then listen and see if you were right.**

A: Where ¹... Joe ²... from?
B: He ³... Manchester.
A: Oh, really? Where does he ⁴... in Manchester?
B: He ⁵... in a small house in the suburbs.
A: ⁶... his favourite school subject?
B: I think he likes Computer science.
A: What sort of music ⁷... he ⁸... ?
B: Well, he likes soul and jazz but he ⁹... pop very much.

b) Ask your partner about two other Teen Work students.

c) Interview two students in your class. Then make similar cards for them.

A: *Where do you come from?*
B: *I come from ... .*

15 📼 Listen

One of the students is missing. Who is it? Listen and note the information for this person.

Joe Phillips

Town/City	Manchester
Home	small house in the suburbs
Favourite school subject	Computer science
Music – like	soul, jazz
– not like	pop

Gabriel Navarro

Town/City	Salamanca
Home	small flat near the main square
Favourite school subject	Physics
Music – like	
– not like	heavy metal slow music

Spike Hunter

Town/City	Brighton
Home	house near the sea
Favourite school subject	Art
Music – like	reggae, rap
– not like	country & western

Sandra Mancuso

Town/City	Milan
Home	large flat in the north
Favourite school subject	English
Music – like	classical, pop
– not like	heavy metal

Adam Wysocki

Town/City	Krakow
Home	flat in the centre
Favourite school subject	History
Music – like	Spanish guitar music
– not like	techno

11

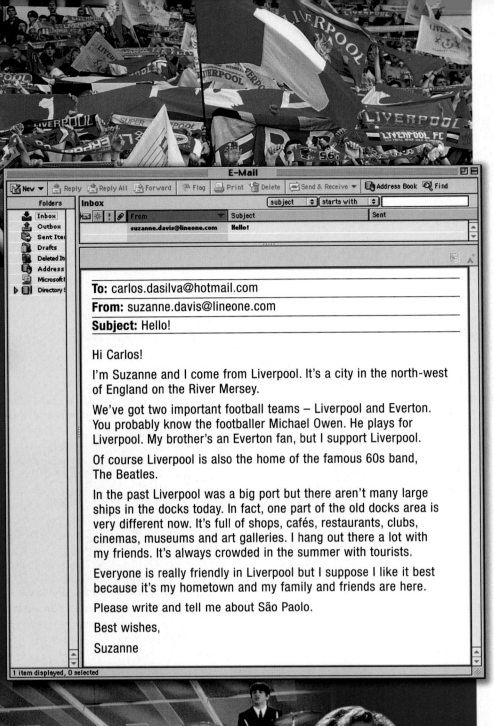

Before you read

What do the pictures tell you about Liverpool?

16 🔊 Read

a) Read the e-mail and put the topic headings below in the same order as the text.

a) Sport
b) Reasons for liking the city
c) Music
d) Location
e) Entertainment

1 Location

b) Find words in the text which you associate with:

- food • drinks • dancing
- historical objects • paintings
- ships • films

Food: restaurants

c) Answer the questions.

1 Where is Liverpool?
2 Which sport and which band is Liverpool famous for?
3 Is Liverpool still a busy port?
4 Why do tourists go to the old docks area now?
5 Why does Suzanne like Liverpool? (Because ...)

17 Write

Write a similar e-mail letter about your hometown.

18 Learn to learn

General advice

1 Ask your teacher about words you don't understand.
2 Write down all new words.
3 Repeat words or phrases when your teacher corrects you.
4 Speak in English as much as possible.
5 Always write out your homework corrections.

E-Mail

New ▼ | Reply | Reply All | Forward | Flag | Print | Delete | Send & Receive ▼ | Address Book | Find

Folders	Inbox		subject ⬍ starts with ⬍	
Inbox	✉ ❋ ! 📎 From	Subject		Sent
Outbox	suzanne.davis@lineone.com	Hello!		
Sent Item				
Drafts				
Deleted It				
Address				
Microsoft				
Directory				

To: carlos.dasilva@hotmail.com

From: suzanne.davis@lineone.com

Subject: Hello!

Hi Carlos!

I'm Suzanne and I come from Liverpool. It's a city in the north-west of England on the River Mersey.

We've got two important football teams – Liverpool and Everton. You probably know the footballer Michael Owen. He plays for Liverpool. My brother's an Everton fan, but I support Liverpool.

Of course Liverpool is also the home of the famous 60s band, The Beatles.

In the past Liverpool was a big port but there aren't many large ships in the docks today. In fact, one part of the old docks area is very different now. It's full of shops, cafés, restaurants, clubs, cinemas, museums and art galleries. I hang out there a lot with my friends. It's always crowded in the summer with tourists.

Everyone is really friendly in Liverpool but I suppose I like it best because it's my hometown and my family and friends are here.

Please write and tell me about São Paolo.

Best wishes,

Suzanne

1 item displayed, 0 selected

On the tour bus

🎞 **Read the story and put the sentences at the bottom of the page in the correct places. Then listen and see if you were right.**

1 Where is everybody?

2 Where's Gabriel?

I'm here.

OK. And where are the others?

_____ .

3 Sorry I'm late.

That's all right. Where are Louise and Sandra?

_____ . They're a bit tired.

OK. Come on. _____ ! Let's get on the bus.

4 Where does the bus go?

_____ . It's a very interesting trip.

5 _____ the _____nese Gate.

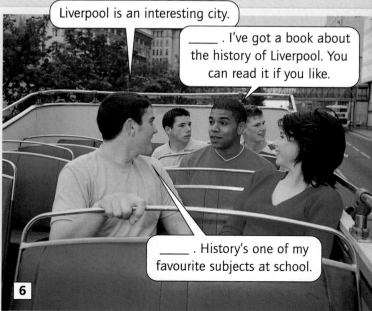

6 Liverpool is an interesting city.

_____ . I've got a book about the history of Liverpool. You can read it if you like.

_____ . History's one of my favourite subjects at school.

• Yes, it is. • Let's go! • It goes round the centre of Liverpool.
• They don't want to come. • Look at • Thank you. • They aren't here yet.

13

2

You mustn't play loud music.

Grammar
there is/there are with *some*
  and *any*
Verbs *must/mustn't, can/can't*
Prepositions of place: *in, on, under,*
  in front of, behind, above, next to,
  opposite, on the left/right (of),
  to the left of … /right of …,
  between, in the corner (of), near

Vocabulary
Parts of a room
Furniture and objects
Patterns and colours

Communication
Check on a situation

1 Vocabulary Parts of a room, furniture and objects

Match the words with the items in the picture.

1 – noticeboard

Which items are not in the picture?

- bed • radio • table
- lamp • wardrobe
- mirror • carpet/• floor
- curtain • desk
- washbasin • armchair
- chair • radiator
- bookcase • wall
- pillow • wastepaper bin
- poster • pictures
- door • noticeboard
- window • duvet
- cupboard • vase
- rug • cassette player

14

Grammar flash

Prepositions of place

in the cupboard
on the table
under the desk
in front of the radiator
behind the curtains
above the armchair
next to the table
opposite the bed
on the left/right (of)
to the left of … /right of …
between the windows
in the corner (of)
near the door

2 Practice

Complete Spike's description of her room with the correct prepositions.

'My room at the hostel is a bit basic but it's OK. The walls are cream and there are some patterned curtains at the window. ¹ *Under* the window there's a bed with a red and yellow checked duvet. I keep my cassette player ²… the table ³… the bed. There's a brown bookcase ⁴… the bed with some books ⁵… it. ⁶… the bed there's a window. ⁷… the room there's a wardrobe. ⁸… the window and the wardrobe there's a purple armchair. ⁹… the wardrobe there's a radiator and ¹⁰… the radiator there's a desk with a lamp ¹¹… it. ¹²… the desk there's a wastepaper bin and there's a green chair ¹³… it. There's a poster ¹⁴… the wall and there's a noticeboard ¹⁵… the desk. There's a mirror ¹⁶… the vase ¹⁷… the bookcase. Oh, I forgot, there's also a plain brown carpet on the floor and a rug ¹⁸… the bed and the table.'

3 🔊 Soundbite Sentence stress

It's **on** the **floor**. It's **under** the **desk**.
(Look at page 130.)

4 Vocabulary

Patterns and colours

Describe the carpet, curtains and furniture, using the words below.

1 It's a green and yellow patterned carpet.

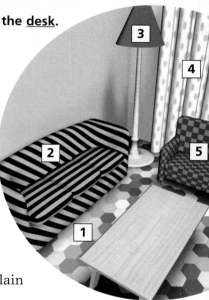

Patterns
* checked • patterned
* striped • spotted • plain

Colours
* beige • black • blue • brown • green
* grey • pink • purple • red • white
* yellow • orange • cream

5 Learn to learn

Organise new vocabulary (1)

1 Write down new words in a separate notebook.

2 Where possible, organise your vocabulary in word groups, e.g. furniture, patterns, colours.

6 Grammar

there is/there are with *some* and *any*

Positive statements
There's a desk in the room.
There ... ... curtains above the bed.

Negative statements
There isn't a TV.
There ... ... pictures on the walls.

Questions
Is ... a washbasin in the room?
... ... books in the bookcase?

Short answers

Positive	Negative
Yes, ... is.	No, there ... .
Yes, there are.	No, there ... .

Think!
Complete the sentences above with the correct words.

7 Practice

Test your memory. Ask and answer about the things in Spike's room on pages 14 and 15.

- desk • wardrobe • poster • carpet
- radio • sofa • bookcase • TV • rug
- washbasin • table • cupboard • lamp
- mirror • pictures • vase • armchair
- chair • books • wastepaper bin

A: *Is there a desk in Spike's room?*
B: *Yes, there is. It's next to the radiator.*
A: *Are there any pictures on the walls?*
B: *No, there aren't.*

8 Interaction

Students A and B

- Draw an outline of your room at home. Draw the bed, doors and windows.

- Exchange outlines with your partner.

- Take turns to ask questions and complete the plan of your partner's room.

9 Write

Write a description of your room.

I (don't) like my room. It's quite/very small. I share it with my brother. The walls are ... . There's a plain red ... and there are some ... .

10 🎧 Listen and read

Mick: Hi! How's it going? How do you like your rooms?
Spike: They're a bit basic but they're OK.
Adam: Yes, they're fine thanks. Just one thing. Can I have some pillows?
Mick: Sure. Sorry about that. I'll get some for you.
Adam: Thanks. And I don't think there's a wastepaper bin.
Mick: No problem. I'll go and get one now. Remember, you can put some posters on the wall if you like but you mustn't use drawing pins.
Spike: OK. Can we move the furniture around?
Mick: Sure.
Spike: Good. I want to put my armchair on the other side of the room.
Mick: Don't forget – you mustn't play loud music after ten thirty at night.
Adam: Yes, we know.

11 Comprehension

Correct the sentences.

There are some pillows on Adam's bed.

There aren't any pillows on Adam's bed.

1 Adam's room has got a wastepaper bin.
2 There are some posters on the wall.
3 They can't move anything in the room.
4 They can play loud music until eleven o'clock.

13 Communication

Checking on a situation

A: Hi! How's it going?
B: Fine thanks. Just one thing. Can I have some coat hangers?
A: Sure. I'll get some for you.

A: Hello! How's everything?
B: OK thanks. Just one thing. I don't think there's a desk lamp.
A: Sorry about that. I'll get one for you.

You are staying with a family in England. Talk to your landlady and make requests.

1 There are no coat hangers.
2 There is no desk lamp.
3 There is no mirror.
4 There are no blankets.
5 There is no towel.

⚡ **Grammar flash** ⚡

must/mustn't, can/can't
(I, you, he, she, it, we, they)

You **must** be quiet after 10.30.
You **mustn't** play loud music after 10.30.
You **can** put some posters on the walls.
You **can't** make coffee in your room.

---

14 Practice

a) Talk about your school rules with *can/can't* or *must/mustn't*.

1 We can use calculators in Maths exams.
2 We mustn't chew gum in class.

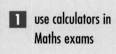 **1** use calculators in Maths exams

 **2** chew gum in class

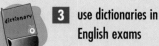 **3** use dictionaries in English exams

4 wear make-up and jewellery at school

 **5** bring personal stereos to school

6 take food or drink into the classroom

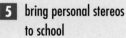 **7** do our homework on time

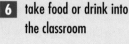 **8** use mobile phones at school

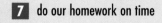 **9** be polite to teachers and other students

12 📼 Useful phrases

Listen and repeat.

• How's it going?
• Just one thing.
• Sorry about that.
• No problem.
• Remember.
• [You can] … if you like.
• Don't forget.

b) Write two more school rules.

Swimming Pool Rules

1 Please have a shower before you enter the pool.

2 Please do not run around the edge of the pool.

3 Please tie your hair back or wear a swimming cap if you've got long hair.

4 You can jump into the pool from the side but not from the diving boards.

5 Never push another person into the water.

6 Please do not take bottles or glasses near the pool.

7 You can use mobile phones in the café but not in the pool area.

15 Read

a) Read the list of rules about the swimming pool. Find the rule which gives information about:

a) long hair
b) mobile phones
c) pushing
d) jumping
e) taking drinks into the pool area
f) having a shower
g) running

b) Explain the rules using *must/mustn't*.

1 You must have a shower before you enter the pool.

16 Over to you

Tell the class about any rules you have at home for:

- using the phone (or your mobile phone).
- playing music.
- watching TV or videos.
- having friends round.
- going out in the evening.

Do you think any of these rules are unfair?

Progress check Units 1 and 2

Grammar

1 Choose the correct part of the verb *to be* to complete the sentences.

... you American?   a) Am   b) <u>Are</u>   c) Is

1 Adam and Gabriel ... both students.
   a) is   b) are   c) be
2 A: Are you from Spain? B: Yes, I ... .
   a) am   b) is   c) are
3 Joe ... American, he's English.
   a) aren't   b) isn't   c) am
4 His name's Sam and ... Katie's brother.
   a) he   b) is   c) he's
5 They ... Joe's bags, they're Spike's.
   a) aren't   b) are   c) isn't
6 Spike ... not her real name.
   a) it's   b) 's   c) it

2 Complete the sentences with the correct form of the verb(s) in brackets.

She ... coffee. (not like)   *She doesn't like coffee.*

1 ... you ... in Liverpool? (live)
2 He ... from Poland. (come)
3 I ... the guitar. (play)
4 We ... her Spike. (call)
5 What ... your mother ...? (want)
6 My parents ... my sort of music. (not like)
7 ... all the students ... from Spain? (come) ·

3 Complete the text with *can, must* or *mustn't*.

'My school is a girls' boarding school. We live at school and there are lots of rules. Everyone ¹ *must* wear a white blouse and a grey skirt. The blouse ² ... have long sleeves and the skirt ³ ... be too short. We ⁴ ... wear make-up in school but we ⁵ ... wear lipstick in the evening. At weekends we ⁶ ... go into town but we ⁷ ... be back by nine o'clock. Of course, we ⁸ ... go into bars or restaurants – that's against the rules.'

4 Complete the sentences with the correct form of *there is* or *there are*.

It's a big house. *There are* six bedrooms altogether.

1 In my room ... a desk next to the bed.
2 ... some posters on the wall and ... also a big mirror.
3 A: ... a phone in your room?
   B: No, ..., but ... one downstairs in the hall.
4 A: ... any good shops near your home?
   B: Yes, ... some quite good ones.
5 I like London because ... lots of parks and trees.

Vocabulary

5 Choose the odd word in each group.

	Italian	<u>Britain</u>	Spanish	French
1	science	jazz	rap	reggae
2	yellow	plain	blue	grey
3	brother	father	girl	daughter
4	black	checked	patterned	striped
5	bedroom	dining room	garden	kitchen
6	carpet	hall	mirror	wardrobe
7	shower	bath	sitting room	washbasin

Communication

6 Work in pairs. Student A:

Ask Student B

• what his/her name and address is.
• how many brothers and sisters he/she has got.
• what sort of music he/she likes and doesn't like.
• to describe his/her bedroom at home.

Now Student B:

Ask Student A

• what his/her telephone number is.
• how many nationalities there are in the class.
• what school subjects he/she likes and doesn't like.
• to describe his/her sitting room at home.

I never drink coffee.

LEARNING GOALS

Grammar
Adverbs/Phrases of frequency
Present simple for routines
Present continuous
Present simple and continuous
  in contrast

Vocabulary
Clock times/Periods of time
Free time activities

Communication
Talk about routines

Jennifer Lopez

Jennifer Lopez (or J. Lo) is a highly successful actor, singer and dancer. Her new films and new albums usually go straight to the top. Jon Adams finds out about her lifestyle.

Hard work

What's a typical working day for J. Lo?
'Making a film is hard work. I usually get up at half past five in the morning and I'm always on the film set at half past six. I never drink coffee and I always have a light lunch – just a green salad. I don't like late nights. I'm usually in bed by half past ten. If I stay out late, I'm too tired the next morning.'

Adam Shankman, a director of one of her recent films, says: 'J. Lo is actually a quiet person. She doesn't like going out all the time. She often stays at home on Saturday night and watches videos.'

Time off

When J. Lo isn't working on a film or making a record, her lifestyle is very different. 'When I've got time off, I'm quite happy to go out. I love New York restaurants and I often go clubbing afterwards. I love dancing. I sometimes dance until three o'clock in the morning!'

A close family

J. Lo's family lives in New York. 'We're a very close family. I usually see my parents every weekend and I always phone them if I have a problem. I've got two older sisters and we get on very well together. They're not just my sisters, they're my best friends.'

Before you read

What do you think is a typical Saturday night out for a pop or film star?

1 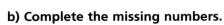 Read

Read about Jennifer Lopez.

er Lopez in a dramatic scene from *My family*

2 Comprehension

Read the article again and correct the notes.

1 Jennifer Lopez is mainly an actor.
   No, she isn't, she's also a singer and a dancer.

2 When she makes a film, she gets up at six o'clock.
   No, she doesn't, she gets up at half past five.

> 1 Jennifer Lopez is mainly an actor.
> 2 When she makes a film, she gets up at six o'clock.
> 3 When she makes a film, she goes to bed at midnight.
> 4 When she stays at home on Saturday night, she usually reads a book.
> 5 She never goes clubbing.
> 6 She usually sees her parents once a month.
> 7 She never talks to them about her problems.

3 Vocabulary Word check

Match the adjectives with an appropriate noun.

1 hard   2 late   3 green   4 best   5 light   6 close

a) salad   b) night   c) family   d) work   e) lunch   f) friend

4 Memory bank Clock times

a) Match the time phrases below with the points on the clock.

o'clock – A

- ten past
- twenty to
- o'clock
- quarter past
- quarter to
- half past

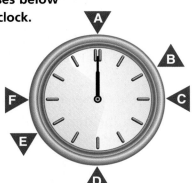

Periods of time

b) Complete the missing numbers.

  15 minutes = a quarter of an hour
1 ... minutes = half an hour
2 ... minutes = three quarters of an hour
3 ... minutes = an hour

5 Over to you

Answer the questions.

What's the time now?
What time do you start school?
What time do you finish school?
How long is your lunch break?
How long is your English lesson?

6 Grammar

Adverbs of frequency
• usually • often • always • never
• sometimes
I'm **always** on the film set at half past six.
I **never** drink coffee.

Put the adverbs in order of frequency starting with *always*.

Phrases of frequency
How often do you see your grandmother?
I see her **once/twice** a week.
How often do you go to the cinema?
I go **three times a month**.

Make rules using *before* or *after*

1 Adverbs of frequency come … the main verb but … the verb *to be*.
2 Phrases of frequency come … the verb (and the object).

7 Practice

Complete the sentences about Jennifer Lopez with *always, never, usually* or *sometimes* and the correct form of the verb.

She (be) … on the film set at half past six.

She's always on the film set at half past six.

1 She (be) … on the film set at half past six.
2 She (drink) … coffee.
3 She (have) … a light lunch.
4 She (be) … in bed by half past ten.
5 She (go) … clubbing.
6 She (dance) … until three o'clock.
7 She (see) … her parents every weekend.

8 🎧 Soundbite

The sounds / ps /, / ts / **and** / ks /

sho*ps*   star*ts*   tal*ks*   (Look at page 130.)

9 Vocabulary Free time activities

Match the verbs with a suitable noun phrase or phrases.

• play • write • visit • go to
• listen to • watch • surf

• football • a video • relatives • the cinema
• letters • TV • friends • computer games
• a disco • CDs • the gym • the Internet
• the radio

play: football/computer games

10 Communication

Talking about routines

A: What do you do after school?
B: I usually do my homework but I sometimes play football. What do you do?
A: I usually go straight home and watch TV.
B: Do you ever go to the cinema?
A: Yes, I do.
B: How often do you go?
A: Once a week, usually on Saturday.

Talk about what you do after school and at the weekend. Use the vocabulary from Exercise 9.

11 Write

Write about a typical week in your life. Or imagine a day in the life of a famous person and write about it.

12 Listen and read

Man: Excuse me, I'm looking for Albert Dock.

Spike: It's here on the map. I'm going there myself.

Man: Oh, really? Do you work there?

Spike: Yes. I'm working on a project. We're helping to make a youth centre.

Later

Mick: Good afternoon, Spike!

Spike: That's not fair! I'm only a few minutes late.

Mick: OK. This is the routine, everybody. We usually work from nine o'clock – or in Spike's case nine fifteen – to three thirty but today we're only working until three.

Spike: Good!

13 Comprehension

Answer the questions.

1 Where does the man want to go?
2 What work are the students doing?
3 How late is Spike?
4 What are the normal hours of work?
5 What's different about today?

14 Useful phrases

Listen and repeat.

- Excuse me.   • That's not fair!
- Oh, really?   • Good!

15 Grammar

Present continuous

Positive statements
I'm staying in a hostel.

Negative statements
I'm not staying at a hotel.

Questions

… you staying in a hostel?
Is he … in a hostel?

Short answers

Positive	Negative
Yes, I am.	No, I … .
Yes, he … .	No, he … .

Think!
Complete the sentences above with the correct words.
Find more examples of the present continuous in the dialogue.

16 Practice

Use the cues to write sentences in the present continuous.

1 Who (you/write to) … ?
2 The students (stay) … in a hostel.
3 Their records (not/sell) … very well in the USA.
4 (your brother/study) … at university now?
5 Louise (not/feel) … very well at the moment.

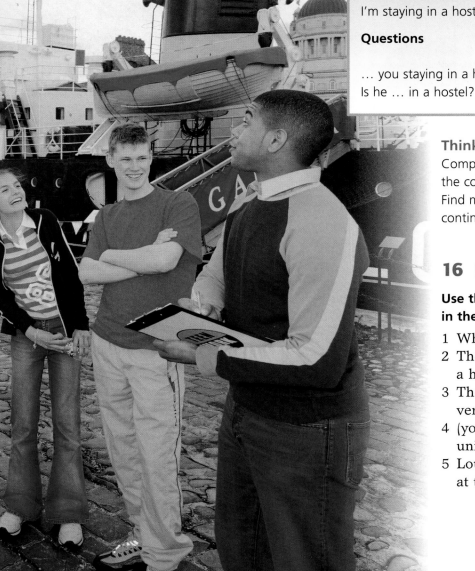

⚡ Grammar flash ⚡

Present simple and continuous in contrast
We usually **work** from 9 o'clock to 3.30 but today we**'re working** until 3.00.
I **live** in Salamanca but at the moment I**'m staying** in Liverpool.

Make rules

1 We use the … for daily routines and fixed times.
2 We use the … for activities which are happening at the time of speaking or for a limited period of time.

17 Practice

Look at the pictures of famous people. What's strange about them? Make sentences using these verbs.

- act • play • sing • ride • drive

1 *In the picture Brad Pitt is singing but he usually acts in films.*

18 Over to you

Talk about:

- the books you usually read. Then say what you are reading at the moment.
- the clothes you usually wear. Then say what you are wearing at the moment.
- the subjects you study at school. Then say what topics you're studying in History and Geography this term.

19 📼 Listen

Listen to the telephone conversation between Louise and her mother and answer the questions.

1 What is Louise doing when her mother phones?
2 What's the news about her father?
3 When is Louise's mother going to phone again?

20 Learn to learn

Test your memory

to interview   excited   to relax
to depend   journalist   to diet

Make sets of small cards with the English word on one side and the translation on the other. Then ask someone to test you.

1 Brad Pitt (films)
2 Enrique Iglesias (songs)
3 Lleyton Hewitt (tennis)
4 Vanessa-Mae (violin)
5 Michael Schumacher (racing cars)

At the hostel after work

Read the story and put the questions at the bottom of the page in the correct places. Then listen and see if you were right.

1 ____? / We're playing *Star Wars*.

2 ____? / I'm winning, of course. / It's not fair. You always win!

3 ____? / I think they're watching TV in the common room. They usually watch *Neighbours* after tea.

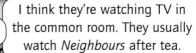

4 ____? / It's five thirty. Why? / I'm waiting for a phone call. / Oh, really! ____?

5 It's OK, Katie! It's for me.

6 ____? / Oh, shut up, Joe. I'm not in the mood.

7 ____?

• Who from? • What's the time? • What are you two doing? • What are all the others doing?
• What's the matter with Louise? • How's it going? • Well, does he still love you?

4

Would you like a sandwich?

LEARNING GOALS

Grammar
Countable and uncountable nouns
Verb *have got* with *some* and *any*
going to future

Vocabulary
Food and drink

Communication
Offer food and drink with
would like

1 Vocabulary

Food and drink

Look at the pictures and match the words with the numbers.

- apple • yoghurt
- bread • cheese
- pasta • egg • beef
- onion • peas • butter
- nuts • milk • orange
- lamb • fish • lettuce
- carrot • potato
- doughnut • banana
- tomato • biscuit
- olive oil
- cucumber
- beans
- lemon
- rice
- mushroom • chicken
- cake • melon
- peach

26

⚡ Grammar flash ⚡

Countable and uncountable nouns

Countable nouns have a plural form:

Singular	Plural
one banana	two bananas

Uncountable nouns have only one form:
coffee   tea   money
I like **coffee** but I don't like **tea**.

2 Practice

a) Say which of these words are countable (C) and which are uncountable (U).

apple C   butter U

- apple • butter • bread • doughnut
- rice • olive oil • spaghetti • biscuit
- beef

b) Which of these foods are good/not good for you? Think about:

- carbohydrates • proteins • fats
- vitamins

3 Learn to learn

Organise new vocabulary (2)

A helpful way to learn words which belong to a large group is to make a word web.

Copy the word web and add the food words from this unit.

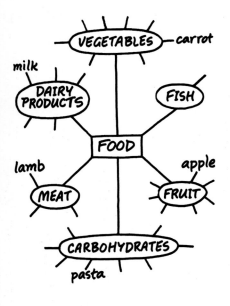

4 Grammar

Verb *have got* with *some* and *any*

Positive statements	Negative statements
I've got some eggs.	I haven't got any biscuits.
She … some coffee.	She … got any fruit.

Questions	**Short form answers**	
	Positive	**Negative**
… you got any potatoes?	Yes, I have.	No, I … .
… she got any milk?	Yes, she … .	No, she … .

Note
We use *some* and *any* with both uncountable and plural countable nouns.

Think!
Complete the sentences above with the correct words.

5 Interaction

Student B: Turn to page 129.
Student A: You are at a supermarket. You want to make a cheese omelette and a mixed salad for lunch. Look at the recipe and phone Student B to ask if the things you need are in the kitchen. Then make a list of things you must buy.

A: *I want to make a cheese omelette and a mixed salad for lunch. Have we got any eggs?*
B: *No, we haven't.*
A: *Have we got any … ?*

Cheese omelette

Ingredients
eggs, butter, cheese, salt, pepper

Mixed salad

Ingredients
lettuce, tomatoes, cucumber, oil, vinegar, salt, pepper

6 Over to you

Write a food diary by making a note of everything you eat and drink during one day. Then compare your diary with your friend's diary. How healthy is your diet?

7 🔊 Listen and read

Mick: OK, everyone! It's twelve thirty.
We're going to have lunch now.

Joe: Great! I'm starving.

Mick: Help yourselves to sandwiches.
We've got chicken, tuna, or cheese
and tomato. What would you
like, Joe?

Joe: I'd like chicken, please.

Mick: What about you, Louise? What are
you going to have?

Louise: Nothing, thanks. I'm not hungry.

Mick: Would you like some fruit?

Louise: No, thanks.

Later

Mick: All right, everyone. It's time to start
work again.

Gabriel: What are we going to do this
afternoon, Mick?

Mick: Clear the yard.

Gabriel: Must we? It's so hot and sunny.

Mick: Sorry, Gabriel. We're here to work!

8 Comprehension

a) Answer these questions.

1 When do they have lunch?
2 What sort of sandwiches are there?
3 Is Louise hungry?

b) Answer T (true), F (false) or DK (don't know).

1 Joe is hungry.
2 There aren't any sandwiches for
vegetarians.
3 There are two sorts of fruit.
4 The weather is fine and sunny.

9 🔊 Useful phrases

Listen and repeat.

- Great!
- I'm starving.
- Help yourself/yourselves to [sandwiches].
- It's time to [start work again].

10 📼 Soundbite

The sounds / tʃ / and / dʒ /

<u>ch</u>eese <u>ch</u>ips <u>j</u>uice <u>j</u>am
(Look at page 130.)

11 Communication

Offering food and drink

A: Would you like a sandwich?

B: Yes, please.

A: What sort would you like?

B: I'd like chicken, please.

A: OK. Help yourself. Would you like something to drink?

B: Yes, please. Have you got any Diet Coke?

Later

A: Would you like another sandwich?/some more coke?

B: Yes, please./No, thanks. I'm fine.

Choose two of the situations and offer your partner things to eat and drink.

• after school at your house

• at a class party • at a picnic

12 Grammar

***going to* future**

Positive statements	Negative statements
We're going to have lunch.	We aren't ... have a big lunch.

Yes/No questions	Short form answers	
	Positive	**Negative**
... we ... have lunch?	Yes, we	No, we ... .

Think!
Complete the sentences above with the correct words.

13 Practice

Complete the dialogue with the correct form of *going to* and the verb in brackets.

Mother: Well, we (watch) [1] ... a video. (you/join) [2] ... us, Gary?

Gary: No, thanks. I (see) [3] ... if Russ is in.

Mother: But he lives on the other side of town. How (you/get) [4] ... there?

Gary: I (cycle) [5] ... . It's not that far!

Mother: Well, take your anorak. I think it (rain) [6] ... .

Gary: OK, OK! See you later!

14 📼 Listen

a) Listen to Michelle, Cindy and Jack talking about what they're going to have for lunch today. Complete the lists.

Michelle: plain yoghurt, ...
Cindy: an egg and tomato sandwich, ...
Jack: a slice of pizza, ...

b) Which person is going to have a healthy lunch?

Birthday treats

What sort of plans have you got for your birthday? Is it going to be just a normal day or are you going to do something special? Our reporter talked to five people about their plans for their next birthday.

Cara, 13

I'm fourteen on Saturday. I'm going to sleep late, and I hope Mum is going to bring me breakfast in bed. My favourite breakfast is a big bowl of cornflakes with sliced banana in it, and toast with butter and honey.

Nicole, 13

It's my fourteenth birthday next Friday. Mum and Dad are going to take me and my two best friends to have a meal at the Hard Rock Café in London. I know what I'm going to have already - a double-decker hamburger and chips, then apple pie and ice cream.

Jack and Emma, 14

My brother and I are twins. We're planning to have a video party for our fifteenth birthday. We're going to rent two or three DVDs from the video shop and watch them with our friends. We all like pizzas and it's easy to order them from the local pizza restaurant. I hope my parents aren't going to be there all the time!

Michael, 15

It's my birthday next Saturday and I'm going to invite two of my best mates from school to a football match to watch Liverpool play Leeds. After the match my dad is going to take us out to an Indian restaurant for a curry.

15 🎞 Read

a) Complete the chart about the birthday plans.

Name	Age next birthday	Special treat	Food
1 Cara	14	Have breakfast in bed	
2 ...			
3 ...			
4 ...			

b) Find words in the text that mean the same as:

1 a deep plate
2 cut into thin, flat pieces
3 on two levels
4 two brothers or sisters of the same age
5 friends

c) Close your books and see if you can remember their plans.

Cara is fourteen on Saturday. She's going to have breakfast in bed. She's going to have a big bowl of cornflakes with ... .

16 Over to you

Make plans for an ideal birthday treat for your next birthday. Tell the class what you are going to do and what special things you are going to eat and drink.

17 Write

Either
a) Write an e-mail invitation to send to friends for your next birthday party.

Hi!

It's my birthday next week and I'm going to have a party on Saturday (March 10th) here at my place from 8 p.m. until late! I hope you can come.

Don't forget to bring your favourite CDs.

See you then.

Josh

Or
b) Write about your plans for your next birthday.

Progress check Units 3 and 4

Grammar

1 Complete the sentences with the correct form of the verb in brackets and write the times in words.

I ... at 7.30 in the morning. (get up)
I get up at half past seven in the morning.

1 She always ... to school by bus. (travel)
2 He usually ... from 8 a.m. until 4 p.m. (work)
3 Carla ... lunch at school. (not have)
4 They ... home from college until 4.15. (not get)
5 He sometimes ... to French classes on Monday. (go)
6 ... she always ... her homework on the bus? (do)
7 The film ... until 8.50. (not start)
8 ... you usually ... before you go to sleep? (read)

2 Choose the correct tense: present simple or present continuous.

Karen *walks/is walking* to school every day.

1 Jack's in the gym. He *plays/'s playing* basketball.
2 Louise *likes/is liking* ballet music very much.
3 Sarah *does/is doing* gymnastics every Thursday evening.
4 Sam and Katie *have/are having* a tennis lesson at the moment.
5 Joe usually *runs/is running* round the park every evening.

3 Complete the sentences with *some* or *any*.

A: Have you got ¹ *any* ice cream?
B: Yes, there's ² ... vanilla ice cream in the fridge.
A: Is there ³ ... milk?
B: No, but I've got ⁴ ... cream.
A: That's fine. Are there ⁵ ... strawberries?
B: No, but there are ⁶ ... bananas.
A: That's no good. I need ⁷ ... strawberries.
B: Why?
A: Because I want to make a strawberry milkshake.

4 Complete the sentences with the correct form of the *going to* future.

They ... across the USA next year. (drive)
They're going to drive across the USA next year.

1 She ... in Ireland next year. (study)
2 We ... in a hotel. (not stay) We ... . (camp)
3 How long ... in Australia? (you and your family/be)
4 I'm ... you the answers. (not tell)
5 Spike's parents ... her next week. (visit)
6 ... the football final on TV? (you/watch)

Vocabulary

5 Choose the correct ending to complete the food words.

• ato • ese • nge • ter • ken • ad • tuce • on

1 butter

1 but   2 oni   3 let   4 pot   5 che   6 chic   7 ora   8 bre

Communication

6 Reorder the sentences to complete the conversation.

A: Would you like something to drink?
B: Yes, please.

a) Sure. What sort would you like?
b) What sort have you got?
c) I'd like a glass of fruit juice, please.
d) No, thanks. This is fine.
e) Orange and apple.
f) Here you are. Would you like some ice?
g) I'd like orange, please.
h) What would you like? There's fruit juice, tea, coffee or mineral water.

7 Work in pairs. Student A:

Ask Student B
• what time he/she usually gets up.
• what his/her mother or father is doing at this moment.
• what he/she is going to do at the weekend.

Now Student B:

Ask Student A
• what time he/she usually goes to bed.
• what your teacher is doing at the moment.
• what he/she is going to do after school.

Self-evaluation Units 3 and 4

How do you rate your progress? Tick the chart.

✔✔✔ Excellent		
✔✔ Good	Grammar	
✔ OK but can	Vocabulary	
do better	Communication	

Camp Wilderness

Camp Wilderness
International Summer Camp
Hillsborough
New Hampshire 03244
USA

July 20th

Dear Scott,

Well, here I am at Camp Wilderness. It's really big and we're in a huge park near a lake. We're a long way from any people or shops.

There are about seventy-five of us here. I'm sharing a cabin with five other boys. Everyone speaks some English but I'm learning a bit of Spanish from José, the Spanish boy. The American, Dan, sleeps in the bed next to me and he snores! The Polish guy is nice. His name is impossible to pronounce. It begins with G so we call him 'Gee'. The Italian boy, Bruno, has got a girlfriend back home in Italy and he always phones her on his mobile first thing in the morning and last thing at night. Sad!!

The day starts early – at half past six! I always get up late so when I get to the showers there's usually no more hot water! We have breakfast in a huge barn. I usually only have Cornflakes and toast but we get waffles and muffins and eggs if we want them. The food's good here.

After breakfast we do our activities. At the moment I'm doing rock climbing in the morning and canoeing in the afternoon. Tonight we're going to have a karaoke party. There's a really nice Italian girl here called Giovanna. I think she likes me because she always smiles at me at meal times. Anyway, I'm going to sit next to her at the party tonight.

I must go. My canoeing lesson starts in five minutes and I mustn't be late.

See you soon.

Greg

1 🎧 Read

a) Read the letter on page 32 and complete the information.

Name of camp:
Number of guests:
Nationalities:
Main language spoken:
Type of accommodation:
Activities:

b) Describe:

- the people in the same cabin as Greg
- the morning routine
- breakfast
- this evening's plans

2 Learn to learn

Dictionary skills: how to find the meaning of a word

A dictionary entry will define a word and explain its meaning. It will also give an example of how to use the word in a sentence.

definition

wil.der.ness / ˈwɪldənəs / **n.** an area in its natural state where there are no signs of humans: *We went camping in the beautiful wilderness of West Virginia.*

usage

Use a dictionary to find the meaning of the words:

- cabin • snore • barn • waffle • muffin

3 Speak

In pairs or groups, plan an ideal day's activity programme at a summer camp in your country. Then tell the class about the programme. What are you going to do on your ideal day?

4 Write

Read Jade's letter to the summer camp organiser. Write a similar letter.

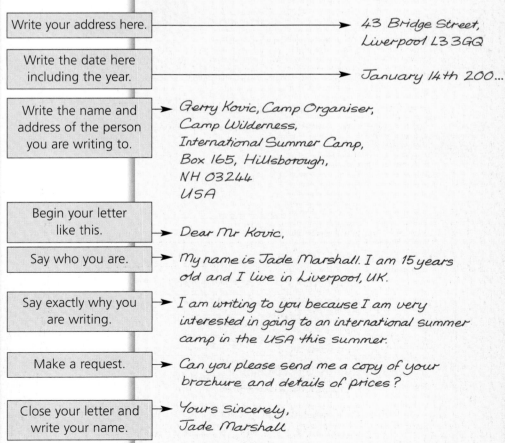

Write your address here. → 43 Bridge Street, Liverpool L3 3GQ

Write the date here including the year. → January 14th 200...

Write the name and address of the person you are writing to. → Gerry Kovic, Camp Organiser, Camp Wilderness, International Summer Camp, Box 165, Hillsborough, NH 03244 USA

Begin your letter like this. → Dear Mr Kovic,

Say who you are. → My name is Jade Marshall. I am 15 years old and I live in Liverpool, UK.

Say exactly why you are writing. → I am writing to you because I am very interested in going to an international summer camp in the USA this summer.

Make a request. → Can you please send me a copy of your brochure and details of prices?

Close your letter and write your name. → Yours sincerely, Jade Marshall

Culture flash 1
Food and meals

Kevin Walker, 15, from Manchester, talks about his mealtimes and his favourite foods.

I have a quick breakfast at 7.45 before I go to school. I just have a bowl of cornflakes, a piece of toast and marmalade and a glass of orange juice. On Saturdays I have a cooked breakfast. My favourite is fried eggs and bacon with fried tomatoes.

I eat lunch in the school canteen. We can choose what we like. I usually have pizza or a meat pie. Some of my friends take a packed lunch.

In the evening, Mum cooks dinner. We usually eat at about half past six. My favourite is spaghetti bolognese or lasagne, but I also like fish and chips. We have fruit or ice cream for dessert. We sometimes have a take-away meal. My favourite is Chinese.

We always have a big Sunday lunch. I like roast chicken or roast beef with potatoes and peas, followed by apple pie and ice cream. I eat most of my meals at home, except school lunch of course, but I sometimes have hamburgers with my friends in town.

Mmm. My favourite breakfast.

Lunch in the school canteen

Sunday lunch at home

Mealtimes in the UK

	On weekdays	At the weekend
Breakfast	7–8.30 a.m.	8–10 a.m.
Lunch	12.30–2 p.m.	1–3 p.m.
Dinner	6–8 p.m.	7–9 p.m.

Take-away meals are very common in the UK. The three top non-British take-away meals are:

1 Chinese   2 Indian   3 Thai

1 Answer the questions.
1 When does Kevin have a cooked breakfast?
2 What does he eat at school?
3 What does Kevin eat with his friends?
4 What non-British take-away meals are popular in the UK?

2 You want to make a typical British Sunday lunch for three friends. Make a list of things to buy.

potatoes

My favourite food

Project A A survey

Do a group survey on your favourite meals and favourite food. Ask:
What is your favourite meal of the day?
What is your favourite main dish/vegetable/dessert?
Make a chart of the results:

	Favourite meal	Favourite main dish	Favourite vegetable	Favourite dessert
1 Gerry	lunch	...	...	...
2 Petra	breakfast			
3 Silvia				
4 Ben				

Talk about the results with other groups.

Project B A recipe

Write a recipe for your favourite meal, snack or drink. Find a picture of your favourite food or drink if you like. Use Lesley's recipe to help you.

Lesley's banana milkshake

My favourite drink is a milkshake.
It's very simple to make.
For two people you need:

• a banana cut into slices
• a quarter of a litre of milk
• a spoonful of honey *
• some ice cubes (optional)

* You can use two scoops of vanilla ice cream instead of honey if you want a luxury milkshake.

Put everything into a blender and blend until smooth.
Pour the milkshake into two tall glasses.
Drink your milkshake through a straw – it tastes better!

6

Who are they playing?

LEARNING GOALS

Grammar
Present continuous as future
Gerund (-*ing* form) after verbs
  like, love, hate, (don't) mind, prefer
Defining relative clauses with *who, which, where*

Vocabulary
Months and dates
Sports/Sports locations

Communication
Make polite requests with *could*

Before you listen

Do you ever go to football matches?
Who do you go with?
Are the tickets expensive?
Who's your favourite team?

1 ▦ Listen and read

Joe: Excuse me, could we look at your *What's On?* magazine, please?

Woman: Sure. Go ahead.

Joe: Thanks. Look! Liverpool are playing at Anfield tomorrow night.

Gabriel: Who are they playing?

Joe: Barcelona. It's a friendly match.

Gabriel: Barcelona! I'd really like to see that!

Adam: Me too.

Joe: Mick, could you get us some tickets for tomorrow's match?

Mick: I'm sorry, I can't. It's too late. But there are sometimes some tickets at the gate, if you don't mind queuing.

Gabriel: I don't mind queuing to see Barcelona. Do you want to come, Sandra?

Sandra: No, thanks. I'm not very keen on football. I prefer swimming.

Spike: Yuk! I hate swimming. I hate putting my head under water!

2 Comprehension

a) Answer the questions.

1 Which two teams are playing at Anfield?
2 What must the group do to get a ticket?
3 Which sport does Sandra prefer?

b) Who wants to go to the match?
Answer Y (yes), N (no) or DK (don't know).

- Joe? • Spike? • Gabriel? • Sandra?
- Adam? • Louise?

3 Grammar

Present continuous as future
We**'re going** to a football match tonight.
Liverpool **are playing** Barcelona tomorrow.

Compare
Do you have more than one way of talking about the future in your language?

4 📼 Useful phrases

Listen and repeat.

- Sure.
- Go ahead.
- Look!
- Me too.
- I'm sorry, I can't.
- I'm not very keen on [football].
- Yuk!

5 Memory bank Months and dates

What are these dates in words?

1 1st Aug 1965 = *the first of August nineteen sixty-five*
2 2nd Sept 1974 =
3 3rd Nov 1980 =
4 14th Oct 1997 =
5 21st Jan 2000 =
6 7th Apr 2003 =

Complete these phrases with the correct prepositions.

7 ... August
8 ... 1965
9 ... 1st August 1965

6 Interaction

Student B: Turn to page 129 and follow the instructions.

Student A: Ask Student B questions to complete your list of sporting events. Then answer Student A's questions.

A: *Who are Brazil playing next?*
B: *They're playing ... .*
A: *When is the match?*
B: *It's on ... .*
A: *Where are they playing?*
B: *At ... .*

Some important future sporting events

Latin-American Football Cup
Teams: Brazil v ...
Date: ...
Place: ...

 = a football

Basketball Major League
Teams: Washington Wizards v New Jersey Nets
Date: 15th September
Place: Madison Square Garden, New York

 = a basketball

Rugby League International
Teams: France v ...
Date: ...
Place: ...

 = a rugby ball

37

SUNBUNNY or SNOWBABY?

What's your rating? Mark the boxes: ✔ = Yes   ✗ = No

Do you like

1 (sunbathe)? □
2 (play) beach games? □
3 (wear) a swimsuit? □

Do you mind

4 (be) on a crowded beach? □
5 (get) sand in your hair? □
6 (feel) hot? □

Do you prefer

7 a) (relax) by the pool? □
   b) (play) volleyball? □

8 a) (lie) in the sun? □
   b) (sit) in the shade? □

9 a) (have) a quick dip? □
   b) (swim) long distances? □

Scoring

1 Yes 1	No 0	**4** Yes 0	No 1	**7** a) 1	b) 0
2 Yes 1	No 0	**5** Yes 0	No 1	**8** a) 1	b) 0
3 Yes 1	No 0	**6** Yes 0	No 1	**9** a) 1	b) 0

Your Sunbunny rating

6–9 You are a number one sunbunny. You love summer, sun and sea. You love getting a tan. But you're a bit lazy! Try to be a bit more active on the beach. It can be fun!

3–6 You like the sun but you don't just want to lie in it. You like being active and sporty. Sitting around isn't for you.

0–3 You hate the sun, sandy beaches and too many people. You don't mind a bit of exercise but you are definitely not a sunbunny! Maybe you're a snowbaby?

Do you like

1 (play) in the snow? □
2 (throw) snowballs? □
3 (ice-skate)? □

Do you mind

4 (wear) thick winter clothes? □
5 (be) outside if it's snowing? □
6 (fall down) in the snow? □

Do you prefer

7 a) (walk) in the snow? □
   b) (do) winter sports? □

8 a) (sit) in a mountain café? □
   b) (ski) or (snowboard) all day? □

9 a) (watch) winter sports on TV? □
   b) (watch) winter sports live? □

Scoring

1 Yes 1	No 0	**4** Yes 0	No 1	**7** a) 0	b) 1
2 Yes 1	No 0	**5** Yes 0	No 1	**8** a) 0	b) 1
3 Yes 1	No 0	**6** Yes 0	No 1	**9** a) 0	b) 1

Your Snowbaby rating

6–9 You are a number one snowbaby. Winter sports are your favourite activity and you love cold weather, snow and fresh air.

3–6 You like winter sports and enjoy a snowy winter but you don't like to feel cold. You're not very energetic and prefer sitting around. Try to take a few more risks!

0–3 Oh dear – you don't like winter or snow! You're not at all interested in winter sports. You don't mind watching them but only in a warm room!

7 Grammar

Gerund (*-ing* form) after verbs *like, love, hate, (don't) mind, prefer*

I like sunbath**ing**.
I love ly**ing** in the sun.
I don't mind be**ing** outside. (= It's OK.)
I hate swim**ming**.
I prefer sit**ting** in the shade.

Make rules

When we use the *-ing* form what happens to the spelling of verbs like:
1 *sit, swim, run, put* and *get*?
2 *have* and *sunbathe*?
3 *lie* and *die*?

8 Practice

a) Complete the questionnaire opposite using the verbs in brackets. Then ask and answer the questions to find your partner's rating.

A: *Do you like sunbathing?*
B: *Yes, I do./No, I don't.*

A: *Do you mind being on a crowded beach?*
B: *Yes, I do. I hate it./No, I don't mind. It's OK.*

b) Tell the class about your partner's answers.

Gianfranco likes sunbathing but he doesn't like being on a crowded beach. He prefers relaxing by the pool to playing volleyball. His Sunbunny rating is 5.

9 Vocabulary **Sports and sports locations**

Name the sports and match them with the places.

1 tennis court

- course - pitch - court - pool - track
- circuit

10 🔊 Listen

Listen to the radio programme about four future sporting events and copy and complete the chart.

Sport	Venue	Date
1	Silverstone	
2	The Millennium Sports Centre	
3	Royal Albert Hall	
4	Crystal Palace National Sports Centre	

11 Over to you

Talk about sport

1 What's your favourite sport?
2 When's the next big match and where is it?
3 Who's playing/competing?

12 🔊 Soundbite **The sound / θ /**

<u>th</u>ird eigh<u>th</u> nin<u>th</u>   (Look at page 130.)

13 Communication

Making polite requests with *could*

A: Could we look at your *What's on?* magazine, please?
B: Sure. Go ahead./Certainly./I'm sorry. I'm afraid I need it.
A: Could you get us some tickets, please?
B: Yes. OK./I'm sorry. I'm afraid I can't.

Make requests for the following situations.

1 You want your teacher to check your work.
2 You want a friend to video *Match of the Day* for you this evening.
3 You want a friend to lend you his/her CD player.
4 You and a friend want to use the school computer after school. Ask your teacher.

Becks is best!

David Beckham is one of football's most famous faces. Beckham – or 'Becks' to use his nickname – plays for Manchester United and is captain of the England football team. He is also a happily married man who adores his family. His wife, Victoria, is the famous ex-Spice Girl singer.

1 ?
No, I love it. I train nearly every day. I never get tired of football. Real Madrid are playing A.C. Milan tonight and I'm going to watch the match on TV.

2 ?
My stupid kick against the Argentinian player Simeone in the World Cup in 1998.

3 ?
To help the England team to win the next World Cup.

4 ?
In a big house in the country outside London but we've also got a house near the stadium where I train.

5 ?
My wife Victoria and my children are my life. I'd do anything for them.

6 ?
Shopping with Victoria, playing with my children – and going on holiday!

7 ?
I can be very moody. When I broke my foot I was very bad company, I'm terrible to live with. And another thing, I always make a mess in the kitchen when I cook.

14 Read

Read the interview with David Beckham and put the questions in the correct places.

a) Have you got any bad qualities?
b) Where do you live?
c) How important is your family to you?
d) What do you like doing in your spare time?
e) Are there any moments which you regret?
f) What's your greatest ambition?
g) Do you ever get bored with football?

Grammar flash

Defining relative clauses with *who, which, where*

He is a happily married man **who** adores his family.
Are there any moments **which** you regret?
We've got a house near the stadium **where** I train.

Make a rule

We use … to refer to people, … to refer to places and … to refer to things.

15 Practice

Complete the sentences with *who, which or where.*

1 Anfield is the name of the stadium … Liverpool FC play.
2 The team … scores the most goals wins the Cup.
3 The coach is the person … trains the players.
4 The shop next to the stadium is one of the places … you can buy photographs of the famous players.
5 The 'player of the season' is usually the one … scores most goals.
6 The competition … attracts most people is the World Cup.

16 Write

Write an interview for a magazine.

Imagine you are a sports journalist. Write a short interview with your favourite sports star.

An afternoon in town

**Read the story and put the pictures in the correct order.
Then listen and see if you were right.** *1 = Picture D*

A

What would you like?

Could I have a hamburger, please?

B

What about you, Louise? Do you want to come?

No, thanks. I'm going back to the hostel.

C

Look! There's a burger van.

Brilliant! I'm starving.

D

Sandra and I are going into town to do some shopping. Adam, are you coming with us?

No, thanks. I don't like shopping. I'm going swimming with Joe.

E

Back to the hostel? What? On your own?

It's OK. I don't mind being on my own.

OK. See you later.

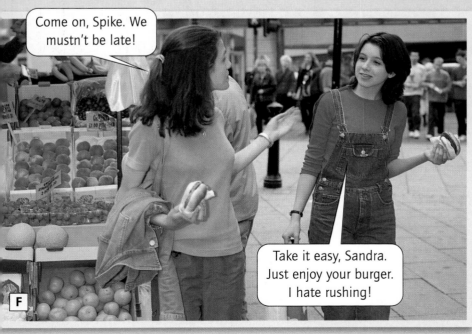

F

Come on, Spike. We mustn't be late!

Take it easy, Sandra. Just enjoy your burger. I hate rushing!

G

Can I help you?

Yes. Could I have a cheeseburger with onions, please?

Yes, certainly.

7

It was all very strange.

LEARNING GOALS

Grammar
Past simple of regular verbs
Past simple of verb *to be*
Possessive pronouns
Question word: *Whose?*

Vocabulary
Common adjectives
School subjects

Communication
Ask and talk about past events

1 🎞 Read and listen

Complete the story with these past tense verbs.
Then listen and see if you were right.

- parked • looked • replied • walked
- decided • weren't • was • arrived
- noticed • burned • appeared • showed
- collected • asked • opened • finished

Last October, when I was in the West Country, I ¹ *looked* in an old guide book and ² ... to visit a beautiful old country house called Compton Hall, dating back to the sixteenth century.

I ³ ... at the house quite late in the day and ⁴ ... the car. I ⁵ ... that there ⁶ ... any other cars in the car park, but that didn't seem strange because it ⁷ ... late in the season. As I ⁸ ... towards the house, the front door suddenly ⁹ ... and a young girl of about eighteen ¹⁰ ... .

'Welcome to Compton Hall,' she called. 'I'm Clarissa Compton. Let me show you the house.' She showed me all the rooms in the house and explained its history. When we ¹¹ ... the tour, I photographed her in front of the door. 'Here. Have this! It's a present for you.' She slipped a small packet into my backpack and disappeared into the house. I returned to my car and unwrapped the packet. Inside there was a small painting of the house. It was all very strange.

In the evening I checked in at a local hotel. 'Did you enjoy your day?' the receptionist

2 Grammar

Past simple of verb *to be*

Infinitive	Past simple
be	I/he/she/it was.
	You/we/they were.

Positive statements	Negative statements
She was young.	She wasn't old.
They were young.	They weren't old.

Past simple of regular verbs

Infinitive	Past simple
love	loved
walk	walked
stop	stopped

Positive statements	Negative statements
He parked the car.	He didn't park the car.

Questions	Short answers	
	Positive	Negative
Did he walk towards the house?	Yes, he did.	No, he didn't.

Note these spelling changes.

stop stop**ped**   hurry hurr**ied**

3 🔊 Soundbite The sounds / t /, / d / and / ɪd /

stopp<u>ed</u>   **climb<u>ed</u>**   **want<u>ed</u>**   (Look at page 130.)

4 Practice

Put the verbs in brackets into the past simple tense. Then write the events in the order in which they happened. Sentences a) and i) are in the correct order.

a) *Last October the man decided to visit Compton Hall.*

b) Later the man (stop) at a small town and (check) in at a hotel.

c) As he (walk) towards the house, the door (open) and a young girl (appear).

d) The hotel receptionist (explain) why Compton Hall (not be) open to the public.

e) She (show) him the house and (talk) about its history.

f) After they (finish) the tour, the man (photograph) the girl.

g) She (introduce) herself as Clarissa Compton and (invite) him on a tour of the house.

h) When he (arrive) the car park (be) empty.

i) *When the man looked at his photographs, there was no picture of Clarissa.*

---

¹² … . 'Yes, I did. Very much,' I ¹³ … . 'I visited Compton Hall and Clarissa Compton ¹⁴ … me the whole place.'

The young man looked puzzled. 'Compton Hall, sir? No, not Compton Hall. The old house ¹⁵ … to the ground five years ago.'

Last week I ¹⁶ … my photographs from the photo shop. When I looked at the photograph of Clarissa there was just a grey mist.

43

5 🎧 Listen and read

Adam: I finished your book last night, Joe.

Joe: Did you enjoy it?

Adam: Yes, I did.

Spike: What book?

Adam: It was a book of ghost stories. It was really good.

Spike: It sounds a load of rubbish!

Joe: You're not in a very good mood, Spike. What's up?

Spike: I'm expecting my exam results today. Have you got yours?

Joe: Yes. Mine arrived yesterday.

Spike: How were they?

Joe: They weren't bad. In fact, I did quite well.

Spike: I'm really worried about mine.

Later

Stella: Oh, Spike. Your father phoned at lunchtime.

Spike: Did he leave a message?

Stella: No, he didn't.

Spike: I bet it was about my exam results.

Gabriel: Go and phone him and find out.

Spike: No! I don't want to know!

Gabriel: Go on, Spike. Do it!

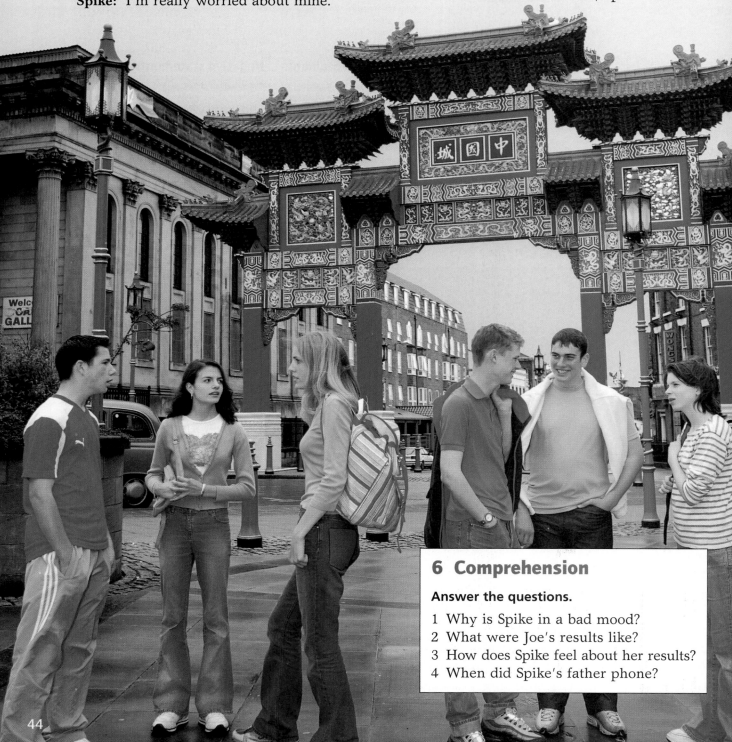

6 Comprehension

Answer the questions.

1 Why is Spike in a bad mood?

2 What were Joe's results like?

3 How does Spike feel about her results?

4 When did Spike's father phone?

7 🔊 Useful phrases

Listen and repeat.

- [It sounds] a load of rubbish.
- [You're not] in a very good mood.
- What's up?
- I'm really worried about [my results].
- I bet [it was about my results].
- Go on.
- Do it!

---

8 Grammar

Possessive pronouns

Singular	Plural
my → **mine**	our → **ours**
your → **yours**	your → **yours**
her → **hers**	their → **theirs**
his → **his**	

Question word: *Whose?*

Whose bag is this? It's mine.

---

9 Practice

Complete the sentences with the correct possessive pronouns.

1 **A:** Sandra, is this your bag?
  B: No, that's … over there.
2 **A:** Which is Spike's room?
  B: … is number five.
3 **A:** Is that Tina and Jeff's flat?
  B: No, it isn't. … hasn't got a balcony.
4 **A:** These are not my books.
  B: That's right. … are in the cupboard.
5 **A:** Is this Adam's guitar?
  B: No, … is a Spanish guitar.
6 **A:** Jack, someone's in our seats.
  B: Let's tell them. Er … excuse me, those seats are … !

---

10 Memory bank

Common adjectives

- big • easy • expensive • new
- boring • late • heavy • awful
- slow • strong • old • tall

Which are the opposite adjectives? Write the pairs in your vocabulary notebook.

1 big – small

---

11 Communication

Asking and talking about past events

exams?/fine/Maths exam/
difficult?/quite easy

A: How were your exams?/What were your exams like?
B: They were fine.
A: Was the Maths exam difficult?
B: No, it wasn't. It was quite easy.

Make conversations with these prompts.

1 Oasis concert?/brilliant/difficult to get tickets?/easy
2 holiday?/OK/weather good?/awful
3 English exam?/all right/questions easy?/quite difficult
4 film?/long/very good?/a load of rubbish

Ask someone in the class about last weekend or a recent event. Ask a general question first, then a second question to get more information. Try to continue the conversation.

---

12 Over to you

Ask the questions below. If the answer is 'Yes', ask another question to find out more details.

Last weekend did you …

- phone a friend?
  (Who? How long/talk for?)
- visit a website on the Internet?
  (Which?)
- watch television?
  (Which programme? What was it like?)
- listen to some new albums?
  (What?)
- play a computer game?
  (Which? What was your score?)
- play a game or sport?
  (What? Where?)
- travel by bus or train?
  (Where to?)

Now tell the class about your partner.

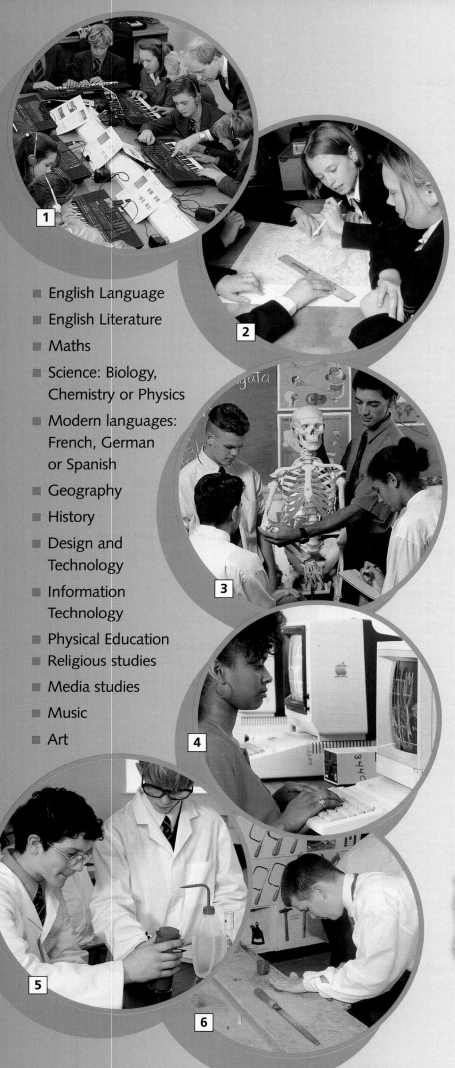

13 Vocabulary

School subjects

Read the list of subjects.

1 Which subjects are the students studying in the pictures?
2 Which of these subjects do you study?
3 What other subjects are on your timetable?

- English Language
- English Literature
- Maths
- Science: Biology, Chemistry or Physics
- Modern languages: French, German or Spanish
- Geography
- History
- Design and Technology
- Information Technology
- Physical Education
- Religious studies
- Media studies
- Music
- Art

14 ▭ Listen

a) Spike phones her father to find out about her exam results. Listen and note her grades.

English Language	☐	Biology	☐
English Literature	☐	History	☐
Maths	☐	Art	☐
French	☐		

b) Answer the questions.

1 Is Spike pleased with her exam results?
2 Why is she upset about her grade in Art?
3 What does Spike want to do?
4 What two suggestions does her father make?
5 What are Spike and her parents going to do when Spike gets home?

15 Learn to learn

Record past tense forms of regular verbs

It is a good idea to note down verbs with their infinitive and past tense forms.

Infinitive	Past tense
point	pointed
stop	stopped
cry	cried

List the verbs in this unit in the infinitive and past tense.

Progress check Units 6 and 7

Grammar

1 Use the present continuous of the verbs in brackets to make sentences about the future.

(you/play) … in the match on Saturday?
Are you playing in the match on Saturday?

1 (My brother/take) … his guitar exam in June.
2 (She/not go) … to England this summer.
3 (they/come) … to your birthday party?
4 (We/travel) … by train, not by car.
5 (I/leave) … on Thursday next week.

2 Complete the text with the verbs in brackets in the past simple tense.

'Helen's birthday party (be) ¹ *was* very good. I really (enjoy) ² … it. There (be) ³ … about fifty people there. I (talk) ⁴ … to a boy called Ricky and we (dance) ⁵ … most of the evening. At midnight everyone (play) ⁶ … silly games but we just (listen) ⁷ … to music. I (miss) ⁸ … the last bus so Mick (walk) ⁹ … home with me. He's nice.'

3 Complete the short answers.

Did Kate go out with Sam? Yes, *she did.*

1 Were you angry with me? Yes, … .
2 Did you go to the cinema last night? No, … .
3 Was the film good? Yes, … .
4 Were the shops open? No, … .
5 Did your parents give you any money? Yes, … .
6 Was Mark wearing his leather jacket? No, … .

4 Use a verb in the *-ing* form to make sentences.

• do • listen to • take • dance • swim • have • get up

My father loves *taking* the dog for a walk every evening.

1 In summer we love … in the lake.
2 She hates … early.
3 I don't like … cold showers.
4 The students all love … history projects.
5 My parents don't enjoy … my CDs.
6 My sister goes to discos a lot because she loves … .

5 Complete the sentences with *which, where* or *who*.

That's the house *where* I was born.

1 Do you know the people … live in the flat next to you?
2 I know a story … is going to make you laugh.
3 Do you know a place … I can learn to scuba-dive?
4 Don't take anything … isn't yours.
5 I've got a friend … goes to school in Paris.
6 There are a lot of restaurants … children are welcome.

6 Complete the sentences with the correct possessive pronoun.

• ours • theirs • mine • yours • his • hers

You've got your own ruler. Don't take *mine.*

1 I haven't got a pen. Can I borrow … , Joe?
2 This isn't Spike's room. … is always untidy!
3 That's not Stella and David's car. … is a Fiat.
4 John wants his sandwiches now but we're going to have … later.
5 No, it isn't Adam's guitar. He keeps … in his room.

Vocabulary

7 Sort the words into four groups: months of the year, sports locations, school subjects and adjectives.

• heavy • Science • November • track • Geography • cheap • pool • July • pitch • May • Maths • court • February • boring • History • early • March • old • Physics • circuit

Communication

8 Work in pairs. Student A:

Ask Student B

• what subjects he/she hates doing at school.
• when his/her birthday is.
• what he/she is doing this evening.
• what he/she did last weekend.

Now Student B:

Ask Student A

• what things he/she likes doing on Sunday.
• what date it is tomorrow.
• what his/her plans are for Saturday evening.
• what he/she watched on TV last night.

Self-evaluation Units 6 and 7

How do you rate your progress? Tick the chart.

✔✔✔ Excellent
✔✔ Good
✔ OK but can do better

Grammar	
Vocabulary	
Communication	

8

I slept on the pavement.

LEARNING GOALS

Grammar
Past simple of irregular verbs

Vocabulary
English money
Places in towns

Communication
Talk about events in the past
Buy things in shops
Ask for and give directions

Fan Mania!

They scream, they cry and they faint at concerts. They shout and cheer at football matches. They put photos and posters on their walls. They send letters, birthday cards and gifts. It's all quite normal behaviour. If you're a fan, it can be hard work!

Star reporter, Jackie Mann, talks to two dedicated fans.

14-year-old, Melanie, from Liverpool

'I've got all Robbie Williams' albums and ten posters of him on my bedroom wall. The other day I made a special tape of my favourite Robbie Williams songs. I play it every day. When he gave a concert in Liverpool last summer, I slept on the pavement for two nights in the queue for tickets! Yesterday I bought a Robbie Williams baseball cap which cost me £15. It was a lot to pay but I didn't mind. He's the best!'

Andy Bolton, 15, from Manchester

'I'm a Manchester United fan. I go to all their matches if I can. Last year they didn't do so well and came third in the League but this year they're brilliant. My dad and I had tickets for the match last Saturday against Liverpool and they won 4-0. It was fantastic. A lot of the Liverpool fans left before the match ended.'

48

Before you read

What sort of music do you like?
Are you a fan of a particular singer, band or football club?

1 🖭 Read

**Read the texts in the magazine article. Which is about:
a) a football club b) an old pop group c) a pop singer?**

Fan mania is not just a modern phenomenon. It was the same forty years ago.

When The Beatles hit the pop scene in the 1960s ...

- The Beatles took the top five places in the Top Ten charts in April 1964.

- 10,000 screaming fans met The Beatles when they landed at JFK airport on their second US tour in 1965.

- Over 50,000 people went to the Shea Stadium in New York and saw The Beatles in concert.

- When a 17-year-old girl wrote to a New York magazine and asked for a penfriend who was interested in The Beatles, she got 4000 replies.

- Fans spent $50 million a year on Beatles souvenirs.

2 Comprehension

a) Answer T (true), F (false) or DK (don't know) about Melanie and Andy.

1 Melanie is a fan of Robbie Williams.
2 There are lots of posters of him on her bedroom wall.
3 She queued for a day to get tickets for his concert.
4 Her dog is called Robbie.
5 The baseball cap was expensive.
6 Andy supports Manchester United.
7 They were the best team last year.
8 The match against Liverpool last Saturday was a disaster.
9 He's got lots of Manchester United posters.

b) Answer the questions about The Beatles.

1 How many Beatles records were in the Top Ten in April 1964?
2 Where did The Beatles land on their US tour and where did they play?
3 How many New York teenagers answered the penfriend letter?
4 How much money did fans spend in one year on Beatles souvenirs?

3 Vocabulary

Word check

Find words in the texts which mean the same as:

1 mad behaviour
2 to lose consciousness for a short time
3 to speak very loudly
4 the part of the street between the road and the buildings
5 people waiting in a line
6 a very unusual event
7 something to remind you of a place, a past event or a person

4 Grammar

Past simple of irregular verbs

Positive statements
They went to the stadium.

Negative statements
They ... to the stadium.

Questions
... they ... to the stadium?

Short answers

Positive	Negative
Yes, they	No, they ... .

Think!
Complete the sentences above with the correct words.
Are there any irregular past tense forms in your language?

5 Practice

a) Find the past tense forms of these verbs in the texts on pages 48 and 49.

buy *bought*

- buy • come • cost • get • give • go • have • see
- make • meet • sleep • take • win • write • spend

b) Complete the dialogue with the correct form of the verbs.

A: What (do) ¹ *did* you *do* at the weekend?

B: I (make) ² ... a cake and (take) ³ ... it to my grandmother for her birthday. How about you?

A: I (not do) ⁴ ... anything special. I (sleep) ⁵ ... until about ten on Saturday and then (write) ⁶ ... some of my project.

B: (you go) ⁷ ... into town?

A: Yes, I (go) ⁸ ... to Tower Records and (buy) ⁹ ... a CD. Then I (meet) ¹⁰ ... Jason and we (have) ¹¹ ... a coffee. I (get) ¹² ... home at about six.

B: (you see) ¹³ ... *The X Files* on television?

A: No, I only (see) ¹⁴ ... the last five minutes. Was it good?

B: Yes, it was really scary.

6 Learn to learn

Learn by heart

Make a list of verbs which have irregular past tenses and learn them by heart. Keep adding to this list. Note that some verbs are the same in the infinitive and past tense.

Infinitive	Past tense
make	made
buy	bought
cost	cost

7 Interaction

Student B: Turn to page 129 and follow the instructions.

Student A: Ask Student B questions to complete the information about his/her Saturday evening. Then answer Student B's questions about your evening.

Where/go/Saturday evening? ...
How much/tickets/cost? ...
Who/you/see? ...
How many photographs/take? ...
Buy/any souvenirs? ...
What time/leave? ...

YOUR SATURDAY EVENING
Event: A film première
Cost of tickets: £15
Stars: Ewan McGregor and Nicole Kidman
Photographs: No – forgot camera!
Souvenirs: Film, poster, T-shirt
Leaving time: 10.30 p.m.

A: *Where did you go on Saturday evening?*

B: *I went to ... .*

A: *How much did the tickets cost?*

8 Memory bank English money*

Notes: £50, £20, £10, £5
Coins: £2, £1, 50p, 20p, 10p, 5p, 2p, 1p

We write	We say
1p	one penny or one p /piː/
3p	three pence or three p
£1.00	a pound (= 100 pence)
£1.50	one pound fifty (pence)
£2.00	two pounds
£3.45	three (pounds) forty-five (pence)
£20	twenty pounds or a twenty pound note

How do you say these prices?

1 59p   2 £1.65   3 £4.90   4 £13.99   5 13p   6 £28.70

*Many countries in the European Union now use the Euro.

9 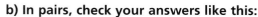 Listen

a) Listen to Louise, Spike and Gabriel and answer the questions.

1 What did they want to find?
2 What did they buy?
3 How much did it cost?
4 What value note did Louise give the assistant?
5 What did the assistant give them as they left?

b) In pairs, check your answers like this:

A: *Why did they go into the shop?*
B: *Because they wanted to ... .*

10 Communication

Buying things in shops

A: Excuse me, how much is this Robbie Williams CD?
B: It's fourteen pounds ninety-nine. (£14.99)
A: OK. I'll have it, please. Have you got change for a twenty pound note?
B: Yes, certainly. Here you are. Five pounds and a penny.

You are shopping in town. Take turns with your partner to buy these things.

1 a poster of Travis – £7.50 (you have a £10 note)
2 a Jennifer Lopez CD – £13.99 (you have a £20 note)
3 a book of crosswords – £4.35 (you have a £5 note)
4 a sweater – £ 39.95 (you have a £50 note)

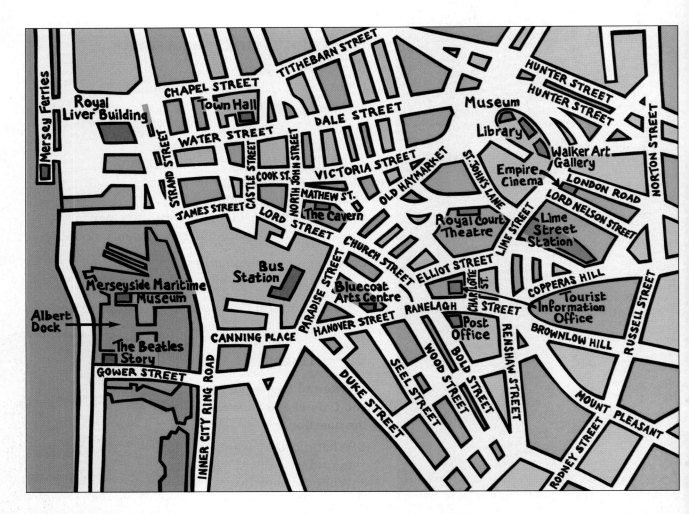

11 Memory bank Places in towns

Which places can you find on the map of Liverpool? Make a list.

railway station, library, …

Add any other places you can think of:

ice rink, …

12 Communication

Asking for and giving directions

A: Excuse me, can you tell me the way to … ?

B: Yes, sure/certainly. | Go down this street.
　　　　　　　　　　　　　 Go straight ahead.
　　　　　　　　　　　　　 Turn left/right (into … Street).
　　　　　　　　　　　　　 Take the first turning on the left.
　　　　　　　　　　　　　 Take the second turning on the right.

A: Is it far?

B: No, you can walk there in five minutes.
　　 The … is | on the left.
　　　　　　　 on the right.
　　　　　　　 in front of you.
　　　　　　　 on the corner of … .

A: Thanks very much.

You are outside Lime Street railway station. Use the map of the centre of Liverpool to ask for and give directions to:

1 the Empire Cinema
2 the tourist information office
3 the Town Hall
4 Albert Dock

13 ▭ Listen

Listen to the dialogues and see if you were right.

14 Over to you

Write down the names of three places near your school that you can walk to:

- in two minutes
- in five minutes
- in ten minutes

Do not show your partner your list. Give directions to the places, and see if your partner can guess what they are.

At the Crazy House Club

Read the story and put the pictures in the correct order.
Then listen and see if you were right. *1 = Picture C*

A

Where exactly is the Crazy House Club?

We're nearly there. We take the next turning on the left.

B

Who's making all that noise down there?

Sssh! It's Stella! We woke her up!

Next time, don't forget your keys!

C

...andra, do you want ...come to the Crazy ...ouse Club tonight?

...es, sure.

What about Adam? Does he want to come? Where is he?

I don't know. I think he went to the cinema with Joe.

D

Joe! Joe! Wake up!

E

Louise! Come on! You're the one who can dance!

It's OK. I prefer to watch.

I'm sure there's something wrong with Louise.

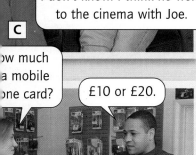

F

...ow much ...a mobile ...one card?

£10 or £20.

OK. I'll have a £10 one, please.

G

Did you remember to bring a key? I didn't.

No, I didn't.

Nor did I.

I think we've got a bit of a problem.

H

Just a minute. I need to get a top up card for my mobile.

9

What was it doing?

LEARNING GOALS

Grammar
Past continuous
Time clauses with *when/while*

Vocabulary
Animals
Rooms and parts of the house

Communication
Describe past events

1 🔊 Listen and read

Katie: Something smells good!
What's going on?

Gabriel: We're making Joe's birthday cake.

Sandra: It's a surprise.

Sam: Guess what? We saw a parrot
on the way home!

Sandra: A parrot! Where?

Sam: We saw it in the park when we were
walking back from the cinema.

Sandra: What was it doing?

Katie: Nothing much. It was just in a tree.

Gabriel: That's strange! Parrots can't live in
the wild in Britain. It's too cold.

Sam: Perhaps it was somebody's pet and it
escaped. Hey! Can I have a taste?

Sandra: No, hands off!

54

2 Comprehension

Answer T (true), F (false) or DK (don't know).

1 Gabriel and Sandra are making a cake.
2 Joe knows about the cake.
3 Katie and Sam saw a parrot in the park.
4 They were on their bicycles.
5 The parrot saw them.
6 There are lots of wild parrots in Britain.
7 Sandra lets Sam taste the cake.

3 🔊 Useful phrases

Listen and repeat.

- Something smells good!
- It's a surprise.
- Guess what?
- Nothing much.
- That's strange!
- Hands off!

4 Vocabulary Animals

a) Name the animals in the pictures on the right. Choose from the following.

- cow • fox • dog • giraffe • cat • lion
- kangaroo • horse • sheep • duck
- goat • tiger • rabbit • chicken • snake
- lamb • rhinoceros • budgie • elephant
- parrot • koala bear • goldfish • crocodile

b) List the animals in different groups under these headings.

Wild animals   Farm animals   Pets
fox

c) Say which part of the world the wild animals come from.

fox = Northern Europe

5 Over to you

Answer the questions.

Have you got any animals at home?

Which animal would you like to have as a pet?

6 🔊 Soundbite

The sounds / ɔː / and / ɒ /

ho̱rse fo̱x   (Look at page 130.)

7 Grammar

Past continuous

Positive statements		Negative statements	
I was	walking.	I wasn't	running.
You were		You weren't	
She was		She wasn't	

Questions		Short answers	
		Positive	**Negative**
Was I	walking?	Yes, you were.	No, you weren't.
Were you		Yes, I was.	No, I wasn't.
Was she		Yes, she was.	No, she wasn't.

Make a similar table with statements, questions and short answers using the pronouns _he, it, we_ and _they_.

Time clauses with _when/while_

While Katie and Sam were walking back from the cinema they saw a parrot.

Katie and Sam were walking back from the cinema **when** they saw a parrot.

What were Katie and Sam doing **when** they saw the parrot?

8 Memory bank

Rooms and parts of the house

- kitchen • bathroom • toilet • dining room
- sitting room • hall • bedroom • study • library
- balcony • garage • patio • garden • pool

9 Practice

A group of film stars were spending the weekend in a Hollywood mansion. At 7 p.m. on Saturday they heard a scream in the garden.

Take turns to ask and answer about the film stars. Say where they were at 7 p.m. and what they were doing.

A: _Where were Heath Ledger and Ben Affleck?_
B: _They were in the study._
A: _What were they doing?_
B: _They were playing chess._

1 Heath Ledger and Ben Affleck/play chess
2 Angelina Jolie/listen to music
3 Cameron Diaz/make a phone call
4 Penelope Cruz and Tom Cruise/walking in the garden
5 Jennifer Lopez/wash her hair
6 Russell Crowe/clean his car

10 Over to you

What were you doing at these times?

1 Yesterday at:
a.m.   7.30   8.15   10.00
p.m.   1.30   7.00   10.00

2 Last Saturday at:
a.m.   9.00   11.00
p.m.   3.00   9.00

At half past seven yesterday morning I was watching The Breakfast Show on TV.

At three o'clock last Saturday afternoon I ... .

1 Heath Ledger/Ben Affleck

4 Penelope Cruz/Tom Cruise

11 Communication

Describing past events

A: There was a robbery in my street this morning.

B: Did you see anything?

A: Yes, I saw two men.

B: What were they doing?

A: They were running out of the bank.

Use the conversation and your imagination to talk about an incident (e.g. a robbery, an accident or a mugging) in one of the following places.

• at a supermarket
• in a games arcade
• at a football match
• in the street

12 📼 Listen

It's Joe's birthday party. Listen to the dialogue and put these events in the correct order.

a) He blew out the candles on the cake.
b) He opened his present.
c) They played a CD.
d) They all said 'Happy Birthday, Joe'.
e) He thanked them for the cake.

13 Learn to learn

Use a dictionary (1)

1 Read the whole text for general meaning.
2 Only look up words and expressions if you can't guess their meaning.
3 Go through all the meanings in the dictionary until you find the right one.
4 With expressions containing several words, look up the main word first.

Now turn to page 58 and try your dictionary skills.

2 Angelina Jolie

3 Cameron Diaz

5 Jennifer Lopez

6 Russell Crowe

Snakes alive!

When fourteen-year-old Kate first saw the boa constrictor in a pet shop it was just a few centimetres long. 'She was very small and I could hold her in my hand,' said Kate. 'I always wanted an exotic pet and I had just enough money to buy her. My parents weren't very happy but I persuaded them. I called my snake Sofia.'

Sofia lived in a tank in the sitting-room but Kate took her out every day for some exercise. Sofia enjoyed exploring all the corners of the room. As the weeks passed, Sofia grew bigger and bigger. One Friday when Kate checked Sofia's tank, she saw that the snake wasn't there. 'I looked everywhere,' said Kate, 'under the bed, in the cupboard, behind the bookcase and under the TV. Then I noticed that one of the windows was open.'

Kate looked for Sofia for a long time but with no luck. 'I can't find her,' she thought desperately. 'She could be somewhere outside.'

The next evening, Kate's best friend, Lizzie, was staying the night in the spare bed in Kate's room. Lizzie was getting into bed when she suddenly screamed. 'There's something cold and alive in my bed!' she said. Kate pulled the duvet back. There, curled up happily, was Sofia. 'Well, you can understand her,' said Kate. 'It was the warmest place in the house!'

After Sofia's adventure, Kate and her parents decided that Sofia was now too big to keep as a pet and they gave her to the local zoo. Kate visits her every Sunday and says that Sofia is very happy in her new home.

Before you read

Why do you think people keep exotic animals as pets?

14 🔲 Read

a) Read the text and guess the meaning of these words and phrases. Check your answers with your teacher or a dictionary.

- boa constrictor • exotic
- tank • to explore • alive
- duvet • curled up

b) Answer the questions

1 How big was Sofia when Kate first saw her?
2 Where did Sofia live at Kate's house?
3 What exercise did she get?
4 Where did Kate search when she saw Sofia was missing?
5 When and where did she find her?
6 Why was Sofia happy under the duvet?
7 What did Kate and her parents finally do with Sofia?

15 Write

Use your imagination or write a story which was in the news recently about an incident involving an animal. Use these questions to help you.

- What kind of animal was it?
- Where did the story take place?
- Who were the people and what were they doing?
- What did the animal do?
- What happened in the end?

Progress check Units 8 and 9

Grammar

1 Complete the sentences with *did, was* or *were*.

The sun *was* shining.

1 When … they arrive?
2 She … having a good time when I saw her.
3 They … n't at school today.
4 I … n't like her at first.
5 … they visiting the USA for the first time?
6 … Gary watching TV when you phoned?

2 Complete the text with the past simple or past continuous form of the verbs.

'Last weekend my mother (take) [1] *took* me and my brother on a trip to Blackpool. My father (work) [2] … so he (not/come) [3] … with us. We (get up) [4] … at 5 a.m. on Saturday morning. It (rain) [5] … when we (leave) [6] … and my mother (not/feel) [7] … in a very good mood. After an hour my brother (begin) [8] … to feel sick so we (stop) [9] … at a motorway café. Then we (turn off) [10] … the motorway and (take) [11] … a small country road. Anyway, we (drive) [12] … along when suddenly we (see) [13] … about twenty sheep in the middle of the road. They (just/stand) [14] … there. We nearly (hit) [15] … one of them. They (not/move) [16] … for an hour so we just (sit) [17] … there! In the end, we (not/get to) [18] … Blackpool until after lunch.'

3 Join the parts of the sentences with *when* or *while* and the correct form of the past tense.

I/have breakfast … // the parcel/arrive. (when)
I was having breakfast when the parcel arrived.

… I/wash my hair // someone/knock at the door. (while)
While I was washing my hair, someone knocked at the door.

1 We/just go out … // it/begin to snow. (when)
2 … she/swim in the sea // she/lose one of her beach shoes. (while)
3 I/do my homework … // all the lights/go out. (when)
4 … they/have dinner // the cat/eat the goldfish. (while)
5 My brother/cycle quite fast … // he/got a puncture. (when)
6 … I/change some money // a robber/run into the bank. (while)

Vocabulary

4 Choose the correct ending to complete the animal words.

• se • ep • oceros • aroo • ar • fish • rot • en
• affe • ant

1 elephant

1 eleph	2 be	3 kang	4 gir	5 chick
6 she	7 gold	8 rhin	9 hor	10 par

Communication

5 Use the map to complete the conversation.

A: Excuse me. Is there a post office [1] … here?
B: Yes, [2] … is. It's [3] … East Street.
A: How do I get to it [4] … here?
B: Walk [5] … this street – King Street – and [6] … at the traffic lights.
A: Those traffic lights over there?
B: That's right. Then take [7] … right into [8] … Street.
A: First turning. OK.
B: The post office is about 50 metres down the street on your [9] … . It's [10] … the police station.

6 Work in pairs. Student A: Ask Student B

• where he/she first went to school.
• what he/she was doing last night at 9 o'clock.
• how much a litre of milk costs.
• how to get to the nearest football ground from school.

Now Student B: Ask Student A

• two things he/she did at the weekend.
• what he/she was doing at 7 o'clock this morning.
• how much a cup of coffee costs.
• how to get to his/her home from school.

POLICE Station Library
NORTH STREET
WEST STREET EAST STREET
Post Office
KING STREET QUEEN STREET
SOUTH STREET
You are here

Self-evaluation Units 8 and 9

How do you rate your progress? Tick the chart.

✔✔✔ Excellent
✔✔ Good
✔ OK but can do better

Grammar	
Vocabulary	
Communication	

A Frightening Escape

A few years ago, an American pilot was flying a small plane from Massachusetts to North Carolina when the engine failed. He jumped out of the plane with a parachute at 14,000 metres.

"For the first few minutes after jumping out of the plane I just fell. I had my oxygen mask and helmet, but it was very cold and I was falling very fast. My left hand was completely numb. I couldn't open the parachute because I was too high and there was not enough air. At last there was more air and I began to go more slowly and suddenly the parachute opened. My nose was bleeding, my right hand was cut, and my left hand was still very cold, but I felt better.

Then I noticed that the clouds were getting dark and I realised I was going into a thunderstorm. All of a sudden there was wind, rain, thunder, lightning and even hail. As I was falling, I closed my eyes to protect them from the lightning.

Slowly the weather got calmer and I was below the storm. I was probably about a hundred metres above the ground when I looked down and saw green fields and knew I was very near to landing. Then I crashed through some trees and landed on the ground. I lay there for a few seconds, cold but still conscious. Soon I was able to move my arms and legs. By some miracle I was all right."

1 🔊 Read

a) Read the text and guess the meaning of these words and phrases. Check your answers with your teacher or dictionary.

- pilot • jump • oxygen mask • helmet • numb
- nose • bleed • cut • thunderstorm • lightning
- hail • protect • below • crash • conscious
- arm • leg • miracle

b) Put the events in order to summarise the story.

1 c) The engine of the pilot's plane failed.

a) The pilot jumped out of the plane.
b) The parachute opened.
c) The engine of the pilot's plane failed.
d) He landed on the ground.
e) He went through a storm.
f) There was more air.
g) He saw some fields.
h) He hit a tree.
i) His parachute didn't open.

2 Learn to learn

Dictionary skills: different parts of speech

You can use a dictionary to find out what part of speech a word is. Sometimes a word can be more than one part of speech e.g. a verb (v) as well as a noun (n).

> **hail¹** / heɪl / *verb*   **1 hail a taxi, hail a cab** to wave at a taxi to make it stop   **2** if it hails, frozen rain falls from the sky
>
> **hail²** *noun*   **1** *[no plural]* frozen rain that falls from the sky   **2 a hail of bullets** a lot of bullets travelling through the air at the same time: *Bonnie and Clyde died in a hail of bullets.*

Use a dictionary to look up *hand*, *arm* and *land*. What do they mean in their different parts of speech?

3 🔊 Listen

Listen to two people discussing the pilot's experience.

1 Where did the pilot land?
2 When did he land?
3 What was the weather like?
4 Was he hurt?
5 Where did he go?
6 Did the first car stop?
7 Did he ever fly again?

4 Write

Write a story about an incident on the road or in the air.

- Say who was there and where he/she was.
- Say what went wrong.
- Say what happened afterwards.

School in the UK

In the UK, children start primary school at the age of five and stay until they are eleven. Then they go to secondary school. At sixteen, students take their GCSE exams (General Certificate of Secondary Education) in about five to ten subjects. When they are sixteen, students can leave school if they want. Many stay in school until eighteen to study for A Levels (Advanced Level).

The British school year starts in early September and finishes in late July. School students have two weeks' holiday at Christmas and at Easter, and six weeks' holiday in the summer.

Students in primary schools sometimes wear a uniform. Most students wear a uniform in secondary school.

Here is Robin Craig's timetable. Robin is fourteen years old.

North Walton Comprehensive School

Name: Robin Craig   **Year:** 9   **Form:** 9G

	Lesson 1 9.00–10.00	Lesson 2 10.00–11-00		Lesson 3 1.30–12.30		Lesson 4 13.30–14.30	Lesson 5 14.30–15.30
Mon	GERMAN	GEOGRAPHY	B	IT	L	IT	HISTORY
Tues	PE	MUSIC	R	ENGLISH	U	MATHS	RE
Wed	DRAMA	SCIENCE	E	FRENCH	N	ART	ENGLISH
Thurs	ENGLISH	MATHS	A	PE	C	SCIENCE	IT
Fri	HISTORY	SCIENCE	K	MATHS	H	FRENCH	GEOGRAPHY

Optional after-school activities: •Drama •Dance •Orchestra •Choir •Chess •Computer Club •Sport

1 Answer T (true) or F (false).

1 British students must stay at school until they are eighteen.
2 Most students take between five and ten GCSE exams.
3 Most students leave school at sixteen.
4 Robin's school day finishes at 2.30.
5 A lesson at Robin's school is one hour.
6 There are two lessons after lunch.
7 Students can learn Italian after school.

2 Think about your school timetable.

1 What time does your school day start and finish?
2 How long is each lesson?
3 How many lessons do you have in one day?
4 What time are the breaks?
5 How long are the breaks?
6 What extra activities can you do after school?

3 Make a timetable, then list any after-school activities that you do.

My school day

Use Robin's information below to help you to write a project about your school day. Include some photographs of your school, classroom, school friends and teachers.

Write what you do before school starts

I get up at 8 o'clock. I have a quick shower and some cereal, and leave the house at 8.30. I walk to school. It takes ten minutes but I like to get there early and chat with my friends.

Write about the morning

Registration is at 8.50 and our first lesson is at 9. My favourite subjects are Geography, Games and IT. We have an hour's lunch break at 12.30. I always have lunch in the school canteen but a lot of my friends take a packed lunch.

Write about the afternoon

We have two lessons after lunch and we finish at 3.30. I stay after school on Tuesdays because I go to the Chess Club.

When I get home from school, I play computer games or watch MTV. Dinner is at 6.00 and after dinner I do my homework. We usually have an hour's homework every day.

Write about the evening

After I finish my homework, I sometimes watch TV downstairs but I usually go up to my room and go on the Internet or read. I go to bed at about 10.30.

11

I've lost
my rucksack.

Grammar
Present perfect simple
Prepositions: *with, on, in*

Vocabulary
Materials and personal possessions
Clothes
Physical description

Communication
Ask about and describe objects
Describe people

1 🔊 Listen and read

The students are going on a day trip to Blackpool.

Spike: Sorry I'm late! Can you hang on a minute? I've lost my rucksack. I've looked everywhere for it.

Mick: Spike, you don't need a rucksack. We're only going on a day trip!

Spike: But I must find it. It's got my camera and a spare T-shirt and lots of other stuff in it.

Mick: When did you last have it?

Spike: I know I had it on Sunday evening at Joe's birthday party. It was with my jacket in the dining room.

Mick: Hey, you lot! Has anyone seen Spike's bag?

Joe: What's it like?

Spike: It's a blue and yellow rucksack.

Adam: Have you asked Stella? Maybe she's put it somewhere.

Gabriel: Stella isn't here. She's gone to town with Katie and Sam.

Spike: Oh, never mind. Let's get going!

Sandra: At last!

2 Comprehension

a) Answer T (true), F (false) or DK (don't know).

1 Spike can't find her rucksack.
2 The rucksack has got Spike's diary in it.
3 Spike lost the rucksack on Sunday morning.
4 Stella is at the hostel.
5 Sandra is pleased when the bus leaves.

b) Complete Spike's entry on the hostel lost property card.

Lost property		Date *19th August*
Name and room	Item lost	Description
J. Hunter Room 8		
Other details *Contents: camera, ...*	When and where last seen	

3 🔊 Useful phrases

Listen and repeat.

- Can you hang on a minute? • Hey, you lot! • What's it like?
- Never mind. • Let's get going! • At last!

4 Grammar

Present perfect simple

Positive statements

I/You We/They	've (have)	seen the bag.
He/She	's (has)	

Negative statements

I/You We/They	haven't	seen the diary.
He/She	hasn't	

Short answers

Questions

Have	you/we/ they	seen the bag?
Has	he/she	

Positive

Yes,	I/we/ they	have.
	he/she	has.

Negative

No,	I/we/ they	haven't.
	he/she	hasn't.

Make a rule

To make the present perfect, we use the present simple of the verb …
and the past participle of the main verb.

Go back and look

Find the past participles in the dialogue in Exercise 1.

Regular verbs		
Infinitive	**Past simple**	**Past participle**
ask	asked	asked
look	looked	looked
pass	passed	passed
search	searched	searched
start	started	started
wait	waited	waited

Irregular verbs		
Infinitive	**Past simple**	**Past participle**
be	was	been
do	did	done
go	went	gone/been
have	had	had
leave	left	left
lose	lost	lost
put	put	put
see	saw	seen
wear	wore	worn

(A full list of irregular verbs is given on page 136.)

Note

Note the difference between past participles *gone* and *been*:
She's **gone** to town. (She's still in town.)
She's **been** to town. (She's gone and come back./She isn't in town now.)

5 Learn to learn

Sort into groups

It can help to learn irregular verb forms if you divide them into groups: verbs which do not change, e.g. *put*; verbs with one change, e.g. *have*; and verbs with two changes, e.g. *go*. Look at the list of verbs on page 136 and write them in your notebooks in the three different groups.

6 Practice

Make conversations using the present perfect.

A: *Why is Sue so happy?*
B: *(She/pass her exams)*

She's passed her exams.

1 A: Why are you hungry?
   B: (I/not have breakfast)

2 A: Why can't they come to the cinema?
   B: (They/not do their homework)

3 A: Everyone says *The Lost World* is great.
   B: Really? (We/not see it)

4 A: Why isn't he playing in the match?
   B: (He/leave his football boots at home)

5 A: Does Alan like his new jacket?
   B: I don't know. He (not/wear it yet)

7 🔊 Soundbite

The sound / h /

<u>h</u>ave   <u>h</u>aven't
(Look at page 130.)

8 Vocabulary

Materials and personal possessions

Material	Object
cardboard	bag
cotton	bracelet
denim	buckle
glass	diary
gold	earring
leather	keyring
metal	necklace
nylon	pencil case
paper	personal stereo
plastic	purse
rubber	ring
silk	rucksack
silver	strap
straw	scarf
wood (adj.wooden)	wallet
wool (adj.woollen)	watch

Use the words in the box and a colour word to describe each object below.

1 It's a pink bag with flowers on the strap.

9 Communication

Asking about and describing objects

A: Excuse me, I've lost my wallet. Has anybody handed it in?
B: What's it like?
A: It's black leather.
B: You're lucky. Here it is./No, I'm afraid we've only got a (brown) wallet.
A: Thanks./Oh, OK. Never mind. Thanks.

Now look at the pictures below and ask and answer about the following lost objects.

1 a blue woollen hat with orange and red stripes on it
2 a blue denim diary with a black strap
3 a silver keyring with a football and a football boot on it
4 a silver and black pen
5 a yellow and black nylon rucksack with animals on it

You left something on the bus, tram or train yesterday. Decide what it was, then roleplay a conversation at the Lost Property Office.

10 Over to you

Describe three personal possessions which you like and three which you don't like.

I've got a green nylon rucksack with a picture of Brad Pitt on it. I like it very much.

I've got a red plastic watch with Mickey Mouse on it. I don't like it at all.

11 🎞 Listen

Listen to the telephone conversation and answer the questions.

1 Describe in detail what the man has found.
2 Where did he find it?
3 What is going to happen?

The man with no name

Who is he? Can you help?

Two weeks ago this man walked into a hospital in Texas, USA, with a bruise on his head and a cut over his left eye. He can't remember his name or where he comes from. In fact, he can remember nothing about his previous life.

He is about 18–20 years old. He is 1.92 metres tall and he's got light brown hair and brown eyes. When he walked into the hospital, he was wearing a red sweatshirt, long beige shorts and black and white trainers.

He has a British accent and speaks French and Italian. He says his name is Roger Staufen but there is no record of a person with this name. We have sent a photograph of him to Missing Persons agencies all over the world but so far no one has recognised him.

Have you seen him before?

If so, please contact the National Missing Persons Helpline on 0800 800 800

What information do you need to find a missing person?

12 📼 Read

Read the article and copy and complete the information.

> Name: *Roger Staufen?*
> Age:
> Physical description:
> What he was wearing:
> Nationality:
> Other details:

13 Memory bank

Hair colour and style

- blonde • brown • dark • fair
- short • long • curly • wavy
- straight

Eye colour

- blue • brown • green • grey

Clothes

- jacket • jeans • trousers
- skirt • sweater • dress • belt
- boots • top • shoes • T-shirt
- pullover • cardigan
- sweatshirt • trainers • shirt

Style of clothes

- baggy • tight
- long-sleeved / short-sleeved / sleeveless

See if you can think of any other words in each of the groups above.

14 Over to you

Close your eyes and describe:

- what your partner looks like.
- what your partner is wearing.

15 Write

Imagine a friend was in a car accident and loses his/her memory. Write a similar poster to help people identify him/her.

Sam is in trouble

📼 **Read the story and try to guess the missing questions. Then listen and see if you were right.**

Mick, I'm still worried about my rucksack.

OK. Let's go and phone Stella.

1

That was Mick on the phone. Spike's lost her bag. _____ ?

No, I haven't. Sorry!

2

Are you sure, Sam?

Mum! I'm trying to watch this programme. _____ ?

3

It's a blue and yellow rucksack.

Oh, that one!

What do you mean, 'Oh, that one'? _____ ?

4

n the garden.

The garden? _____ ?

5

We needed a goalpost! We were playing football.

I don't care what you were doing! Go and get it at once!

6

12

It's the tallest tower in Britain.

Grammar
Present perfect simple with *never* and *ever*
Comparative and superlative of short and long adjectives
Question word: *How?* + adjective

Vocabulary
Adjectives of measurement: *fast, heavy, tall, long, wide*

Communication
Ask and talk about experiences
Make comparisons

1 🔊 Listen and read

Joe: It says here that Blackpool Tower is the tallest tower in Britain.

Louise: Are you coming to the top with us, Spike? There's a lift.

Spike: No, thanks.

Joe: Why not? Are you scared of heights?

Spike: No, of course not. Let's face it, there are more interesting things to do than go to the top of a tower!

Joe: Oh, come on.

Spike: No. I'm just not in the mood. That's all.

Louise: Well, we're going up.

Spike: OK. Suit yourselves!

Gabriel: Have you ever been up the Eiffel Tower in Paris, Joe?

Joe: No, I haven't. But I've been on the London Eye.

Adam: What's that? I've never heard of it.

Joe: It's a huge wheel on the bank of the River Thames in London.

Adam: Is it taller than this?

Joe: No, but it's better because it moves.

Spike: Here, have some candyfloss, Adam. Have you ever tasted it?

Adam: Yes, I have. It's horrible. It's very sweet.

Spike: I know. Just like me!

2 Comprehension

Correct the sentences which are not true.

1 There's a lift to the top of Blackpool Tower.
2 Spike wants to go up the tower.
3 Joe has never been up the Eiffel Tower.
4 Adam has heard of the London Eye.
5 Blackpool Tower is taller than the London Eye.
6 Adam likes the taste of candyfloss.

3 🎧 Useful phrases

Listen and repeat.

- Why not?
- No, of course not.
- Let's face it.
- I'm just not in the mood.
- That's all.
- Suit yourselves!
- I've never heard of it.
- Just like me!

> ## ⚡ Grammar flash ⚡
>
> **Present perfect simple with *never* and *ever***
> I've **never** been to Paris.
> Have you **ever** been to Paris?

4 Communication

Asking and talking about experiences

A: Have you ever been to a theme park?
B: Yes, I have. I've been to Disneyland Paris.
A: When did you go?
B: I went last summer.
A: What was it like?
B: It was exciting/fun/horrible/boring/expensive.

B: Have you ever flown in a helicopter?
A: No, I haven't but I'd like to./No, I haven't and I don't want to!

a) Use the prompts to ask and talk about your experiences.

- go to a theme park   • meet anyone famous
- hit anybody   • fly in a helicopter/small plane
- see anyone famous   • act in a play
- break your arm or leg   • play in a band
- drink goat's milk   • eat raw fish

b) Now tell the class about your partner's experiences.

Carla has been to a theme park. She went last August. It was exciting but very expensive.

5 Write

Write five sentences about your experiences.

I've never flown in a helicopter but I've been in a small six-seater plane.

6 Grammar

The comparative and superlative of short and long adjectives

Adjective	Comparative	Superlative
tall	taller	tallest
big	bigger	biggest
heavy	heavier	heaviest
frightening	more frightening	most frightening
terrifying	more terrifying	most terrifying

Irregular adjectives

good	better	best
bad	worse	worst
far	further	furthest

The London Eye is the newest/most popular attraction in London.
The Eiffel Tower is taller/more beautiful than Blackpool Tower.

7 🔲 Soundbite

Sentence stress

It's the <u>tall</u>est <u>tow</u>er in <u>Brit</u>ain.
(Look at page 131.)

8 Practice

a) Compare the cars, using the comparative form of the adjectives.

estate car/sports car/reliable

The estate car is more reliable than the sports car.

1 sports car/hatchback/expensive
2 estate car/sports car/safe
3 hatchback/sports car/big
4 sports car/estate car/fast
5 sports car/hatchback/exciting to drive

b) Complete the questions with the correct superlatives.

Which is ... to drive?

Which is the most exciting to drive?
The sports car. It's got a five-star rating.

1 Which is ... ?   The estate car. It's got six seats.
2 Which is ... ?   The sports car. It can go at 220 km/h.
3 Which is ... ?   The estate car. It costs £22,000.
4 Which is ... ?   The hatchback. It's got a four-star rating.
5 Which is ... ?   The estate car. It's got a five-star rating for safety.

	HATCHBACK	ESTATE CAR	SPORTS CAR
Price	£15,900	£22,000	£19,500
Top speed	180 km/h	200 km/h	220 km/h
Number of seats	4	6	2
Safety (top rating ★★★★★)	★★★	★★★★★	★★
Exciting to drive? (top rating ★★★★★)	★★★	★★	★★★★★
Reliable (top rating ★★★★★)	★★★★	★★★	★★

9 Learn to learn

Check spelling

Some English words are often wrongly spelt by students. Rewrite the following words correctly, then check them in a dictionary.

- exiting • intresting • dificult • beautifull
- exspensive • funnyer • frigtening

10 Over to you

a) Make a list of three:

- dangerous sports, e.g. bungee jumping, paragliding, whitewater rafting
- makes of car
- films or videos which you have seen this year
- TV programmes
- school subjects

b) Compare the three things in each category using some of these adjectives.

A: *Bungee jumping is more dangerous than whitewater rafting.*

B: *Yes, but it's more exciting.*

- fast • slow • expensive • cheap
- dangerous • safe • boring • interesting
- exciting • frightening • good • bad
- funny • popular • easy • difficult

11 🖭 Listen

Louise has had another phone call from her mother. Listen and answer the questions.

1 Who comforts Louise after the phone call?
2 What's the news?
3 How is the news going to change Louise's career?
4 Who interrupts them?

The Smartest Pet on the Planet

By Lucy Parfitt, technology reporter

Many dogs can fetch a ball in their teeth, but only one dog can stand on its head and read e-mails at the same time. The dog's name is RoboDog.

RoboDog is the world's largest and most advanced robot pet. It is 80 cm long, 65 cm tall and 35 cm wide – about the same size as a labrador – and weighs more than 12 kilos. The British designers say that RoboDog is more sophisticated than a similar robot dog in Japan.

Inside the electronic pet there are sixteen motors, a computer and a video camera, which is the dog's 'eye'. RoboDog can chase balls, climb stairs, wag its tail, and lie down like a real dog. It can also wave and shake its owner's hand! RoboDog's battery lasts 90 minutes and then it goes to sleep.

Why would anyone want RoboDog when they can have a real dog? One reason is because it is a brilliant home watchdog. It uses its computer to connect to the Internet so that you can operate it from a computer anywhere in the world. If you are out of the house,

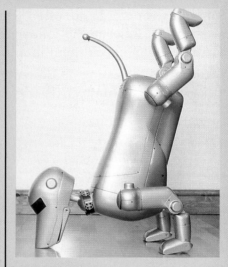

you can use a mouse to move RoboDog round your home. The video camera inside the dog can show you if everything is all right. It can also connect to your e-mail, read any messages and then speak them.

RoboDog costs £20,000 so it's not the cheapest pet around, but it's certainly one of the easiest to look after. It doesn't need food or water and you don't need to take it out for a walk!

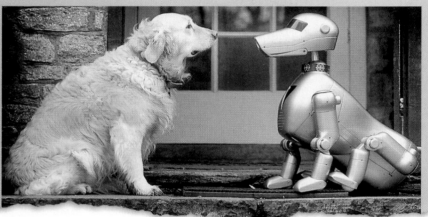

12 🔲 Read

Answer the questions.

1 What similar things can RoboDog and a real dog do?
2 Why is RoboDog useful for a house owner?
3 Why is RoboDog easier to look after than a real dog?
4 How can you control it from a distance?

13 Vocabulary

Nouns and adjectives of measurement

Nouns: height width length weight duration
Adjectives: heavy tall long high wide

a) Match each noun with its correct adjective(s).

height = tall, high

b) Read the text again and complete the technical details.

Technical details		
Length:	Height:	Width:
Weight:		
Duration of battery:		

14 Speak

Ask and answer technical questions about RoboDog, using the correct adjective. Ask about its:

- length • height • width
- weight

1 A: *How long is RoboDog?*
  B: *It's 80 cm long.*

15 Write

Invent your own robot. Then send an e-mail to a friend, describing your robot and what it can do.

Hi!
Guess what? I've just invented my own robot for my bedroom. It's quite big. It's about … tall. It's great because it can … .

Progress check Units 11 and 12

Grammar

1 Complete the sentences with the correct form of the present perfect simple.

… to Madrid three times. (I/be)
I've been to Madrid three times.

1 … anybody famous? (you/ever/meet)
2 … that film. (Sally/see)
3 … to London. (I/never/be)
4 … the train. (they/miss)
5 … this book? (you/read)
6 … abroad? (your father/ever/work)

2 Complete the dialogue with the past simple or present perfect tense of the verbs.

Ben: What's the matter, Jenny?
Jenny: I¹ *'ve lost* my passport. (lose)
Ben: When ² … you … it? (last use)
Jenny: When I ³ … to France last summer. (go)
Ben: Maybe Mum ⁴ … it. (see)
        Mum, ⁵ … Jenny's passport? (you/see)
Mum: ⁶ … in all her drawers? (she/look)
Jenny: It's OK. I ⁷ … it. (find)
        It ⁸ … in my rucksack all the time! (be)

3 What does 's stand for in the sentences: *is* or *has*?

She's tired. *is*   She's had lunch. *has*

1 It's hot.   4 He's looking for his diary.
2 It's arrived.   5 She's hurt her hand.
3 She's lost her bag.   6 It's a great film.

4 Complete the sentences with *on*, *in* or *with*.

There are some lovely pictures *in* this book.

1 He's got a motorbike … red and silver stripes … it.
2 Her jeans have got a big hole … them.
3 I want to buy a denim jacket … a star … the back.
4 I've got a T-shirt … two parrots … the back.
5 Laura is the only girl … red hair … the class.

5 Complete the sentences with the adjectives in their comparative or superlative forms.

A mile is … a kilometre. (long)
A mile is longer than a kilometre.

1 I'm … my father. (tall)
2 What's … film on at the moment? (frightening)
3 Is Spanish … French? (easy)
4 The book is … the film. (interesting)
5 The new U2 CD is … their last one. (good)
6 The final was … match of the season. (bad)

Vocabulary

6 Sort the words into three groups: size, material, possessions.

• woollen • high • rucksack • large • bracelet • deep
• small • plastic • keyring • short • leather • wide
• cotton • belt • huge • tiny • denim • wallet
• long • tall • enormous

7 Choose the correct adjective in each sentence.

How *long/far* does it take to get from Oxford to London?

1 Is it very *far/long* from the station to the school?
2 How *tall/high* are you?
3 Don't dive. The swimming pool isn't very *wide/deep*.
4 The window wasn't open very *wide/deep*, but he managed to get in.

Communication

8 Work in pairs. Student A:

Ask Student B

• to describe him/herself and say what he/she is wearing.
• if he/she has ever been to the USA.
• to compare two subjects he/she does at school.

Now Student B:

Ask Student A

• to describe a personal possession.
• if he/she has ever been to Britain.
• to compare two films he/she has seen this month.

Self-evaluation Units 11 and 12

How do you rate your progress? Tick the chart.

✔✔✔ Excellent
✔✔ Good
✔ OK but can do better

Grammar	
Vocabulary	
Communication	

13

You shouldn't move it.

LEARNING GOALS

Grammar
Verb *will*/*won't* for predictions
  and decisions
Verb *should*/*shouldn't* for advice
  and obligation

Vocabulary
Parts of the body

Communication
Talk about injuries
Make decisions
Give advice

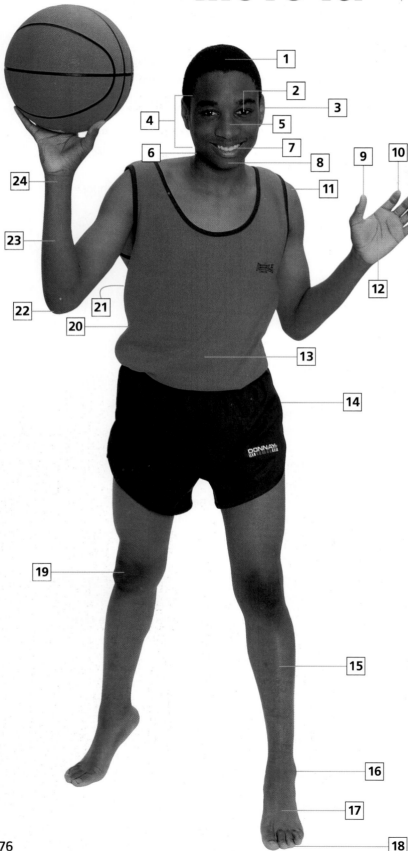

1 Vocabulary

Parts of the body

- arm • finger • hand • ear • head
- face • stomach • knee • leg • wrist
- hip • mouth • nose • thumb • toe
- shoulder • waist • neck • back • eye
- chin • ankle • foot (*pl.* feet) • elbow

a) Match the numbers with the parts of the body.

1 – head

b) List the words in four groups.

the head	the leg	the arm	the body
ear	*knee*	*finger*	*shoulder*

c) Add any other words you know to the groups.

2 Practice

a) Which parts of the body can you break, sprain or twist?

You can break your arm or leg.

b) Where do you wear the things in the list below? Make sentences about them using the prepositions *in*, *on* or *round*.

You wear shoes on your feet.

- shoes • earrings • a tie • make-up
- a scarf • gloves • tights • a ring
- a watch • a hat • a ribbon
- a rucksack • a belt

76

3 🎙️ Listen and read

Louise: What a view!
Joe: I'll take a photo. Say 'cheese'!
Sandra: Joe! Look out!

Joe: Aagh!
Louise: Are you OK, Joe?
Joe: I've hurt my ankle. It's very painful. I think I've sprained it.
Boy: Are you all right?
Spike: You shouldn't ride so fast.
Boy: I'm really sorry.
Joe: I'll try and walk on it.
Sandra: No, no. You shouldn't put any weight on it. Perhaps we should take him to hospital.
Boy: I'll go and get help. There's a farmhouse down there.
Adam: No, hang on. I've got an idea. Gabriel, join hands with me and we'll make a seat. We'll carry him to the farmhouse.
Gabriel: OK. All right, Joe? It won't be long now.
Louise: Will he be all right?
Spike: Don't worry. He'll be fine.

4 Comprehension

Answer the questions.

1 What part of his body did Joe hurt?
2 Where was the boy on the motorbike riding?
3 What did the boy offer to do?
4 How did Joe get to the farmhouse?

5 🎙️ Useful phrases

Listen and repeat.

- What a view!
- Say 'cheese'!
- Look out!
- I've got an idea.
- Don't worry.
- He'll be fine/all right.

77

6 Grammar

Verb *will/won't* for predictions and decisions

Positive statements	**Negative statements**
I'll (I will) take a photo.	It won't (will not) be long.
We'll (we will) carry him.	

Question	**Short answers**	
	Positive	**Negative**
Will he be all right?	Yes, he will.	No, he won't.

Note
Will and *won't* are the same for all persons.

7 ▭ Soundbite The sound / l / in final position

I'**ll** he'**ll** (Look at page 131.)

8 Practice

Complete the conversation using *will*, *'ll* or *won't*.

Tim: I want to go walking with Ruth in the Lake District. Is that OK?

Father: The Lake District? That's a long way. How (you get) ¹ ... there?

Tim: We (go) ² ... by bus. It (not take) ³ ... very long.

Father: What time (you be) ⁴ ... back?

Tim: I don't know but we (not/be) ⁵ ... very late.

Father: Fine. I (keep) ⁶ ... some supper for you.

Tim: Thanks.

Father: Now, (you be) ⁷ ... all right?

Tim: Of course we ⁸ ... ! Don't worry about us. We (be) ⁹ ... fine!

9 Learn to learn

Practise speaking

1 In 'Communication' exercises, always change parts at the end to get as much practice as possible.

2 In freer-speaking practice don't worry too much about making mistakes.

10 Communication

Talking about injuries and making decisions

A: What's the matter?
B: I've twisted my ankle.
A: Is it very painful?
B: Yes, it is.
A: OK. I'll call a doctor.

Now use the cues to make similar conversations.

Injury	**Part of the body**
• twisted	• finger
• hurt	• wrist
• cut	• ankle
• broken	• knee
• sprained	• hand

Decision

• get some help
• call a doctor
• get a bandage
• put a plaster on it
• get an ice pack

11 Over to you

Talk about these questions with your friends.

1 Have you ever had an accident?

2 What part of your body did you hurt?

3 Did you go to hospital?

4 Have you got a scar anywhere? How did you get it?

12 Grammar

Verb *should/shouldn't* for advice and obligation

Positive statements
We should take him
to hospital.

Negative statements
He shouldn't put any
weight on it.

Questions

Should we call a doctor?

Short answers

Positive   **Negative**

Yes, we should.   No, we shouldn't.

Notes
1 *Should* and *shouldn't* are the same for all persons.
2 *Should* is not as strong as *must*.

13 Practice

Choose two phrases to talk about each picture below using *should* or *shouldn't*.

1 He shouldn't take the lift. He should walk up the stairs.

- get up and go out
- watch TV
- drop litter
- stand on a chair
- read a book
- eat fruit instead
- lie in bed all day
- use a step ladder
- eat biscuits
- put it in a bin
- lie in the sun
- take the lift
- read in the dark
- walk up the stairs
- sit in the shade
- turn the light on

14 ▭ Read

Read and complete the
questionnaire.

15 Write

Use the correct answers from Exercise 14 to write a list of First Aid
tips to deal with the four situations. Then add some tips to deal
with a burnt hand and a cut finger.

First Aid Advice   1 Fainting If someone faints, you should … .

How much do you know about First Aid?

Find out by choosing the best answer a), b) or c) for each situation, then check the answers below.

1 Fainting

**It's a very hot afternoon at school and one of the
girls in your class faints.**

Should you:
a) throw some water on her face?
b) open the window and loosen any clothes round her
   neck and waist?
c) call an ambulance?

2 A nose bleed

You suddenly notice that your nose is bleeding.

Should you:
a) blow your nose really hard?
b) lie down on your back?
c) sit down with your head between your knees and
   squeeze your nose with your finger and thumb?

3 A twisted ankle

**A member of your basketball team twists his ankle
badly and is in great pain.**

Should you:
a) see how far he can walk on the ankle?
b) put an ice pack round the ankle and take him to
   hospital for an X-ray?
c) lift his leg and foot on to a chair and call a taxi to
   take him home?

4 A black eye

**In an exercise class you accidentally hit a girl very
hard in the eye.**

Should you:
a) put an ice pack on her eye?
b) wash her eye with cold water?
c) tell her to make an appointment to see her doctor?

Answers: 1 b 2 c 3 b 4 a

Joe goes to hospital

📼 **Read the story and try to guess the missing words.
Then listen and see if you were right.**

1

My name's Joe Phillips. I've _____ .

OK. I'll just take some details.

2

Take a seat. The doctor _____ .

Thank you.

3

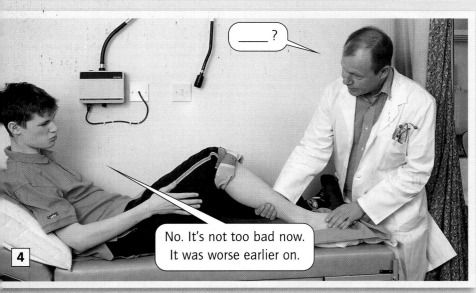

_____ ?

No. It's not too bad now. It was worse earlier on.

4

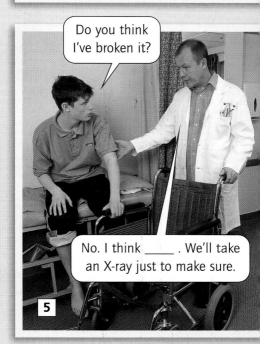

Do you think I've broken it?

No. I think _____ . We'll take an X-ray just to make sure.

5

good or bad news?

Well, _____ . But you have sprained it badly.

6

Can I walk on it?

No. _____ rest it as much as possible.

7

_____ , Joe?

Yes, don't worry. I'm fine.

8

14

Do I have to?

LEARNING GOALS

Grammar
Verb *have to* (present and past simple)
Vocabulary
Household jobs
Occupations
Communication
Talk about jobs

1 Vocabulary Household jobs

Use the verb phrases in the box to say what each person is doing.

1 He's doing the cleaning.

> • do the washing • wash the car • do the vacuuming
> • do the shopping • do the washing-up • empty the rubbish
> • make the bed • do the cleaning • do the ironing • tidy up

82

Crosstalk

by Millie Banks

Parents v Children

In this week's Crosstalk, we talk to fourteen-year-old Luke Meadows and his mother, Anthea.

LUKE

'I hate doing household jobs. I don't mind washing the car or taking the dog for a walk but I don't like emptying the rubbish. It always smells foul. And I hate tidying my room. That's the most boring part of Saturday.

I like my room. The walls are full of photos of Liverpool football team and I've got a big poster of Sarah Michelle Gellar on the ceiling and a fish tank in the corner with some tropical fish in it. There's lots of stuff on the floor and on my desk but I know where everything is.

My sister, Tania, has to help quite a lot in the house but she's older. She has to empty the dishwasher every day and she sometimes has to go shopping at the supermarket but that's all. She goes bananas if Mum asks her to do more than that.'

ANTHEA – LUKE'S MOTHER

'My husband, Jeff and I both work full-time so everyone has to help a bit in the house. Luke has to take the dog for a walk and empty the rubbish twice a week. And Jeff sometimes asks him to wash the car but he gets extra pocket money for that.

Let's face it – no one likes doing housework. I don't mind doing the shopping and cooking but I really hate washing and ironing. There's always so much. I sometimes ask Luke and Tania to iron their own jeans and T-shirts but they never do it.

Luke's room is always a mess. It's a typical boy's room. There are footballs and computer games all over the place and clothes, of course. He always drops them on the floor in a heap. He has three jobs to do every Saturday – he has to tidy his room, clean the fish tank and put his dirty clothes into the wash. It's not much to ask but I always have to ask him two or three times.'

2 Read and listen

Listen to Luke and his mother while you read the magazine article.

3 Comprehension

Make a list of all the jobs which Luke and Tania do to help their parents.

4 Vocabulary

Word check

Find words or phrases in the text which mean the same as:
- horrible • things • remove plates from
- very untidy • a pile

5 Useful phrases

Listen and repeat.
- It smells foul. • lots of stuff
- (She) goes bananas • all over the place
- It's not much to ask

6 Grammar

Verb *have to* present simple

Positive statements

| I have to | take the dog for a walk. |
| He has to | |

Negative statements

| I don't have to | empty the dishwasher. |
| He doesn't have to | |

Questions

| Do you have to | take the dog for a walk? |
| Does she have to | |

Short answers

Positive	Negative
Yes, I do.	No, I don't.
Yes, she does.	No, she doesn't

Think!

Make similar statements, questions and short answers with *he* and *they*.

7 Practice

a) Use the list you made in Exercise 3 to say what jobs Luke has to do at home.

Luke has to walk the dog and tidy his room. He also … .

b) Ask and answer about the jobs which Tania has to do.

A: *Does Tania have to …?*
B: *Yes, she does. / No, she doesn't. / I don't know.*

- make her bed   • do the shopping
- tidy her room   • take the dog for a walk
- do the ironing

8 Over to you

a) Make lists of the jobs you have to do and those you don't have to do at home.

Which jobs: • do you hate doing?
             • really get on your nerves?
             • don't you mind doing?

b) Find out the jobs your partner has to do. Are they the same as the jobs you have to do?

A: *Do you have to make your bed?*
B: *Yes, I do. / No, I don't.*

Name	Amy Lane	Rory Grant	Ray Sharman	Jenny Trim
Job	In a children's play group	?	At the post office	?
Duties	Helping the children with activities Tidying up toys	?	Sorting the letters for delivery Working in the parcels collection office	?
Uniform	No	?	Blue shirt, navy blue tie and trousers	?
Hours	8.30–3.30	?	6.00–2.00	?

Ray

9 Interaction

Student B: Turn to page 129.

Student A: Find out from Student B about the jobs Rory and Jenny are doing on work experience and complete the chart. Then answer Student B's questions.

A: *Where is Rory doing work experience?*
B: *At a hospital.*
A: *What does he have to do?*
B: *…*
A: *Does he have to wear a uniform?*
B: *…*
A: *What time does he have to start?*
B: *…*

Amy

10 Grammar

Verb *have to* past simple

Positive
I had to do my homework last night.

Negative
I didn't have to tidy up my room.

Question
Did you have to do your homework?

Short answers

Positive	Negative
Yes, I did.	No, I didn't.

11 Practice

Complete the dialogue with the correct past form of *have to*.

Nicky: Where did you work last week?

Craig: At a supermarket.

Nicky: What ¹ *did you have to* do?

Craig: I ² ... put things on shelves.

Nicky: Is that all? What else ³ ... do?

Craig: I ⁴ ... collect all the trolleys and put them back at the entrance.

Nicky: What time ⁵ ... start in the morning?

Craig: At 8 o'clock. So I ⁶ ... get up at 6.30. Can you believe it!

Nicky: What time did you finish?

Craig: At 4 o'clock.

Nicky: ⁷ ... wear a uniform?

Craig: Yes, ⁸ ... . That's the worst part. I ⁹ ... wear a red nylon jacket and black trousers.

14 occupations

1 engineer
2 secretary
3 cashier
4 nurse
5 electrician
6 wait___
7 reception___
8 doct___
9 plumb___
10 carpent___
11 beautic___
12 dent___
13 hairdress___
14 clean___
15 sales assist___

12 Vocabulary Occupations

Choose the correct ending to complete the occupations in the list above.

• er • or • ian • ist • ant

Now match each picture with an occupation.

13 📼 Soundbite Word stress

<u>doc</u>tor   beau<u>ti</u>cian   (Look at page 131.)

14 Communication

Talking about jobs

A: What does your father do?
B: He's an electrician. He's got his own business.
A: What does your mother do?
B: She's a hairdresser. She works in a beauty salon.
A: What about your brother?
B: He hasn't got a job. He's still at school.

Now talk about your family.

15 Learn to learn

Improve your listening skills

When you listen to a cassette in class:

1 Look first at the task in your book and think about what you are going to hear.
2 Try to listen for the main ideas first. Don't worry if you do not understand every word.
3 Focus on the words with the main stress. These are often the important words.

Now use the Learn to learn to help you understand Exercise 16.

16 📼 Listen

Listen to Anne talking about an amusing incident and answer the questions.

1 When did the incident happen?
2 What did Anne and her friends have to do?
3 Describe the curtains in the two rooms.
4 Why did the girl in the superstore laugh at Anne?

Progress check Units 13 and 14

Grammar

1 Complete these sentences with will, 'll or won't.

Will you be home before six o'clock?

1 We're really busy, so we … go out tonight.
2 Excuse me, where … I find a copy of last week's *Smash Hits*?
3 There aren't any sandwiches left so I … have a biscuit.
4 I … have any more coffee, thanks. I've got a headache.
5 The city centre has really changed. You … be surprised!
6 The children are so excited. I expect they … sleep tonight.

2 Complete the conversation with will, 'll or won't and the verb in brackets.

Jill: Do you want to come to the tennis club disco on Saturday? It (be) ¹ *'ll* be good.
Tim: OK. What time does it start?
Jill: Seven thirty.
Tim: Fine. I (meet) ² … you at your house at six thirty.
Jill: Promise you (not/be) ³ … late.
Tim: No, I ⁴ … .
Jill: (you/come) ⁵ … by bus?
Tim: No, I ⁶ … . My cousin (give) ⁷ … me a lift.
Jill: OK. I (see) ⁸ … you at six thirty.

3 Complete the advice with should or shouldn't.

You *should* look both ways before you cross the road.

1 You … eat with your mouth full.
2 She … cycle without lights.
3 You … eat at least one piece of fruit a day.
4 … I write a letter to thank them?
5 You … try to answer every question in the exam.
6 People … throw litter on the streets.

4 Complete the sentences with the correct form of have to.

The students at summer camp *have to* get up at 6 a.m.

1 You … (not) go if you don't want to.
2 … you … stand up when you speak to your teacher in class?
3 She … (not) wear a uniform when she went to summer school in Spain.
4 He's hurt his arm so he … go to hospital for an X-ray.
5 … people … get a visa for a trip to Australia?
6 … he … to drive on a motorway when he took his driving test?

Vocabulary

5 Choose the odd word in each group.

hand	finger	waist	wrist
1 ankle	arm	foot	knee
2 finger	eye	ear	mouth
3 shoulder	hip	back	toe
4 ear	thumb	eye	nose

6 Complete the name of the job.

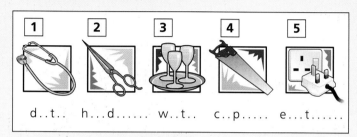

d..t..   h...d......   w..t..   c..p.....   e...t......

Communication

7 Work in pairs. Student A:

Ask Student B

• what you should do (you've cut your finger).
• to make a prediction about his/her favourite sports star or team.
• about some of the household jobs he/she has to do.
• about his/her father's or mother's job.

Now Student B:

Ask Student A

• what you should do (you've got a black eye).
• to make a prediction about his/her favourite TV personality or show.
• about a household job he/she has to do but hates doing.
• about his/her father's or mother's job.

Self-evaluation Units 13 and 14

How do you rate your progress? Tick the chart.

✔✔✔ Excellent
✔✔ Good
✔ OK but can do better

Grammar	
Vocabulary	
Communication	

87

Time to spare?

1 Have you ever had a problem deciding which CD to buy, which film to see or which video to rent? If the answer is 'yes', maybe you should go online and click on to the *'Time to spare'* website. This tells you about the latest films, videos and CDs and gives ratings for each: ✓✓ = Yes! ✓ = OK, ✗ = Forget it! There is also a chat room for people to exchange their own comments on films and CDs.

2 The website is the idea of three fifteen-year-old students from Leeds City High School. A year ago Carla Wells, Amajit Ray and Benny Lewis were sitting in Carla's house wondering what film to see at the cinema. 'The reviews in the newspaper weren't very good,' said Carla, 'so we decided to start our own website.' In the next few weeks, the three teenagers found five interested friends to join their team, write reviews and help to run the site.

3 The team meets once a week to decide what they are going to review and to discuss any problems. It is important to keep the site fresh so they have to update the reviews every two weeks. Because there are eight of them, they can share the work.

1 🎞 Read

a) Read about some teenagers who started their own website. In which paragraph is each question answered?

a) Who are the key people who started the Time to spare website?

b) What does the website offer?

c) When, why and how did the teenagers start it?

d) How does the team work?

e) What is going to happen in the future?

f) Why is the site popular?

b) Now answer the questions above.

2 Vocabulary

Complete the sentences with these words to do with the Internet.

- website • online • click • chat room
- visitors

1 This is a very useful ... if you want to find out about cheap travel.

2 It attracts thousands of ... every day.

3 You can find the information by phone or you can go ... .

4 If you aren't sure what to do next, ... on the word *Help*.

5 If you want to exchange ideas or just talk to others, you can join a ... .

Nicola, who is a regular visitor to the site, says: 'The Time to spare website is brilliant. It's quick and very easy to use, and I really like their reviews. They're shorter and funnier than in most newspapers and magazines. A lot of my friends use the site and they really like it too.'

What about the future? At the moment they have no plans to expand. The site will probably close at the end of the summer, because they all have important exams next year. 'It's been great fun and we've learnt a lot,' says Benny, 'but the trouble is, we haven't got any more time to spare!'

---

3 Learn to learn

Dictionary skills: how to pronounce a word

As well as telling you the meaning of a word, a dictionary will also tell you how to pronounce the word. It shows the number of syllables, the main stress and the phonetic spelling.

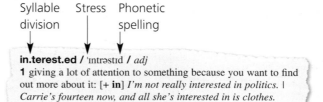

Syllable division   Stress   Phonetic spelling

in.terest.ed / ˈɪntrəstɪd **/** *adj*
1 giving a lot of attention to something because you want to find out more about it: [+ **in**] *I'm not really interested in politics.* | *Carrie's fourteen now, and all she's interested in is clothes.*

Look up the words *information, visitor* and *immediately* in a dictionary and find out how to pronounce the words.

4 🎞 Listen

Listen to a teenager talking about some websites he has visited recently and complete the information.

Name or type of site	Reason
1	
2	
3	

5 Speak

Mark the statements on a scale from 1 to 5. Then compare your ratings with your friends.

1 = I don't agree at all   5 = I agree strongly

1 It is very important nowadays to have computer skills.

2 You need to be very intelligent to learn how to use a computer.

3 Parents are usually quicker at using a computer than their children.

4 If you don't like computers, you haven't got a chance of a successful job.

5 It is quite easy and cheap to start your own website.

6 Write

Write a letter to some teenagers in another country. Tell them what's hot – and what's not – at the moment among you and your friends. Think about:

- films • music • TV programmes • clothes

Rooms and possessions

If it's possible, teenagers in Britain like to have their own room. They think parents should knock before they go in.

1 Look at the rooms which belong to Catherine, 14, and Ross, 15. Find the following things in the rooms.

• bed • desk • wardrobe • chair • dressing table • bookcase • chest of drawers • bookcase • computer • poster • sports bag • trainers • tennis racket • weights • soft toy • shelf • music system • CDs • hairbrush • make up • magazines • radio alarm • photos

Which things are not in the rooms?

2 Discuss in groups.

How do you know that the rooms belong to teenagers not adults?
How do you know the teenagers are British?
Is there anything in the rooms you really like or don't like?

3 Do a class survey to find out the top five possessions in your class.

My room

Use Sherry's description to help you write a project about your room. Draw a picture or take a photo to illustrate it.

Sherry Moore, 15, from Ohio describes her room.

Describe the furniture

My bedroom is quite big, about 4 by 3 metres. The walls are pale pink and the window and door frames are purple. I painted it myself. It's plain but I like it.

The bed is near the door. I usually have a patterned duvet on it – and my favourite soft toys! There's a desk near the bed with a computer and a telephone on it. I don't use the desktop computer much now because I got a laptop for my birthday. I keep all my make-up and things on the desk because I haven't got a dressing table. Opposite my bed there's a music system. I've got a lot of CDs. I've got a purple beanbag to sit on next to the music system. It's more comfortable than an armchair. I haven't got anything special on the floor, just a small rug near my bed.

Describe the walls

On the walls there are some posters, photos, postcards and also my swimming certificates. There's a small window above the desk. It hasn't got a curtain so I've hung a scarf over it.

Give any other information

I've tidied my room three times since I decorated it. Mum says she's never seen it look so tidy.

16

What would you like to do?

What's on in ...

Liverpool

17th – 23rd August

❶ Summer Sounds

A concert of popular classical music
performed by the Liverpool Youth Orchestra at

Kings Dock
Friday 21st August and Saturday 22nd August

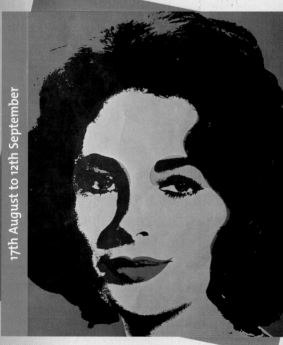

Friday 21st and Saturday 22nd August

17th August to 12th September

❷ The Best of Pop Art

An exhibition of 1960s pop art including
paintings by Andy Warhol and Roy
Lichtenstein

Tate Liverpool
17th August to 12th September

1 Comprehension

Which event or events would be interesting for someone who likes these things?
- sport and outdoor activities
- modern art
- musicals
- classical music

2 🔊 Listen

a) Listen to the *What's On?* programme and list the events in the order the presenters talk about them.

b) Listen again and answer the questions.

1 What nationality is Andy Warhol?
2 What time does the football match start?
3 Is the go-karting track open on Sunday?
4 How many of Abba's songs are in *Mamma Mia*?
5 How much are the cheapest tickets for the classical concert?

❸ *Go-Karting Experience*

Go-Karting Track, Virgil Street

a.m. – 7 p.m.   £2 for 4 laps

All summer

❹ *Pre-Season Football Friendly*

Liverpool v Real Madrid

Watch Liverpool warm up for the season against a top Spanish team

Anfield Stadium
Saturday 22nd August

Saturday 22nd August

❺ *Mamma Mia*

Don't miss the chance of a great night at the theatre. Follow the story of a young girl's search for her father, with songs by Abba.

The Liverpool Empire
Every night 7.30 p.m.
Last performance Saturday 22nd August

Every night 7.30 p.m.

93

3 🔊 Listen and read

Mick: OK. Have you all seen the *What's On?* magazine?
Spike: Yes, we have, thanks.
Mick: So ... What would you like to do on Saturday?
Sandra: I'd like to go to the pop art exhibition.
Spike: And me.
Joe: I'd rather go to the football match.
Adam: Me too.
Gabriel: Yes, I'd prefer to go to the football too.
Mick: What about you, Louise?
Louise: I'd like to go go-karting.
Joe: Yes, I'd quite like to do that too. We could go in the morning before the football.
Mick: OK. What about Saturday evening? Would you prefer to go to the classical concert or the Abba musical?
All: The musical!
Mick: All right. But don't be disappointed if I can't get tickets. It's a very popular show. See you all at supper!
Louise: OK. What shall we do now? I feel like some exercise. How's your ankle, Joe?
Joe: It's better, thanks. Why don't we go for a walk?
Louise: Yes, I'd love to.

4 Comprehension

Complete Mick's booking list.

Event	Name
1 Classical music concert	*Nobody*
2 Pop art exhibition	
3 Go-karting	
4 Football match	
5 Musical	

5 🔊 Useful phrases

Listen and repeat.

- What's on?
- So ...
- Me too.
- Don't be disappointed.
- I feel like (some exercise).
- I'd love to.

6 🔈 Soundbite

I like / aɪˈlaɪk / and **I'd like** / aɪdˈlaɪk /
I like your jacket.   I'd like your jacket.
(Look at page 131.)

7 Memory bank

Leisure activities

- a concert • bowling • a party • a picnic
- sightseeing • a basketball match • a disco
- the sports centre • swimming • sailing
- the theatre • cycling • the cinema
- the beach • a wildlife park • a barbecue
- a games arcade • the circus • ice-skating
- skateboarding • go-karting • shopping
- a football match

a) Group the words under the following verbs. Some words can go in more than one group.

go to	go	have
a concert	*bowling*	*a party*

b) Which activities are better for the evening?

⚡ Grammar flash ⚡

would rather/would prefer to

I/He They	'd (would) rather go bowling.
I/He They	'd (would) prefer to go cycling.

Make rules by choosing *with* or *without*

1 *Would rather* is followed by a verb in the infinitive with/without *to*.
2 *Would prefer* is followed by a verb in the infinitive with/without *to*.

8 Communication

Suggestions and preferences

A: What shall we do on Saturday evening?
B: Why don't we go bowling?
C: No, not bowling. I'd rather/prefer to go to a disco or the cinema.
D: Yes, I'd like to go to the cinema.
A: OK. Let's see what's on.

In groups of four, use the leisure activities in the Memory bank and some ideas of your own to discuss what to do on Saturday or Sunday.

9 Write

Write an e-mail message to a friend to ask if he/she would like to go with you to a show or an event in your town.

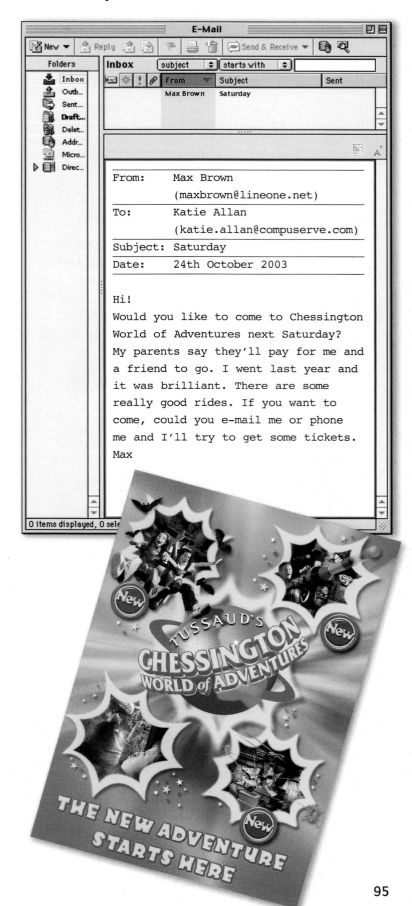

E-Mail

New ▾ Reply · · · · Send & Receive ▾

Folders | Inbox   subject ▸ starts with ▸
Inbox | From ▾ | Subject | Sent
Outb... | Max Brown | Saturday
Sent...
Draft...
Delet...
Addr...
Micro...
Direc...

From: Max Brown
          (maxbrown@lineone.net)
To: Katie Allan
          (katie.allan@compuserve.com)
Subject: Saturday
Date: 24th October 2003

Hi!
Would you like to come to Chessington
World of Adventures next Saturday?
My parents say they'll pay for me and
a friend to go. I went last year and
it was brilliant. There are some
really good rides. If you want to
come, could you e-mail me or phone
me and I'll try to get some tickets.
Max

0 items displayed, 0 sele...

TUSSAUD'S
CHESSINGTON
WORLD of ADVENTURES

THE NEW ADVENTURE
STARTS HERE

Carnival

The carnival is fun but beware of thieves and pickpockets. It's best to go to the carnival with a group of friends.

- Don't wear smart clothes or expensive jewellery. If you have an expensive watch, leave it at home.

- If you want to carry things like a sweater for the evening, wear a small rucksack.

- Always keep your money in a money belt if you've got one. Never take a lot of money out with you.

- You should never try to be a hero. If someone stops you and demands money, give it to them. Don't fight them! They're probably stronger than you.

10 🔲 Read

Read about the carnival and look at the pictures. Are the people doing the right (✓) or wrong (✗) things?

⚡ Grammar flash ⚡

The imperative for instructions and advice
Always keep your money in a money belt.
Never take a lot of money with you.
Don't wear expensive jewellery.

11 Over to you

Talk about these questions.

Do you have a festival or a carnival in your city?
If so, what time of year is it?
What advice would you give to visitors?

Always / Never / Don't … .
You should / shouldn't … .

12 Learn to learn

Use a dictionary (2)

A good dictionary shows you:
1 how to pronounce a word.
2 what part of speech it is.
3 the meaning of the word.
4 an example of how the word is used.

|1| |2|

author/ ˈɔːθə / *n.*
someone who writ‹
books: *Agatha Chr*
is a British author.

|4|

At the football match

Read the story and try to guess the missing words.
Then listen and see if you were right.

1
Our seats are F61 to 66.

I'd like to sit next to you.

OK.

2
_____ near the end.

Me too.

3
I'm going to get a programme. _____ ?

Yes, please.

4
_____ , Sandra, and your change.

Thank you, Joe.

5
I'm really looking forward to the match.

_____ .

6
I told my Dad about your father.

Why? _____ do?

He works for a computer company.

7
This is really great!

_____ .

97

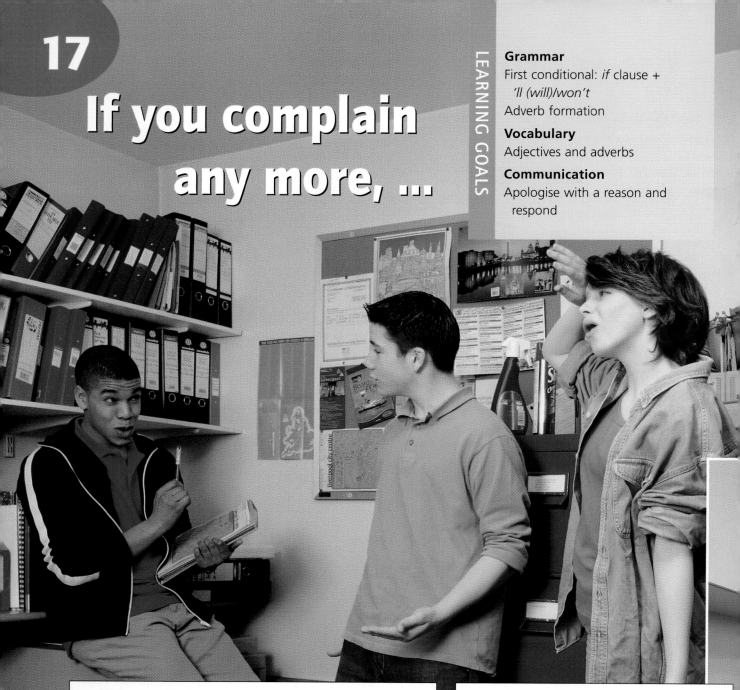

17

If you complain any more, ...

LEARNING GOALS

Grammar
First conditional: *if* clause +
'*ll (will)/won't*
Adverb formation

Vocabulary
Adjectives and adverbs

Communication
Apologise with a reason and
respond

1 🔲 Listen and read

Gabriel: We've finished the cleaning job, Mick.
Mick: Good. You've got time to do one more job.
Spike: But it's so hot!
Mick: It's for an old lady. She wants you to paint her kitchen.
Spike: Paint her kitchen! Very interesting!
Mick: If you go now, you'll have lots of time. You'll do it easily in an afternoon.
Spike: Why do Gabriel and I always get the boring jobs!
Mick: Spike, if you complain any more, I'll give you a really difficult job.
Spike: Thank you very much. See you!

(She slams the door.)

Mick: What's got into her?

Later

Mrs Hunt: Oh, dear. It's the wrong colour. I wanted blue not yellow.
Spike: *(under her breath)* I don't believe it!
Mrs Hunt: I'm sorry I didn't check the colour before you started painting.
Gabriel: That's all right, Mrs Hunt. Don't worry about it. If you get the right colour, we'll come back again tomorrow.
Spike: Hmmph!

2 Comprehension

Answer T (true), F (false) or DK (don't know).

1 The cleaning job was easy.
2 Mick has another job for Spike and Gabriel.
3 The weather is quite cold.
4 Spike is in a good mood.
5 Mrs Hunt lives alone.
6 They painted the kitchen the wrong colour.

3 📼 Useful phrases

Listen and repeat.

- It's so hot!
- See you!
- What's got into (her)?
- I don't believe it!

4 Vocabulary

Adjectives and adverbs

Regular		Irregular	
Adjective	**Adverb**	**Adjective**	**Adverb**
angry	angrily	early	early
bad	badly	fast	fast
careful	carefully	good	well
loud	loudly	hard	hard
quick	quickly	late	late
slow	slowly		
terrible	terribly		

Make a similar chart for these regular adjectives and write the adverbs.

- beautiful
- careless
- cheap
- easy
- (un)happy
- quiet
- sad
- (un)tidy

5 Practice

Complete the sentences with the correct adverb from Exercise 4.

I hate getting up … .

I hate getting up early.

1 Please talk … in the library.
2 Remember to read the instructions … .
3 He was driving too … when the police caught him.
4 He did … in the Maths exam. He only got two answers correct.
5 Susie's studying very … for her exams.
6 I don't understand, so please speak … .

6 Over to you

Answer the questions below about yourself. Then check and see if your partner agrees.

A: *(I think) I write tidily. Do you agree?*
B: *Yes, I do. / No, I'm afraid I don't. I think you write very untidily!*

Do you:
- write tidily or untidily?
- speak loudly or quietly?
- usually arrive late or early for everything?
- do things carefully or carelessly?
- like films to end happily or sadly?
- sing badly or well?
- eat quickly or slowly?

7 Grammar

First conditional if clause + 'll (will)/won't

If clause	Main clause
If you complain any more,	I'll (will) give you a really difficult job.
If you go now,	it won't (will not) take long.

Note

The clauses can be reversed:

If you go now, it won't take long.

It won't take long if you go now.

Make a rule

In first conditional sentences, the verb in the *if* clause is in the … tense and the verb in the main clause is in the future tense.

8 📼 Soundbite

Intonation in conditional sentences

If you go *now*, you'll have lots of *time*.

(Look at page 131.)

9 Practice

Use the cues in each picture to say what the people are thinking.

Giles is waiting for a phone call from a girl he has met at a party.

10 Communication

Apologising with a reason and responding

A: I'm sorry I didn't phone you last night. I was really busy.

B: Never mind. It doesn't matter.

A: Sorry I forgot your birthday. I lost my diary last week.

B: That's OK. Don't worry about it.

In pairs, apologise in the following situations and give a reason. You:

- didn't do your homework last night.
- missed a goal in an important match.
- forgot to phone your best friend.
- haven't got your Maths textbook.

Anyway, I want to phone Granny.

How long are you going to be?

(phone be engaged/ Linda probably not ring again)

Hi, Giles, Linda here. Would you like to go to the school disco with me on Saturday?

Uh ... uh ... er ... er ...

OK. Never mind.

(he not want to come/ask someone else)

I don't believe it! I've blown it again!

11 Write

Send a message apologising to a friend.

Last night you and some friends arranged to meet at a pizza restaurant and then go to the cinema but you couldn't get there. Look at the example and send a message to one of your friends.

- Apologise.
- Give a reason why you did not go.
- Say when you will see them again.

```
Tony,

I'm really sorry I didn't meet
you at the pizza restaurant last
night, but I had to stay at home
and look after my younger sister.
I'll see you at school on Monday.

Chris
```

12 📼 Listen

Joe has some news for Louise. Listen and choose the best answer.

1 Joe's father wants Joe to phone him about:
   a) the project.
   b) a job for Louise's father.
   c) a problem at home.

2 The company is looking for:
   a) software experts.
   b) people to sell soft toys.
   c) computer salesmen.

3 Louise decides to phone her father:
   a) this evening.
   b) tomorrow.
   c) immediately.

The Power of Music

Selina Roberts reports

'Don't come near us. If you do, you'll be sorry.' Two rival gangs are facing each other with knives at opposite ends of a parking lot in the town of Lowell, Massachusetts, USA. One gang is Cambodian, the other is Afro-Caribbean. According to Arn Chorn Pond, a human rights worker who lives there, gang fighting is quite common.

Arn knows about violence. He grew up in Cambodia in south-east Asia and lost all his family at the age of fifteen in the Cambodian civil war at the end of the 1970s. He now lives and works in Lowell, where many Cambodian refugees and their families also live.

Arn hates str[eet] violence and wants [to] stop it. He has notic[ed] one thing whi[ch] brings together t[he] rival gangs, and tha[t's] dance music. 'If th[ey] like the music, th[ey] will dance happ[ily] together,' he sa[ys]. 'They won't p[lay] sports together, b[ut] they will dance.'

Not long ago [he] collected some reco[rd]ing equipment a[nd] started a small recording studio. 'This way the gangs c[an] make hip-hop CDs together,' said Arn. 'If they can lea[rn] how to work creatively, they won't want to fi[ght] each other.'

Now, three months later the street gangs are mak[ing] their first CD and are learning to live peacefully togeth[er]. Things are slowly getting better.

13 🔘 Read

a) Read the text and find words and phrases which mean the same as the following:

1 a group of young people who spend time together and sometimes fight other groups
2 a place to park your car
3 the basic rights which every person has
4 a war between people who live in the same country
5 behaviour which hurts other people physically

b) Answer the questions.

1 What is a problem in Lowell, Massachusetts?
2 Why does Arn Chorn Pond know about violence[?]
3 What did Arn discover recently?
4 How did he help the street gangs?
5 What has been the result?

14 Over to you

Talk about these questions.

Are there any street gangs in your town?
Are they violent? What sort of things do they do?
How could people help them?

Progress check Units 16 and 17

Grammar

1 Match the clauses to make sentences.

1 d) If you go to the concert early, you'll get good seats.

1 If you go to the concert early,
2 You'll get there faster
3 If you don't leave now,
4 I won't go into the water
5 If he leaves his bike outside,
6 If you eat too much chocolate,

a) you'll get spots.
b) if it's too cold.
c) someone will steal it.
d) you'll get good seats.
e) you'll miss the bus.
f) if you go by bike.

2 Complete the sentences with the correct form of the verbs in brackets.

If it … very expensive, I … it. (be; not buy)
If it's very expensive, I *won't buy* it.

1 If he … some tickets, he … us to the final. (get; take)
2 If you … Katie, … her to phone me? (see; you/ask)
3 We … late for the film if we … now. (be; not/leave)
4 The dog … if you … the bell. (bark; ring)
5 … me if there … any problems? (you/phone; be)
6 He … ready in time if he … . (not/be; not/hurry up)

3 Complete the sentences with *would rather* or *would prefer*.

I'd *prefer* to go swimming.   I'd *rather* go swimming.

1 Which … you … to do?
2 They … go by train.
3 We … have a disco than a barbecue.
4 She … to sleep in the small room.
5 Would you like to go out or … you … stay in?
6 I … to telephone her rather than write to her.

Vocabulary

4 Complete the sentences with the correct word.

 I love *sunbathing* on the beach.

 1 I'm going … next weekend.

 2 We went … yesterday afternoon.

 3 I've never been … . Is it difficult?

4 Would you like to come … with us?

5 Write the adverb of the word in brackets to complete the sentences.

1 (quick)   I want you to do this *quickly*.
2 (angry)   Why are you looking at me so … ?
3 (early)   I don't like going to bed … .
4 (late)   She arrived … for the exams.
5 (slow)   Could you please say it again … ?
6 (hard)   They tried very … to win the cup.
7 (good)   He doesn't play tennis very … .
8 (careful) Please read this … before you sign.

Communication

6 Reorder the sentences to complete the conversation.

A: What shall we do this evening?

a) So would I. What time does the disco start?
b) Let's go and get ready. It's already seven o'clock.
c) Let's see what's on at the cinema.
d) Well, if you want to do something different, there's a disco at the art college. I'd really like to go.
e) Eight thirty.
f) Oh no, not the cinema. I'd prefer to do something different.

7 It is your friend's birthday on Sunday. You meet in a café but you are late. Follow the instructions.

A: *Hi, Chris. Sorry I'm late. I had to … .*

A: Greet your friend and apologise for being late. Give a reason.
B: Accept the apology.
A: Invite B to do something for the evening.
B: Disagree and state your preference.
A: Agree. Ask what B hopes to get from his/her parents for a birthday present.
B: Reply.
A: Ask what B will buy if he/she gets some money.
B: Reply.

The scenes are filmed here.

Grammar
The passive: present simple

Vocabulary
Jobs in the media
Types of films

Communication
Remind and reassure people
with *will/won't*

Before you listen

Have you got a favourite TV programme? What is it?

What questions would you like to ask the director of a TV soap opera?

Have you ever visited a TV studio?

1 🔲 Listen and read

The group are visiting a TV studio.

Paul: Hello. Welcome everybody. My name's Paul. I'm your guide this morning. Please don't forget to wear your security badges at all times.

Sandra: Don't worry, we won't.

Paul: This is the main studio. Most of the scenes are filmed here.

Gabriel: Are the episodes made a long time in advance?

Paul: Yes, they're made about five or six weeks before they're shown on TV.

Spike: What happens when an actor is ill?

Paul: Well, if someone's ill for a long time, the storyline's changed.

Louise: Do you ever go abroad to film?

Paul: Yes. Last year we went to France to film a couple of episodes. Hi, Richard! How are you?

Spike: *(whispering to Adam)* He's one of the actors.

Louise: Go on, Spike! Ask him for his autograph.

Adam: Remember to smile nicely!

Spike: Shut up, Adam!

Adam: Too late! He's gone!

2 Comprehension

Answer the questions.

1 What does Paul remind the group to do?
2 Where does Paul take the group first?
3 What question does the group ask about the actors?
4 Why was last year different?
5 Who does Paul greet in the studio?
6 What does Louise want Spike to do?

3 🔲 Useful phrases

Listen and repeat.

• Don't worry, we won't.
• How are you?
• Shut up!
• Too late!

4 Vocabulary

Jobs in the media

Match the jobs below with the pictures.

Number 1 is a camera operator.

• actor/actress • director • journalist
• scriptwriter • camera operator
• sound engineer • make-up artist

5 Over to you

Answer the questions.

Would you like to do any of these jobs. Why?

I'd like to be a camera operator because I'm interested in photography.

105

1 First an idea for a film (develop) [1] *is developed* by a film company. Then a director and a scriptwriter (employ) [2] ... and the script (write) [3] ... .

2 When the producer has found the money to make the film, the actors (choose) [4] ... .

3 Then the sets and costumes (design) [5] ... and (make) [6] ... . Finally, technicians (employ) [7] ... .

How a film is made

4 Film acting is quite difficult because a film script (never film) [8] ... in the correct order of events. Actors (often/ask) [9] ... to act the same scene many times over.

5 When filming (finish) [10] ... , the film (put together) [11] ... from thousands of separate shots.

6 Grammar

The passive: present simple
The TV programme **is made** in Liverpool.
The indoor scenes **are filmed** in this studio.

Make a rule
To make the present simple passive we use the ... tense of the verb *to be* and the ... participle of the main verb.

Go back and look
Find examples of the present simple passive in the dialogue in Exercise 1.

7 Practice

Describe how a film is made using the present passive of the verbs in brackets.

106

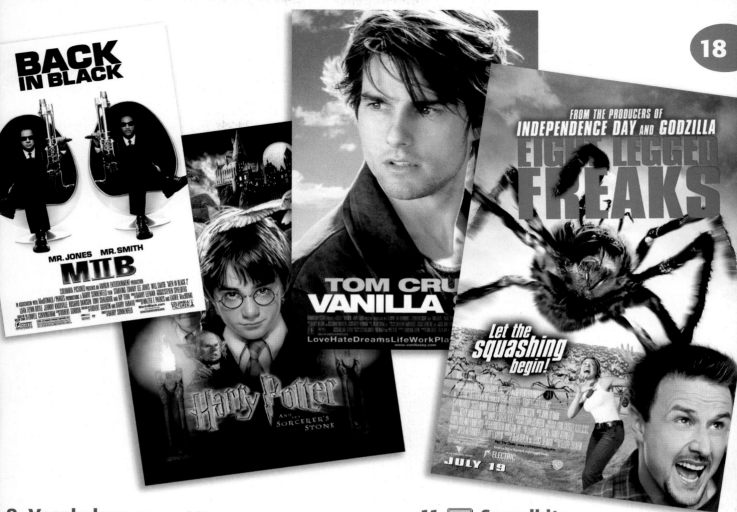

8 Vocabulary Types of films

Can you name a film of each type?

1 'Star Wars' is a science fiction film.

1 science fiction film	6 horror film	11 musical
2 historical film	7 action film	12 comedy
3 gangster film	8 love story	13 cartoon
4 disaster film	9 western	14 courtroom
5 fantasy film	10 thriller	drama

9 Over to you

Think of a film title. In pairs, ask questions to find out the title of your partner's film.

- What sort of film is it? • Who's in it? • What's it about?

10 🎞 Listen

Listen to a cameraman talking about working in films and answer the questions.

1 What's the name of a recent big film he worked on?
2 Who was in it?
3 What sort of films does he prefer?
4 What can go wrong when making a film?
5 In what way do film directors differ?
6 Why do they often shoot the same scene many times?

11 🎞 Soundbite

Fall–rise intonation

Don't worry, I won't. (Look at page 131.)

12 Communication

Reminding and reassuring people

A: Remember to record the film on Channel 4 for me this evening.
B: Don't worry, I will.
A: Thanks. And don't forget to switch off the TV when you go to bed.
B: No, I won't.
A: And if anyone phones, don't forget to take a message.
B: No, I won't, I promise.

Use the cues to remind your brother/ sister to do things while you are away, then add some more instructions.

- record (the film)
- switch off (the TV)
- feed (the cat)
- take phone messages
- set the alarm

THE LORD OF THE RINGS

The Lord of the Rings is a series of three fantasy films. They are based on J.R.R.Tolkien's best-selling books. The three films are directed by Peter Jackson, a New Zealander.

Peter Jackson is interviewed by Dale Burns.

Why do you think *The Lord of the Rings* is so successful?
It's one of the greatest fantasy books of the twentieth century and, of course, everybody loves a fantasy story.

Where is the story set and what's it about?
The story is set in a magical place called 'Middle Earth' where a group of little people called 'Hobbits' live. The three films tell the story of a young Hobbit called Frodo Baggins. He wants to fight and destroy the powers of the Dark Lord, Sauron, who intends to rule Middle Earth. Frodo is helped by a wizard called Gandalf, and lots of strange creatures. The main theme of the story is the fight between Good and Evil.

Are there many special effects in the films?
Yes. There are lots of special effects. Computer technology is used to create Middle Earth and also to create all sorts of fantastic creatures. In one scene there are 15,000 extras wearing armour. The armour is actually made out of knitted string, but computer effects are used to make the string look like metal. The computer is also used to make the 15,000 extras look like an army of 100,000!

Where did you make the films?
I made them in New Zealand. I chose New Zealand because it has green valleys, lakes and mountains and not many people. It is the perfect setting for 'the land of Middle Earth'.

13 Learn to learn

Reading in class

1 Read the title of the text and use the pictures to help you to predict the content.
2 Keep the reading task or question in mind while you read.
3 Read in whole phrases, not word by word.
4 Try to guess the meaning of new words from the context.

Now try your reading skills.

Before you read

Do you know about the films of *The Lord of the Rings*?

Why do you think this type of fantasy film is popular?

14 📼 Read

Read the text and answer the questions.

1 Where is the story set?
2 Who are the Hobbits, Gandalf and Sauron?
3 Who is Frodo?
4 What does he want to do?
5 What is the main theme of the films?
6 Why is New Zealand a good place to make the films?

15 Write

Write a paragraph about a film you have seen recently and enjoyed.

Last week I saw *Minority Report* on DVD. It's a science fiction thriller directed by Steven Spielberg. It's set in New York in the future. It's about people who are arrested before they commit a murder. Tom Cruise plays the part of a New York policeman. The film is really exciting.

A party

🔊 **Read the story and try to guess the missing words. Then listen and see if you were right.**

1.
I really enjoyed the visit to the V studios today.

Yes, it was great. Mick wasn't there!

2.
____ Mick this morning? What's he done wrong?

I wanted to have a party. And Mick said no!

3.
Let's ____ this evening anyway!

Good idea.

Don't forget to bring your guitar.

Don't worry, I won't.

4.
____ glasses!

I think they're kept in here.

5.
____ in my room! Now!

Great! I'll bring some of my CDs.

6.

7.
Let's dance!

No, ____ .

It doesn't matter if we make a noise. We're all going home soon.

8.
What on earth is going on?

They were sent here after prison.

LEARNING GOALS

Grammar
The passive: past simple
much, many, a lot of

Vocabulary
Food and drink in a restaurant

Communication
Order food and drink in a restaurant

Before you read

Ask your teacher or use a dictionary to find the meaning of these words and phrases.

• to coil ropes • to hoist the sails • to scrub the decks • rigging • hammock

1 Read

Read the article about Reform Ships.

Prison or adventure?

The chance to live on a large ship and to learn how to sail could seem like a big adventure for people today. But in Liverpool in the nineteenth century, sailing ships were often used by the authorities to help reform young criminals. They were called 'Reform Ships'.

2 Comprehension

a) Complete the journalist's notes

Name of ship:
Age of criminals:
Length of time on board:
Schooling:
Training:

b) Answer the questions.

1 What did they use the Reform Ships for?
2 What did young teenage boys learn on the *Akbar*?
3 Where did they sleep?
4 Who paid their living expenses?
5 What happened to some of the boys?

c) Find words in the text which mean the same as the following:

- the people who run the legal system
- people who commit a crime
- how to control your behaviour
- clean with a brush
- the cost of food and clothing
- live through
- an illness
- opportunity

3 🔊 Listen

Listen to Mel talking about a week she spent on a big sailing ship and complete the ratings chart. (1 = not good   2 = OK   3 = very good)

> Sailing lessons:
> Other activities:
> Food:
> Sleeping arrangements:
> Weather:
> Overall impression:

4 Over to you

Last week five young people were punished by their parents for playing truant from school for two days. In groups, look at the list of punishments below and say which you think is the worst and which is the best.

> **Punishments for playing truant**
>
> 1 Jack and his brother Max were 'grounded' and told to stay at home every evening for a week.
> 2 Lisa was not given her weekly pocket money.
> 3 Hassan was forbidden to use the computer for a week.
> 4 Prem's mobile phone was taken from her for a fortnight.
> 5 Declan was asked to help in the house for an hour every day for ten days.
> 6 Natalie was not allowed to use her CD player for a week.

A: *I think the worst punishment is Number 1 because … .*
B: *I'm not sure. For me the worst is … .*

One well-known 'Reform Ship' was called the *Akbar*. Young criminals between the ages of twelve and sixteen were sent there for three years after prison to learn discipline.

Life on board the *Akbar* was hard and the boys were often hungry and cold. They were taught school subjects for three hours a day and the rest of the day they were trained to be sailors. They were shown how to coil ropes, climb the rigging, hoist the sails and scrub the decks in summer and in winter. They also had to make and repair their own clothes. At night they slept in hammocks.

Time on the *Akbar* was not considered to be a punishment so parents were asked to give money for the boys' living expenses. Most parents agreed because they thought the training would be useful for the boys later in life.

Some boys didn't survive. Some died of disease, others fell off the ship and were drowned and some died in accidents. But for a young criminal in the nineteenth century, life on the Akbar was still better in many ways than life on land. Thanks to ships like the *Akbar*, thousands of young Liverpool boys were rescued from a life of crime and given a second chance in life.

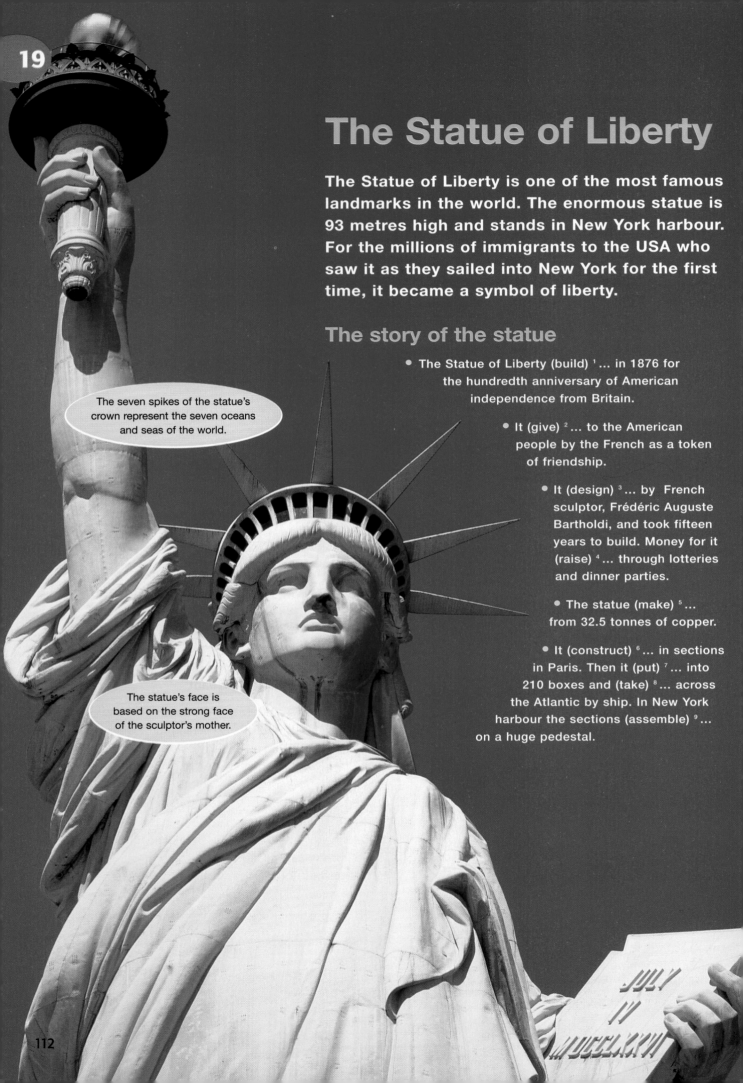

The Statue of Liberty

The Statue of Liberty is one of the most famous landmarks in the world. The enormous statue is 93 metres high and stands in New York harbour. For the millions of immigrants to the USA who saw it as they sailed into New York for the first time, it became a symbol of liberty.

The story of the statue

- The Statue of Liberty (build) ¹... in 1876 for the hundredth anniversary of American independence from Britain.

- It (give) ²... to the American people by the French as a token of friendship.

- It (design) ³... by French sculptor, Frédéric Auguste Bartholdi, and took fifteen years to build. Money for it (raise) ⁴... through lotteries and dinner parties.

- The statue (make) ⁵... from 32.5 tonnes of copper.

- It (construct) ⁶... in sections in Paris. Then it (put) ⁷... into 210 boxes and (take) ⁸... across the Atlantic by ship. In New York harbour the sections (assemble) ⁹... on a huge pedestal.

The seven spikes of the statue's crown represent the seven oceans and seas of the world.

The statue's face is based on the strong face of the sculptor's mother.

5 Grammar

The passive: past simple
One ship **was called** the *Akbar*.
The boys **were taught** school subjects.

Make a rule
To make the past simple passive we use the ... tense of the verb
... and the ... participle of the main verb.

6 Practice

a) Read about the Statue of Liberty and use the past passive form of the verb in brackets to complete the information.

b) In pairs, use the cues to make questions about the Statue of Liberty. Then ask and answer them.

A: *Why was the Statue of Liberty given to the people of the USA?*
B: *It was given by the people of France as a token of friendship.*

1 Why/the Statue of Liberty/give to/the people of the USA?
2 What/it/build for?
3 Who/statue/design by?
4 What/the statue/make of?
5 How/it/take/across the Atlantic?

7 Soundbite   The sound / ə / (schwa)

w**a**s (used)   w**e**re (taken)   (Look at page 131.)

The neutral vowel in unstressed syllables and weak forms is the most common vowel sound in English.

8 Interaction

Student B: Turn to page 129.
Student A: Use one of the verbs below to complete the quiz questions. Then ask Student B the questions.

A: *Where was the Statue of Liberty designed?*
B: *It was designed in France.*

• assassinate • build • design • write • invent

1 Where ... the Statue of Liberty ...?
2 When ... the Pyramids ...?
3 When ... the Morse Code ...?
4 Who ... Oliver Twist ... by?
5 Where ... Abraham Lincoln ...?

Now choose the correct answer for Student B's questions.

• By a volcanic eruption • Beethoven • In 1869
• Picasso • In 1927

Grammar flash

much, many, a lot of

Positive statements
There was **a lot of** room.
There were **a lot of** men.
A lot of people died.

Negative statements
There was**n't much** room.
There were**n't many** women and children.
Not many people survived.

Questions
Was there **much** water?
Were there **many** children?

Notes
1 We generally use *much* and *many* in negative statements and questions.
2 We never use *much* in positive statements.

Make rules about countable and uncountable nouns
1 We use *much* with ... nouns.
2 We use *many* with ... nouns.
3 *A lot of* can be used with both ... and ... nouns.

9 Practice

Complete the sentences with *much, many* or *a lot of*.

1 Let's hurry. We haven't got ... time.
2 How ... tickets do you need?
3 Do you have ... trouble with pronunciation?
4 Are there ... cinemas in your town?
5 There was ... noise at the party.
6 There weren't ... students in class today.
7 ... money was made in Liverpool from the slave trade.

WELCOME TO

WORLD FAMOUS

Barry Marsden's

FISH AND CHIP RESTAURANT

TRY BARRY'S SPECIAL
Fish, chips, peas or beans,
bread and butter and a
choice of tea, coffee or
a soft drink

£6.25

~STARTERS~
Soup £1.95
Orange juice or Tomato juice £1.50

~MAIN COURSES~
Fish or fish cakes £4.00
Scampi £4.20
Roast beef £4.50
Hamburger £2.50
Vegeburger £2.50

~SIDE ORDERS~
Green salad £1.95
Chips £1.50
Peas £1.95
Beans £1.95

~SWEETS~
Apple pie £2.75
Ice cream (chocolate, vanilla
or strawberry) £2.50

~DRINKS~
Coke/Diet Coke £1.20
Sparkling mineral water £1.30
Lemonade £1.20
Tea £1.00
Coffee £1.25
Milk 80p

10 📼 Listen

Listen to the group ordering a meal at Barry Marsden's. Say whether the sentences are T (true), F (false) or DK (don't know).

1 The fish and chip restaurant is famous.
2 The group have got a lot of time left in Liverpool.
3 Fish and chips is an unusual meal to have in Britain.
4 Louise has a Diet Coke and Sandra orders a sparkling mineral water.
5 Everyone has the same dish.
6 Barry's Special is the cheapest dish on the menu.
7 Everyone is going to pay separately for his/her meal.

11 Communication

Ordering food and drink in a restaurant

A: What would you like to start with?
B: Can I have the soup, please?
A: And to follow?
B: I'll have the fish cakes, please.
A: Any side orders?
B: Yes. Chips, please.
A: Would you like a sweet?
B: No, thank you. That's fine.
A: What about something to drink?
B: Can I have a Coke, please?

In groups, order a meal from the menu.

12 Learn to learn

English outside the classroom

Here are some things you can do to improve your English.

1 Look out for English words in shops, in the street, and on menus in cafés and restaurants.
2 Buy British or American magazines or comics.
3 Speak to tourists if you have an opportunity.
4 Write down the words of English or American pop songs.
5 Watch video films which have subtitles and are not dubbed.
6 Use the Internet.

Progress check Units 18 and 19

Grammar

1 Complete the sentences with a present or past passive of the verb in brackets.

Jaws by Steven Spielberg. (direct)

'Jaws' was directed by Steven Spielberg.

1 Tea … in Sri Lanka. (grow)
2 Our flats … in the 1980s. (build)
3 Their school exams … always … in June. (hold)
4 … your cousin … during the match? (hurt)
5 The men … two days after the robbery. (catch)
6 His wallet … when he was in the market. (steal)
7 … your computer … to the Internet now? (connect)

2 Write sentences with *there was/there were* and *much/many/a lot of.*

(✔) noise in the street last night.

There was a lot of noise in the street last night.

1 (✔) … really good films on TV last week.
2 (✗) … people at Anna's party.
3 (?) … good exhibitions in Liverpool last year?
4 (?) … money in the wallet?
5 (✗) … food left after the barbecue.
6 (✔) …things to do in the evening.
7 (✗) … time to go sightseeing.
8 (✔) …people at the pop concert.

3 Correct the underlined verb phrases in these sentences.

<u>We work</u> on a project in Liverpool at the moment.

We are working on a project in Liverpool at the moment.

1 <u>I'm like</u> modern ballet.
2 This watch <u>was make</u> in Switzerland.
3 <u>Have you gone</u> to the cinema last night?
4 <u>She worked</u> in the garden when I met her.
5 <u>My parents was</u> in London three times before.
6 <u>I phone</u> you tomorrow if I have time.
7 If it <u>will rain</u>, we'll go to the museum.
8 Why <u>not we have</u> a rock 'n' roll party?

4 Write the short form answers.

Are you English? (No) *No, I'm not.*

1 Can you speak Russian? (No)
2 Have you got a lot of money with you? (Yes)
3 Do they live in London? (Yes)
4 Does your sister like going to parties? (No)
5 Will it be cold in Spain in November? (No)
6 Have you both finished your homework? (No)
7 Should I get a new computer? (Yes)

Vocabulary

5 Complete the definitions.

A person who writes for a newspaper is a *journalist*.

A person who:
1 acts in plays is an … .
2 directs a play is a … .
3 records the sound for a film is a … .
4 writes a film script is a … .
5 operates a camera is a … .
6 changes an actor's appearance is a … .

Communication

6 Reorder the sentences to complete the conversation in a restaurant.

A: *What would you like to start with?*

a) And to follow?
b) What would you like with your fish?
c) Can I have soup to start with, please?
d) Chips, please.
e) I'll have the fish, please.
f) Can I have a Diet Coke, please?
g) No, thank you. That's fine.
h) OK. Chips. And a green salad?
i) What about something to drink?

7 Work in pairs. Student A:

Ask Student B
• what food products your country is known for.
• where they are produced or grown.
• when your school was built.

Now Student B:

Ask Student A
• where he/she thinks the best cars are made.
• where the best sports clothes are sold in your area.
• when a famous building in your country was built.

NURSE IN A WAR ZONE

Sophie Baud is a French nurse. She recently worked for MSF (Médecins Sans Frontières – a medical aid agency) in a refugee camp. Here are extracts from her diary.

Sunday Aug 4th

When I arrived last week, I couldn't believe the number of people and tents. There are more than 25,000 refugees here, and hundreds of tents.

Tuesday Aug 6th

Sometimes it's hard to imagine that I'm in a war zone. Everyone dresses normally in jeans, T-shirts and trainers. Children and teenagers play football and basketball in the spaces around the tents. They play for hours because they are bored. There isn't much to do in a refugee camp. There is no TV to watch or cinema to go to.

Monday Aug 12th

My work here is very hard. There are no fixed hours. At the beginning, I was working over fifteen hours a day with almost no break. But I'd rather work than sit and do nothing.

Wednesday Aug 14th

Today was particularly hard. It was very hot and a lot of old people fainted from the heat. Then a girl of fifteen called Mira was brought in to see me. She has a liver disease and is very ill. If she doesn't get to hospital soon, I think she will die.

Friday Aug 16th

Fortunately, many of the medical cases are only minor. People often cut their fingers and mouths on the sharp edges of the food tins.

Monday Aug 19th

There is a mental health team here too because a lot of people have psychological problems. They have seen some terrible things.

Wednesday Aug 21st

I've managed to send Mira to a hospital. This is very good news.

Friday Aug 23rd

Today was my last day. When I left the camp, my jeep was followed by hundreds of people saying goodbye. I'd like to come back again soon. It's good to know that I've been of some use here.

1 🔊 Read

a) Read and guess the meaning of the following words.

- war zone • aid • agency • refugee
- fixed • break *(n)* • liver • medical case
- minor • sharp • edge • tin • jeep

b) Match each topic with the day on which the nurse writes about it. Then put the topics in the correct order.

a) The nurse's working hours   *August 12th*
b) A very difficult day
c) What the refugees wear
d) Small medical problems
e) How people pass the time
f) The day she left
g) The size of the camp
h) People's mental health
i) The weather

1 August 4th.   (g) The size of the camp

c) Use the topic headings in Exercise 1b) in the correct order to help you summarise Sophie's experiences.

Sophie was a nurse in a large refugee camp. There were over 25,000 refugees and hundreds of tents.

2 🔊 Listen

Listen to a man talking about his diary. Note his answers to these questions.

1 What is his job?
2 What sort of things did he write as a teenager?
3 How long has he kept a diary?
4 What sort of things does he write in his diary nowadays?
5 Why does he enjoy keeping a diary?

3 Speak

In pairs, discuss these questions.

Have you ever kept a diary? If so, what sort of things did you write in it?
What sort of things do you think are boring to write about?

4 Learn to learn

Dictionary skills: how to find different meanings of words

The same word can often have several different meanings. A dictionary will tell you each meaning with an example.

part of speech   definition   usage

ex.tract / 'ekstrækt **/ n 1** a short piece of writing, music etc. taken from a particular book, piece of music, etc to show what it is like: *I've only seen short extracts from the film.* **2** a substance taken from another substance by using a special process: *vanilla extract*

Use a dictionary to find how many meanings there are of the nouns *heat, break, head*.

5 Write

Write a diary extract for an imaginary week. Say what has happened and how you feel.

Monday
Today has been a really good/bad day … .

117

Famous places in the UK

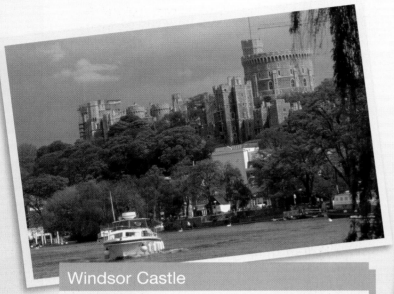

Windsor Castle

Windsor Castle is the official home of Queen Elizabeth II. It is west of London on the River Thames. William the Conqueror began to build the castle in the 11th century and it is now one of the most famous royal palaces in Europe.

Edinburgh Castle

Edinburgh Castle is in the centre of Edinburgh, in Scotland. It is built on top of a huge rock. The oldest part of the castle dates back to 1100. Inside the castle walls, there are many interesting things to see, including the crown jewels and the royal apartments. On a clear day there are wonderful views of the city.

Blackpool Tower

Blackpool is a lively seaside resort in the north-west of England. Blackpool Tower is famous. The tower is 518ft high and was built in 1894 as a rival to the Eiffel Tower in Paris. It contains an aquarium, a zoo, a circus and a dance hall. In autumn, people travel miles to see the lights of the tower and the town at night.

1 Complete the chart with information about the places on pages 118 and 119.

Name	What?	Where?	Why Important?
Windsor Castle	*castle*		
Blackpool Tower			
Edinburgh Castle			
Stonehenge			
Stratford			

2 Make a list of three interesting places to visit in your country and complete a similar chart about them.

Stratford-upon-Avon

Stratford-upon-Avon is a pretty market town on the River Avon. It is about 100km north-west of London and it is famous because it is the birthplace of William Shakespeare (1564-1616). People come to Stratford to see Shakespeare's plays performed in the Royal Shakespeare Theatre and to visit Shakespeare's birthplace, which is now a museum.

Stonehenge

Stonehenge is a circle of huge grey stones on Salisbury Plain in the west of England. It is one of the oldest prehistoric monuments in Europe. It was built between 2000BC and 4000BC. Many historians think that it was built as a temple to the sun.

Project 4   A favourite place to visit

Write about a famous or favourite place to visit in your country. Find photographs to include with your work.

Say where it is situated	The Empire State Building is probably the most famous skyscraper in the world. It is situated in New York, in midtown Manhattan.
Say when it was built	The building was started in 1929 and opened as an office building in 1931.
Say what it looks like	It has 102 floors and a 46-metre-high TV and radio mast. From the observation deck at the top, you can get wonderful views of New York.
Say why it is famous	It is one of the symbols of New York and has appeared in many Hollywood films, from King Kong to Independence Day.

Thanks for everything!

Read the story and try to guess the missing words. Then listen and see if you were right.

At John Lennon Airport, Liverpool

Where's Spike?

_____ . She was standing here a few minutes ago.

1

Sandra, if I send you an e-mail, _____ ?

Don't be silly, Sam!

Yes, of course I will.

2

Goodbye, Mr Burns. _____ .

Oh, you mean the Don't worry. It was last night, after

3

The flight's leaving in an hour.

How are you getting home, Joe?

My father's coming from Manchester to pick me up.

4

_____ .

Next week? No, phone me tonight!

5

Cheers, Gabriel! Have a good trip. _____ Spain, I'll visit you.

That would be great

6

Come on Spike! Your flight's leaving soon. Hurry up!

Or do you want to stay here and work for another week?

No, thanks!

7

Bye, everyone!

Bye! Thanks for everything!

8

120

The 1950s

Blue Suede Shoes

Well it's one for the money, two for the [1] …
Three to get ready, now go cat [2] …
But don't you step on my blue suede shoes.
You can do anything but lay off my blue
suede shoes

You can knock me down, step on my [3] …
Slander my name all over the [4] … .
Do anything that you wanna do
But uh uh honey lay off of them shoes.
Oh don't you step on my blue suede shoes.
You can do anything but lay off my blue
suede shoes.

Well you can burn my house, steal my [5] …
Drink my liquor from an old fruit [6] …
Do anything that you wanna do
But uh uh honey lay off of my shoes.
But don't you step on my blue suede shoes.
Well you can do anything but lay off my blue
suede shoes.

Well it's one for the money, two for the [7] …
Three to get ready, Now go go [8] …
But don't you step on my blue suede shoes.
You can do anything but lay off my blue
suede shoes.

Well it's blue, blue, blue suede shoes
Blue, blue, blue suede shoes yeh!
Well blue, blue, blue suede shoes
Blue, blue, blue suede shoes
Well you can do anything but lay off my blue
suede shoes

Elvis Presley

Elvis Presley, the 'King of Rock and Roll' was probably the greatest rock star of the twentieth century. The young Elvis had everything – good looks and a unique voice. He started his career in 1954 and after two years he was an international sensation. He sold over one billion records and acted in many, often bad, films. He died in 1977. To celebrate the twenty-fifth anniversary of his death, all his songs were re-released. For millions of people *Blue Suede Shoes* is the first great rock and roll hit.

Note

cat = a music fan
wanna = want to
yeh = yes

1 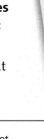 **Listen and put these pairs of rhyming words in the correct verse.**

- car/jar   • show/go
- face/place   • show/go

2 Find words or phrases that mean the same as:

1 don't touch
2 say bad things about
3 girl
4 glass container

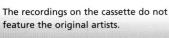

The recordings on the cassette do not feature the original artists.

The Beatles

The Beatles are perhaps the greatest pop musicians of the twentieth century. Many of the songs which were composed by Lennon and McCartney are classics, including *Yesterday*. The Beatles produced a total of fourteen albums. In 2001 the release of a CD of their number one hits went straight to the top of the charts.

Yesterday

Yesterday
All my troubles [1] ... so far away
Now it looks as though they're here to stay
Oh I believe in yesterday
Suddenly, I'm not half the man I used to be
There's a shadow hanging over me
Oh yesterday [2] ... suddenly
Why she [3] ... go
I don't know, she wouldn't say
I [4] ... something wrong
Now I long for yesterday
Yesterday
Love [5] ... such an easy game to play
Now I need a place to hide away
Oh I believe in yesterday
(repeat)
Why she [6] ... go I don't know
She wouldn't say
I [7] ... something wrong
Now I long for yesterday
Yesterday
Love [8] ... such an easy game to play
Now I need a place to hide away
Oh I believe in yesterday.

1 🎵 **Listen and put these words in the correct place. Some of the words are used twice.**

• was • said • came • had to • seemed

2 Answer the questions.

1 Why is the singer sad?
2 What does he want to do now?

The 1970s

Fleetwood Mac

Fleetwood Mac is one of the great names of rock music. The band developed from a 1960s British blues band into a massive international bestseller of soft rock during the 1970s and 1980s. *Don't Stop*, one of Fleetwood Mac's classic songs, comes from the album *Rumours* (1976), which sold over 25 million copies. *Don't Stop* was written by the band's singer, Christine McVie, when she and her husband, John McVie, the band's bass guitarist, were breaking up.

Don't Stop

If you wake up and don't want to [1] ...
If it takes just a little [2] ...
Open your eyes and look at the [3] ...
You'll see things in a different [4] ...

Don't stop thinking about tomorrow,
Don't stop, it'll soon be here,
It'll be better than before,
Yesterday's gone, yesterday's gone.

Why not think about times to [5] ...
And not about the things that you've [6] ...
If your life was bad to [7] ...
Just think what tomorrow will [8] ...

Don't stop *etc*.
All I want is to see you smile,
If it takes just a little while,
I know you don't believe that it's true,
I never meant any harm to you.

Don't you look back
Don't you look back

Christine McVie

1 🔊 **Listen and put these words into pairs which rhyme. Then put them in the correct place.**
• way • come • you • do • smile • day
• while • done

2 **Which of these sentences best describes the message of the song?**
1 Forget what has happened in the past because the future will be different.
2 Everything about our past relationship was terrible so let's start again.
3 Don't believe that life tomorrow will be better.

We Are The Champions

I've ¹ … my dues –
Time after time –
I've ² … my sentence
But committed no crime –
And bad mistakes
I've ³ … a few
I've had my share of sand kicked in my face –
But I've ⁴ … through

   We are the champions – my friends
      And we'll keep on fighting – till the end –
       We are the champions –
       We are the champions
      No time for losers
     'Cause we are the champions – of the world –

    I've ⁵ … my bows
  And my curtain calls –
You've ⁶ … me fame and fortune and everything that goes with it –
I thank you all –

But it's ⁷ … no bed of roses
No pleasure cruise –
I consider it a challenge before the whole human race –
And I ain't gonna lose –

We are the champions – *etc*

Queen

Queen, with lead singer Freddie Mercury, was one of the great 'Glam-Rock' bands of the 1970s. Their stage concerts were full of amazing special effects. In 1977 they released their album *News of the World* which included the hit song *We Are The Champions*. It became an instant classic and is often played and sung at international football matches. Queen broke up in 1991 when Freddie Mercury died, but many of their songs have become classics.

Note
cause = because   *I ain't gonna lose* = I'm not going to lose

1 🎞 **Listen and put the past participle form of these verbs in the correct place. They are in this order.**
• pay • do • make • come • take • bring • be

2 Choose the correct answer.

1 'I've paid my dues' means
   a) I've been honest about everything.
   b) I've paid my taxes.

2 'I've done my sentence' means
   a) I've accepted my punishment.
   b) I've finished my homework.

3 'I've had my share of sand kicked in my face' means:
   a) I've played football on the beach.
   b) I've had many disappointments in life.

4 'I've taken my bows' means
   a) I've been famous.
   b) I've acted on the stage.

5 'No bed of roses, no pleasure cruise' means
   a) No one has given me flowers or a free holiday.
   b) Life hasn't been easy for me.

The 1970s

ABBA

One of the most successful pop groups of the seventies was the Swedish group, Abba. They had eight consecutive number one albums – which was a record. Their music is popular again today and they have many 'tribute groups' who copy their music and style. There is now a hit musical called *Mamma Mia* which contains twenty-seven of their songs and which audiences are enjoying all over the world.

Mamma Mia

I've been cheated by you since I don't know when
So I made up my mind, it must come to an [1] ...
Look at me now, will I ever learn
I don't know how but I suddenly lose control
There's a fire within my [2] ...
Just one look and I can hear a bell ring
One more look and I forget [3] ... , o-o-o-oh

Mamma mia, here I go again
My my, how can I resist you?
Mamma mia, does it show again?
My my, just how much I've missed you
Yes, I've been broken hearted
Blue since the day we [4] ...
Why, why did I ever let you go?
Mamma mia, now I really [5] ...
My my, I could never let you go.

I've been angry and sad about the things that you do
I can't count all the times that I've told you we're
[6] ...
And when you go, when you slam the door
I think you know that you won't be away too long
You know that I'm not that [7] ...
Just one look and I can hear a bell ring
One more look and I forget everything o-o-o-oh

Mamma mia, here I go again *etc*

Mamma mia, even if I say
Bye bye, leave me now or never
Mamma mia, it's a game we [8] ...
Bye bye doesn't mean forever

Mamma mia, here I go again *etc*

---

1 📼 **Listen and put these words in the correct place.**

- strong   • soul   • know   • play
- everything   • through   • end   • parted

2 Which of these statements are true?

a) Her boyfriend often has to go away.
b) She has broken up with her boyfriend many times.
c) Her boyfriend never leaves her.
d) She knows she should end the relationship.
e) She always goes back to her boyfriend.
f) Her boyfriend wants to end the relationship.

3 Find words and expressions in the song which mean:

1 you go out with other girls
2 very sad
3 we're finished as a couple

The 1980s

Billy Joel

The American rock singer, Billy Joel, whose songs are often about the city of New York, was a top singer-songwriter of the 1980s. His style is a mixture of Elton John and Bruce Springsteen. *Uptown Girl* was his biggest hit single. It was re-recorded in 2001 by the Irish boyband, Westlife.

Uptown Girl

Uptown girl
She's been living in her uptown world
I bet she never had a back street guy
I bet her [1] *mama* never told her why.

I'm gonna try for an uptown girl
She's been living in her white bread world
As long as anyone with hot blood can
And now she's [2] *looking* for a downtown man
That's what I am.

And when she [3] *discovers* what she wants from her time
And when she wakes up and makes up her mind
She'll see I'm not so [4] *tough*
Just because I'm in love with an uptown girl.

You know I've seen her in her uptown world.
She's getting tired of her [5] *top* class toys
And all her presents from her uptown boys
She's got a choice.

Uptown girl
You know I can't afford to [6] *buy* her pearls.
But maybe one day when my ship comes in
She'll understand what kind of guy I've been
And then I'll win.

And when she's walking
She's looking so [7] *fine*
And when she's talking
She'll say that she's mine

She'll say that I'm *etc*

Note

Uptown, Midtown and Downtown are different sections of Manhattan. 'Uptown' is an exclusive part of the city, and in the USA, an 'uptown lifestyle' is better than a 'downtown' one.

1 🎞 **The words in italics are wrong. Listen and correct the words.**

2 Find expressions in the song which mean the same as:

1 in a rich and comfortable world
2 strong emotions
3 haven't got the money to
4 when I get lucky

3 Choose the correct answer.

1 An 'uptown girl' is a) rich and smart
   b) poor and ordinary
2 The singer is a) an uptown man
   b) a downtown man
3 He a) doesn't like uptown girls
   b) is in love with her
4 The girl gets lots of presents from
   a) rich boys   b) him
5 He hopes that some day
   a) he's going to win some
   money   b) she's going
   to fall in love with him

The 1990s and onwards

ROBBIE WILLIAMS

Robbie Williams began his career as the lead singer in one of the most successful boy bands of the 1990s, Take That. When the band split up in 1995, Robbie went on to have a hugely successful solo career with massive hits like *She's The One, Rock DJ* and *Angels*. He has regularly won top Britpop music awards, and is one of the UK's most successful singers.

Angels

I sit and wait
Does an angel contemplate my fate
And do they know
The places where we go
When we're [1] …
'cos I have been told
That salvation lets their wings unfold
So when I'm lying [2] …
Thoughts running through my head
And I feel the [3] …
I'm loving angels instead

And through it all she offers me protection
A lot of [4] …
Whether I'm right or wrong
And down the waterfall
Wherever it may take me
I know that life won't [5] …
When I come to call she won't forsake me
I'm loving angels instead

When I'm feeling weak
And my pain walks down [6] …
I look above
And I know I'll always be blessed with love
And as the feeling grows
She breathes flesh [7] …
And when love is dead
I'm loving angels instead

And through it all she offers me protection *etc*

And through it all she offers me protection *etc*

1 📼 **Listen and put these phrases in the correct place.**

a) love and affection
b) break me
c) grey and old
d) love is dead
e) to my bones
f) in my bed
g) a one way street

2 **Answer the questions.**
1 Who does the singer turn to when 'love is dead'?
2 How do the angel or angels help him when he's feeling sad?

The 1990s and onwards

Craig David

Craig David, the talented British singer and songwriter, first appeared at the end of the 1990s when the public were getting bored with all-boy and all-girl bands.

Aged 18, he became the youngest British male singer to have a number one hit. His attractive smoky voice and his easy blend of R&B, pop, hip-hop, and British dance floor styles have brought him international success and he has won awards in many countries around the world.

Walking Away

I'm walking away from the troubles in my life
I'm walking away oh to find a better day
I'm walking away from the troubles in my life
I'm walking away oh to find a better day
I'm walking away

Sometimes some people get me [1] *wrong/angry*
When it's something I've said or done.
Sometimes you feel there is no [2] *hope/fun*
That's why you turn and run.
But now I truly [3] *realise/understand*
Some people don't wanna compromise.
Well, I saw them with my own eyes spreading those [4] *stories/lies*
And well I don't wanna live my life, too many sleepless nights
Not mentioning the fights I'm sorry to say lady.

I'm walking away … *etc*

Well, I'm so tired baby.
Things you say you're driving me [5] *away/home*.
Whispers in the powder room, baby.
Don't listen to the games they play.
Girl, I thought you'd [6] *understand/realise*
I'm not like them other guys
Coz I saw them with my own eyes.
You should've been more [7] *careful/wise*.
And well I don't wanna live my life too many sleepless nights
Not mentioning the fights I'm sorry to say lady.

I'm walking away … *etc*

Note
wanna = want to
them other guys = those other boys
coz = because

1 🔲 **Listen and choose the correct word.**

2 Find a word or phrase which means the same as:

a) don't understand me
b) you try to escape difficult situations
c) passing on untrue stories
d) gossip in the ladies' toilet
e) angry arguments

3 Which of these sentences is not true for the singer?

1 I'm breaking up with you because you make me unhappy.
2 You believe everything other people say about me.
3 I'm leaving you because I've met someone else.

Student B section

Unit 4   5 Interaction

Student B: Use the checklist of things you've got in the kitchen to answer Student A's questions.

CHECKLIST

In kitchen butter oil salt and pepper lettuce
Not in kitchen eggs cheese vinegar tomatoes cucumber

Unit 6   6 Interaction

Student B: First use the information below to answer Student A's questions about future sporting events. Then ask Student A questions to complete your list of sporting events.

B: *Who are Washington Wizards playing next?*
A: *They're playing ... .*
B: *When is the game?*
A: *It's on ... .*
B: *Where are they playing?*
A: *At ... .*

Some important future sporting events

Latin-American Football Cup
Teams: Brazil v Argentina
Date: 19th July
Place: Parque Antártica, São Paulo

Basketball Major League
Teams: Washington Wizards v ...
Date: ...
Place: ...

Rugby League International
Teams: France v Wales
Date: 3rd May
Place: Millennium Stadium, Cardiff

Unit 8   7 Interaction

Student B:

First use the information in your chart to answer Student A's questions about Saturday evening. Then ask Student A questions to complete your information.

Where/go/Saturday evening? ...
How much/tickets/cost? ...
Who/you/see? ...
How many photographs/take? ...
Buy/any souvenirs? ...
What time/leave? ...

YOUR SATURDAY EVENING

Event: A pop concert
Cost of tickets: £25
Stars: Ricky Martin and Jennifer Lopez
Photographs: 36
Souvenirs: A CD and a pop poster
Leaving time: 11.00 p.m.

A: *Where did you go on Saturday evening?*
B: *I went to ... .*
A: *How much did the tickets cost?*

Unit 14   9 Interaction

Student B: Use the information below to answer Student A's questions about Rory and Jenny. Then find out from Student A about the jobs Amy and Ray are doing on work experience and complete the chart.

B: *Where is Amy doing work experience?*
A: *In a children's play group.*
B: *What does she have to do?*
A: *...*
B: *Does she have to wear a uniform?*
A: *...*
B: *What time does she have to start?*
A: *...*

Name	Amy Lane	Rory Grant	Ray Sharman	Jenny Trim
Job	?	At a hospital	?	In an office
Duties	?	Serving tea and coffee Making beds	?	Answering the phone Stamping letters and taking them to the post office
Uniform	?	White nylon	?	Jacket, blouse and dark skirt
Hours	?	7.30–3.30	?	9.00–5.00

Unit 19   8 Interaction

Student B: Choose the correct answer for Student A's questions.

A: *Where was the Statue of Liberty designed?*
B: *It was designed in France.*

• Charles Dickens   • In France   • In a theatre
• Between 2000 and 1000 BC   • In 1838

Now use one of the verbs below to complete the quiz questions. Then ask Student A the questions.

• destroy • paint • compose • make • open

1 When ... the first solo flight across the Atlantic ...?
2 When ... the Suez Canal ...?
3 How ... Pompeii ...?
4 Who ... Guernica ... by?
5 Who ... the 1912 Overture ... by?

129

Soundbite exercises

Unit 1 9 📼 Soundbite

The sounds / sp /, / st / and / sk /
<u>Sp</u>ike <u>St</u>ella <u>sch</u>ool

a) Listen and repeat.

/ sp / **Sp**ike / st / **St**ella / sk / **sch**ool
This is **Sp**ike and that's **St**ella.
Gabriel's a **st**udent from **Sp**ain.

b) Now listen and repeat the sentences.

Spike is at the station.
He likes skiing and skating.
Some English students study Spanish at school.

Unit 2 3 📼 Soundbite

Sentence stress It's <u>on</u> the <u>floor</u>. It's <u>under</u> the <u>desk</u>.

a) Listen to the sentences and mark the stressed words or syllables.

It's <u>on</u> the <u>floor</u>. It's <u>on</u> the <u>bed</u>. It's <u>in</u> the <u>box</u>.
It's <u>on</u> the <u>table</u>.
It's <u>under</u> the <u>desk</u>. It's <u>next</u> to the <u>bed</u>. It's <u>under</u> the <u>bed</u>.
It's be<u>hind</u> the <u>bed</u>. It's a<u>bove</u> the <u>desk</u>.
It's in <u>front</u> of the <u>door</u>. It's in <u>front</u> of the <u>house</u>.

b) Listen again and repeat the sentences.

Unit 3 8 📼 Soundbite

The sounds / ps /, / ts / and / ks / sho<u>ps</u> star<u>ts</u> tal<u>ks</u>

a) Listen and repeat.

/ ps / sho**ps** sto**ps** ho**pes** dro**ps**
/ ts / star**ts** visi**ts** wai**ts** ha**tes** no**tes**
/ ks / tal**ks** wor**ks** wal**ks** li**kes** ma**kes** ta**kes**

b) Now listen and repeat the sentences.

She shops and shops until she drops!
He paints cats, boats and hats.
Sally says she likes chocolates, crisps and cakes.
But Sharon says she likes sweets and nuts.

Unit 4 10 📼 Soundbite

The sounds / tʃ / and / dʒ / <u>ch</u>eese <u>ch</u>ips <u>j</u>uice <u>j</u>am

a) Listen and repeat.

/ tʃ / **ch**eese **ch**ocolate **ch**ips **ch**icken **Ch**ina sandwi**ch**
/ dʒ / **j**uice **j**ust **j**am **J**anuary **J**ill oran**ge**

b) Now listen and repeat the sentences.

John wants a cheese sandwich and an orange juice for lunch.
The children have jam sandwiches and orange juice after school.
Shelley usually chooses chocolate chip ice cream.

Unit 6 12 📼 Soundbite

The sound / θ / <u>th</u>ird eigh<u>th</u> nin<u>th</u>

a) Listen and repeat.

/ θ / **th**ird eigh**th** nin**th**
October the nin**th**
July the four**th**

b) Now listen and repeat the sentences.

I was born on January the fifteenth 1987.
It's his sixteenth birthday this Thursday.
Theo and Thelma are both thirteen on Thursday.

Unit 7 3 📼 Soundbite

The sounds / t /, / d / and / ɪd /
stopp<u>ed</u> climb<u>ed</u> want<u>ed</u>

a) Listen and repeat.

/ t / stopp**ed** watch**ed** lik**ed** talk**ed**
/ d / climb**ed** rain**ed** stay**ed** play**ed**
/ ɪd / want**ed** hat**ed** start**ed** visit**ed**

b) Now listen to the verbs in these sentences. Which ending can you hear: / t /, / d / or / ɪd /?

1 She liked the book.
2 He stopped the car.
3 They hated the film.
4 It rained all day.
5 We wanted to go home.
6 They played a match.
7 The class started late.

c) Listen again and repeat the sentences.

Unit 9 6 📼 Soundbite

The sounds / ɔː / and / ɒ / h<u>or</u>se f<u>o</u>x

a) Listen and repeat.

/ ɔː / h**or**se s**aw** m**or**e of c**our**se f**our** w**or**e
/ ɒ / f**o**x h**o**t g**o**t n**o**t T**o**m w**ha**t sh**o**p

b) Now listen and repeat the sentences.

We saw four white horses.
Oh, what a lot of popcorn you've got.
They haven't got what I want in the shop.

Unit 11 7 📼 Soundbite

The sound / h / <u>h</u>ave <u>h</u>aven't

a) Listen and repeat.

/ h / **h**ave **h**aven't **h**as **h**asn't
how **wh**o **h**eard **h**it **h**ope

b) Now listen and repeat the sentences.

How many horses has Harry got?
I haven't had a letter from him. Have you?
Have you had a holiday in Havana?
They haven't had a hit single for a year.

Unit 12   7 🔊 Soundbite

Sentence stress   It's the <u>tallest</u> <u>tower</u> in <u>Britain</u>.

Listen and repeat the sentences. Make sure you stress the important words and syllables.

It's the <u>tallest</u> <u>tower</u> in <u>Britain</u>.
He's the <u>cleverest</u> <u>boy</u> in the <u>school</u>.
It's the <u>fastest</u> <u>car</u> in the <u>world</u>.
It's the most <u>beautiful</u> <u>place</u> on <u>earth</u>.
It's the most <u>interesting</u> <u>film</u> this <u>year</u>.

Unit 13   7 🔊 Soundbite

The sound / l / in final position   I'<u>ll</u>   he'<u>ll</u>

a) Listen and repeat.

/ l /   I'**ll**   he'**ll**   she'**ll**   it'**ll**   we'**ll**   you'**ll**   they'**ll**

b) Now listen and repeat the sentences.

I'll be fifteen tomorrow.
He'll phone her tomorrow.
We'll ask her to lunch.
They'll be twenty minutes late.
You'll feel better soon.

c) Say these pairs of sentences. Then listen and check your pronunciation.

I see her every day.	I'll see her every day.
We have lunch at two.	We'll have lunch at two.
They arrive after breakfast.	They'll arrive after breakfast.

Unit 14   13 🔊 Soundbite

Word stress   <u>doc</u>tor   beau<u>ti</u>cian

a) Listen and repeat. Put the stress on the first syllable of each word.

<u>doc</u>tor   <u>plum</u>ber   <u>wai</u>ter   <u>den</u>tist   <u>clea</u>ner   <u>sec</u>retary   <u>car</u>penter

b) Listen and repeat. Put the stress on the second syllable of each word.

beau<u>ti</u>cian   re<u>cep</u>tionist   as<u>sis</u>tant

c) Now listen and repeat the sentences.

We need a <u>plum</u>ber and a <u>car</u>penter.
I'd like to be a <u>doc</u>tor and my <u>sis</u>ter would like to be a <u>den</u>tist.
My <u>bro</u>ther's a hotel re<u>cep</u>tionist.
I'd like to be a <u>hair</u>dresser or a beau<u>ti</u>cian.

Unit 16   6 🔊 Soundbite

I like / aɪˈlaɪk / and I'd like / aɪdˈlaɪk /

I like your jacket.   I'd like your jacket.

a) Listen and say which sound you hear each time:

Sound 1 **like** or Sound 2 **'d like** (the short form of **would like**).

a)   b)   c)   d)   e)   f)

	Answers
a) I'd like to go to the cinema.	Sound 2
b) I like your bike.	Sound 1
c) They like classical music.	Sound 1
d) We'd like a coffee, please.	Sound 2
e) We like your flat.	Sound 1
f) They'd like to see the exhibition.	Sound 2

b) Listen again and repeat the sentences.

I'd like to go to the cinema.
I like your bike.
They like classical music.
We'd like a coffee, please.
We like your flat.
They'd like to see the exhibition.

Unit 17   8 🔊 Soundbite

Intonation in conditional sentences

If you go now, you'll have lots of time.

a) Listen and repeat.

If you go now, ...
If I go out, ...
If I see Joe, ...
If we don't book now, ...

b) Now listen and repeat the sentences.

If you go now, you'll have lots of time.
If I go out, Linda will probably phone.
If I see Joe, I'll give him your phone number.
If we don't book now, we won't get any tickets.

Unit 18   11 🔊 Soundbite

Fall–rise intonation   Don't worry, I won't.

Listen and repeat.

Don't worry, I won't.
I won't, I promise.
Never mind, it's OK.
I'll do it, it's all right.
I will, don't worry.

Unit 19   7 🔊 Soundbite

The sound / ə /   w<u>as</u> (used)   w<u>ere</u> (taken)

The neutral vowel in unstressed syllables and weak forms is the most common vowel sound in English

a) Listen and repeat.

/ ə /   w**as** used   w**ere** taken

b) Now listen and repeat the sentences.

It was closed.
They were closed.
When was it built?
When was it abolished?
Where were they made?
Where were they taken?

Vocabulary and expressions

Unit 1

Family members

Types of music

Countries and nationalities

Art
art gallery
Best wishes
Come over
Computer science
cool (That's cool)
crowded
different
docks
English
everyone/body
fan
flat
football team
footballer
friendly
group
hang out
History
home town
hostel
if (you like)
important
in fact
in the past
late
main square
many
much
others (the others)
Physics
play for
port
probably
project leader
Really?
restaurant
ship
slow
subject
suburbs
summer
support
suppose
teach
tired
tourist
trip
turn down
university
warden
welcome
what about?
with

Unit 2

Colours

Prepositions of place

Parts of a room, furniture and objects

armchair
blanket
bookcase
calculator
carpet
cassette player
coathanger
cupboard
curtain
door
drawing pin
duvet
floor
lamp
mirror
mobile phone
noticeboard
personal stereo
pillow
poster
radiator
rug
towel
vase
wall
wardrobe
washbasin
wastepaper bin
window

Patterns

checked
patterned
plain
spotted
striped
___
area
around
basic
bring
chew
cream
diving board
edge
enter
exam
forget (forgot)
gum
jewellery
jump
must
No problem.
polite
push
remember
rules
side
sure

swimming cap
swimming pool
tie (v)
time (on time)

Unit 3

Clock times/Periods of time

Free time activities

afterwards
all the time
next
until
___
act
actor
actually
after
album
case
close (adj)
clubbing (go clubbing)
common room
depend
diet
director
drive
excited
Excuse me
fair
film set
get on (well)
gym
happy to (+ vb)
highly
How's it going?
interview
lifestyle
light
look for
lunch break
make
moment (at the moment)
mood (in the mood)
once
person/people
quiet
racing car
relatives
relax
ride
routine
salad
stay out
still
straight (= directly)
surf (the Internet)
times (three times)
twice
typical

violin
wait for
wear
What's the matter (with)?
win
youth centre

Unit 4

Food and drink

apple
apple pie
banana
beans
beef
biscuit
bread
butter
cake
carbohydrate
carrot
cheese
chicken
chips
cornflakes
cucumber
curry
dairy product
doughnut
egg
fats
fish
fruit
hamburger
honey
ice cream
lamb
lemon
lettuce
meat
melon
milk
mineral water
mixed salad
mushroom
nuts
olive oil
omelette
onion
orange
pasta
peach
peas
pepper
pizza
potato (roast)
protein
rice
salt
sandwich
soup
Spaghetti (Bolognese)
strawberry
toast
tomato

tuna
turkey
vegetable
vinegar
vitamin
yoghurt
___
anorak
bowl
breakfast
clear (v)
flat (adj)
food
help yourself
hope
hungry
ingredients
invite
join
later
local
mate
meal
normal
order (v)
picnic
piece
plate
recipe
rent
slice of (n)
something
special
starving
take someone out
treat
twins
vegetarian
yard

Unit 5

Wideangle

activities
barn
begin with
brochure
cabin
camp
canoeing
early
first thing
huge
impossible
interested in
lake
last thing
long way
muffin
park (n)
price
pronounce
rock climbing
sad
share
showers
sincerely (Yours)

smile at
snore
tonight
waffle
wilderness

Unit 6

Months and dates

Sports

adore
against
bored with
break – broke
brilliant
captain
certainly
cheeseburger
circuit
coach
company
competition
cook
course
court
definitely
die
dip (n)
distance
energetic
fall down
feel (hot)
foot
Go ahead
goal
head
ice-skate
keen on
kick (n)
lazy
lie (v)
live (adj)
married
mess
mind (v)
moody
more
Oh dear
on my own
pitch
player
prefer
put
quality
queue (v)
regret
risk
rush
sand
sandy
score
season
shade
sit around
ski

snowball
sporty
stadium
stupid
sunbathe
sunbunny
swimsuit
Take it easy
tan
team
terrible
thick
throw
track
train (v)
van
winter

Unit 7

School subjects

Possessive pronouns

Common adjectives

awful
backpack
balcony
beautiful
bet
borrow
century
country house
date back to
ghost
ground
guide book
inside
message
mist
packet
painting
park (v)
present (n)
puzzled
receptionist
result
rubbish (a load of rubbish)
slipped
suddenly
towards
untidy
whole
whose

Past tense regular verbs

appear – appeared
arrive – arrived
ask – asked
burn – burned
check – checked
collect – collected
decide – decided
disappear – disappeared
expect – expected
explain – explained

finish – finished
hurry – hurried
introduce – introduced
notice – noticed
open – opened
park – parked
reply – replied
return – returned
seem – seemed
show – showed
unwrap – unwrapped
visit – visited
walk – walked

Unit 8

English money

Places in towns

ahead
airport
behaviour
change (= money)
cheer
concert
corner
crossword
cry
dedicated
disaster
end (v)
faint
fantastic
key
land (v)
left
million
noise
pavement
phenomenon
phone card
remind
right
scary
scream
send
shout
souvenir
tape
turning
unusual

Past tense irregular verbs

buy – bought
cost – cost
meet – met
pay – paid
send – sent
sleep – slept
spend – spent
take – took

Unit 9

Rooms and parts of the house

Animals

boa constrictor
budgie
cow
crocodile
duck
elephant
fox
giraffe
goat
goldfish
horse
kangaroo
koala bear
lamb
lion
parrot
rabbit
rhinoceros
sheep
snake
tiger

a long time
adventure
alive
arcade
blow – blew
cake
candle
chess
curled up
desperately
escape
everywhere
exotic
explore
farm
feel sick
grow – grew
Guess what?
Hands off!
hold
just enough
library
luck
middle
motorway
mugging
Nothing much!
parcel
pass (v)
patio
perhaps
persuade
pet
right
robbery
search
smell
somebody
something
somewhere
stand
strange
study
surprise

tank
taste (n)
think – thought
traffic lights
tree
turn off (a road)
understand
wash
wild
zoo

Unit 10

Wideangle

able (be able)
above
air
all of a sudden
arm
at last
below
bleed
bullet
cloud
completely
conditions
conscious
crash
cut (v)
engine
equipment
even
eye
fail – failed
field
fly (v)
frightening
hail
hand
helmet
high
leg
lie – lay
lightning
miracle
nose
numb
oxygen mask
parachute jump
pilot
plane
protect
rain
realise – realised
soon
still
through
thunder
thunderstorm
weather
wind

Unit 11

Clothes

Materials

cardboard
cotton
denim
glass
leather
metal

nylon
paper
plastic
rubber
silk
straw
wood (en)
wool (len)

Personal possessions

bracelet
buckle
diary
earring
key ring
necklace
pencil case
purse
ring (n)
rucksack
scarf
strap
wallet
watch

agency
all over
anyone
at once
beige
bruise
care (I don't care)
contact
get going
goalpost
hang on
lose
lost property
material
memory
national
need
never mind
no one
over (all over the world)
pass (v)
previous
pullover
recognise
record
search
sleeve
sleeveless
so far
stuff
sweatshirt

Unit 12

act
advanced
bank (of river)
battery
candyfloss
chase
climb
connect
dangerous
difficult
duration

electronic
estate
exciting
fetch
frightening
hatchback
height
helicopter
horrible
last (v)
length
Let's face it
lift (n)
message
motor
mouse (computer)
move
operate
owner
plane
play (= show)
popular
price
rating
raw
reason
reliable
robot
round (prep)
safe
safety
scared of
seat
shake (v)
size
sophisticated
speed
sports (car)
Suit yourself
sweet (adj)
tail
teeth
theme park
tower (n)
wag (v)
watchdog
wave (v)
weigh (v)
weight
wheel
wide
width

Unit 13

Parts of the body

ankle
arm
back
chin
ear
elbow
eye
finger
foot/feet
hand
head
hip
knee
leg
mouth
neck

nose
shoulder
stomach
thumb
toe
waist
wrist

accidentally
appointment
badly
bandage
bin
bleed
blow (your nose)
carry
down (down there)
drop
faint
farmhouse
fine (= OK)
first aid
gloves
hospital
hurt
ice pack
idea
injury
join
litter
loosen
motorbike
painful
plaster
possible
rest (n)
ribbon
ride
shade
should
sprain (v)
squeeze
step ladder
tie (necktie)
turn on/off
twisted
view
X-ray

Unit 14

Household jobs
do the cleaning
do the ironing
do the shopping
do the vacuuming
do the washing-up
empty the rubbish
make the bed
tidy up
wash the car

Occupations
beautician
carpenter
cashier
cleaner
dentist
doctor
electrician
engineer
hairdresser

nurse
plumber
receptionist
sales assistant
secretary
waiter

beauty salon
believe
ceiling
collection
delivery
dirty
dishwasher
empty (v)
entrance
experience
fish tank
foul
full-time
go bananas
heap (n)
nerves (get on
   your nerves)
parcel
pile
plate
pocket money
remove
shelf/ves
smell (v)
sort (v)
supermarket
trolley
tropical
uniform
untidy

Unit 15

Wideangle
chat room
click
comments
discuss
exchange
expand
fresh
high school
keep (something
   fresh)
online
rent (v)
review
share
site
trouble (The
   trouble is...)
update
visitor
website
wonder

Unit 16

Leisure activities
bowling
circus
games arcade
go-karting
ice-skating
musical

picnic
sightseeing

beware
carnival
chance
concert
demand
disappointed
exhibition
festival
fight
hero
including
jewellery
lap
Look forward to
money belt
performance
pickpocket
pop art
pre-season
rather (would
   rather)
show (n)
supper
thief/ves
warm up
What's on

Unit 17

Adverbs
angrily
badly
carefully
careless(ly)
creatively
early
easily
fast
happily
hard
late
loudly
peacefully
quickly
quietly
sadly
slowly
terribly
tidily
well

according to
arrange
blow it
breath (under your
   breath)
civil war
common
complain
engaged (phone)
face (v)
gang
Granny
   (= grandmother)
human rights
knife/ves
lady
notice (v)
power

probably
recording studio
refugee
ring (v)
   (= telephone)
rival
slam
straightaway
violence

Unit 18

Jobs in the media
actor/actress
camera operator
director
journalist
make-up artist
scriptwriter
sound engineer
technician

Types of films
action
cartoon
comedy
courtroom drama
disaster
fantasy
gangster
historical
horror
love story
musical
science fiction
thriller
western

abroad
advance
   (in advance)
alarm (n)
all sorts
armour
army
arrest
autograph
badge
based on
best-selling
commit murder
correct
costume
couple (a couple of)
create
creature
destroy
develop
earth
employ
episode
evil
feed
film (v)
finally
guide (n)
knitted
look like
magical
nicely
order (n)
part (= role)

producer
put together
record (v)
rule (v)
scene
script
security
set (n and v)
set (the alarm)
setting
shoot
shot
Shut up!
special effects
storyline
string
switch off
theme
valley
What on earth?
whisper
wizard
worry (Don't worry)

Unit 19

accident
adventure
agree
allow
anniversary
assassinate
assemble
authority/ies
brush (n)
build
coil (v)
consider
construct
copper
crime
criminal
crown (n)
deck
design (v)
die
discipline
disease
drown
enormous
eruption
face
fall off
forbid
fortnight
friendship
grounded
hammock
harbour
hoist
immigrant
independence
inner
invent
landmark
legal system
liberty
living expenses
lottery
millions
ocean

on board
opportunity
pedestal
prison
punishment
raise (money)
reform
repair
rescue
rigging
rope
sail (n)
sailor
scrub
sculptor
section
slave trade
spike
statue
survive
symbol
teach – taught
thanks to ...
thousands
token
train (v)
truant (play truant)
useful
volcanic
weekly

Unit 20

Wideangle
almost
beginning (at the
   beginning)
break (n)
bring – brought
contain
diary
edge
extract (n)
fixed
fortunately
hard (adj)
heat
imagine
jeep
keep (a diary)
lively
liver
manage to
medical
medical case
mental health
minor
mouth
news
normally
official
particularly
psychological
refugee
sharp
space
tent
tin
use (n) (of some
   use)
war zone

Irregular verbs

Infinitive	Past simple	Past participle
be	was	been
become	became	become
begin	began	begun
bite	bit	bitten
blow	blew	blown
break	broke	broken
bring	brought	brought
build	built	built
buy	bought	bought
catch	caught	caught
choose	chose	chosen
come	came	come
cost	cost	cost
cut	cut	cut
do	did	done
draw	drew	drawn
drink	drank	drunk
drive	drove	driven
eat	ate	eaten
fall	fell	fallen
feed	fed	fed
feel	felt	felt
fight	fought	fought
find	found	found
fly	flew	flown
forget	forgot	forgotten
get	got	got
give	gave	given
go	went	gone
grow	grew	grown
have	had	had
hear	heard	heard
hit	hit	hit
hold	held	held
hurt	hurt	hurt
keep	kept	kept
know	knew	known
learn	learnt	learnt

Infinitive	Past simple	Past participle
leave	left	left
lend	lent	lent
lose	lost	lost
make	made	made
meet	met	met
pay	paid	paid
put	put	put
read	read	read
ride	rode	ridden
ring	rang	rung
run	ran	run
say	said	said
see	saw	seen
sell	sold	sold
send	sent	sent
shine	shone	shone
shut	shut	shut
sing	sang	sung
sit	sat	sat
sleep	slept	slept
speak	spoke	spoken
spend	spent	spent
split up	split up	split up
stand	stood	stood
steal	stole	stolen
swim	swam	swum
take	took	taken
teach	taught	taught
tell	told	told
think	thought	thought
throw	threw	thrown
understand	understood	understood
wake (up)	woke (up)	woken (up)
wear	wore	worn
weep	wept	wept
win	won	won
write	wrote	written

Acknowledgements

We are grateful to the following for permission to reproduce copyright material:

Blue Suede Shoes by Carl Lee Perkins. © 1956 Hi-Lo Music Inc. USA. Public performance rights for USA and Canada controlled by Unichappell Music Inc. (Rightsong Music, publisher). All rights reserved – Carlin Music Corp. London NW1 8BD. Lyrics reproduced by kind permission of Carlin Music Corp. London NW1 8BD. Yesterday Words and music by John Lennon and Paul McCartney © 1965 Northern Songs/Sony/ATV Music Publishing Don't Stop Words and music by McVie. © Fleetwood Mac Music/NEM Entertainment Corp/BMG Songs Inc. All rights reserved. Used by permission. We Are The Champions Words and music by Freddie Mercury © 1977 Queen Music Ltd, London WC2H 0QY Reproduced by permission of International Music Publications Ltd. All rights reserved. Mamma Mia © BOCU Music Limited. Uptown Girl Words and music by Billy Joel. © 1983 Joel Songs. All rights reserved. International copyright secured. Used by permission. Angels Words and music by Chambers/Williams. © BMG Music Publishing Ltd. All rights reserved. Used by permission. Walking Away Words and music by Craig David and Mark Hill © 2000 Warner /Chappell Music Ltd and Windswept Pacific Music Ltd. Warner/Chappell Music Ltd. Griffin House, 161 Hammersmith Road, London W6 8BS (50%)/Windswept Music (London) Ltd. Hope House, 40 St Peter's Road, London W6 (50%)/.Reproduced by permission of International Music Publications Ltd & Music Sales Ltd. All rights reserved. International copyright secured.

We are grateful to the following for permission to reproduce copyright photographs:

Ace Photo Agency for 40 centre, 86 figure D; A1/Britstock-IFA for 12 bottom left, 30 top right, 40 centre right below, 58 inset, 86 (figures A, E), 96 bottom right, 119 bottom right; All Action for 20 left, 50-51; Allsport/Michael Steele for 97 bottom right; Big Pictures for 57 bottom right; Bridgeman Art Library for 92 right; Bubbles for 48 top left, 48 centre; Camera Press for 30 centre right above, 46 centre above, 40 bottom right; Capitol Pictures for 127 top; Chessington World of Adventures (www.chessington.com) for 95 bottom right; Corbis UK Ltd for 49, 58 top, 96 centre right, 102 bottom right, 116 inset, 118 all, 119 top and centre, 121 both, 122 centre above and centre below, 123 both, 125 bottom, 126 bottom; Empics for 30 bottom right, 36-7, 93 bottom; Greg Evans International for 46 top, 46 bottom left, 68; Getty Images for 97 bottom; Getty Images/Stone/Ken Fisher for 72-73; /Corinne Woods for 91; Ronald Grant Archive for 107 top centre left; Robert Harding Picture Library for 32-33 background; Hulton Getty for 122 bottom; Idols Licensing and Publicity Ltd for 57 top right; Image State for 12 right, 30 top left, 55 (figures 1, 4, 5, 8, 9, 12), 93 top left, /Pictor International for 112; Interlocken Center for Experimental Learning, Hillsborough, USA (www.interlocken.org) for 32-33 bottom; IPG/Pål Hansen for 96t; Kobal Collection for 21 top, 107 top left, top centre right and top right, 108; Life File for 30 bottom left, 86 (figure G); Link Picture Library for 85 centre right; London Features International for 12 centre left, 21 bottom, 24 top left, 56 bottom right, 57 top left, 93 right; Jeff Moore for 30 centre below; Network Photographers for 85 top, 102 top; NHPA for 55 (figure 6); PA News Photos for 24 top centre left, 24 centre right, 40, 116-117 background, 117 top and bottom; ©Pearson Education/Trevor Clifford for pages 34 (top and bottom), 35 and 90; Photographers Library 30 left centre above, 86 (figures B, F, H); Pictures Colour Library for 55 (figures 3, 7, 10, 11), 96 left; Popperfoto for 12 top, 48 bottom left; Powerstock for 2-3 background; Redferns Music Picture Library for 122 top, 124, 125 top, 126 top; Retna for 20 right, 24 bottom left, 56 top left, bottom left; Rex Features for 24 right, 48 top right, 55 (figure 2), 56 top right, 57 bottom left, 74 both, 92 left, 126 top, 127; © The Sun, Lowell, Mass., USA/Tory Germann for page 102 bottom left; Superstock for 86 figure C; Topham Picturepoint for 85 bottom, 128 both.

We have been unable to trace the copyright holders of the photographs on page 110 from the website www.royalnavy.co.uk/akbar and we would be very grateful for any information that might enable us to do so.
All photographs not listed above are ©Pearson Education/by Peter Lake

Cover photographs: Corbis UK Ltd (top right); Image State (bottom left and right); Powerstock (top).

Our special thanks to the following for their help during location photography:
Anglia Television Ltd; Bishop's Stortford YMCA; Bowl Xtra; Krazy House, Leyton Orient Football Club; Liverpool Airport plc; Maghull Coaches; Mersey Ferries; Mobile Phone Centre; The Princess Alexandra Hospital: The Rivers Hospital; WildTracks; YHA, Cambridge.